TO LEAD AN HONORABLE LIFE

Invitations to think about Client-Centered Therapy and the Person-Centered Approach

A COLLECTION OF THE WORK OF

JOHN M. SHLIEN

EDITED BY PETE SANDERS

PCCS BOOKS
Ross-on-Wye

First published in 2003

PCCS BOOKS
Llangarron
Ross-on-Wye
Herefordshire
HR9 6PT
United Kingdom
Tel (01989) 77 07 07
website www.pccs-books.co.uk
email contact@pccs-books.co.uk

**To Lead an Honorable Life: Invitations to think about
Client-Centered Therapy and the Person-Centered Approach**

ISBN 1 898059 46 2

Cover photograph by Maggie Taylor-Sanders
Cover design by Old Dog Graphics
Printed by Bath Press, Bath, United Kingdom

Contents

Forewords

GODFREY ('GOFF') BARRETT-LENNARD
Honorary Fellow, School of Psychology, Murdoch University, Melbourne, Australia.

John stands out in my memory, especially as a friend, a supporter when I needed one, a good listener, a person to share ideas with, someone who tended to speak his mind on matters of principle. I am sure he influenced me, and that this came to work both ways. I looked up to him in my time in Chicago (1954–58) but not as a hero (such as Carl then was to me), or from a position as follower. The siblings in my large family of origin were mostly brothers and older than me. In Chicago, John was something like an older brother, eight years my senior *to the day*. When I 'left home' our relationship attenuated for a time, later growing strong again, and symmetrical.

My bulging file of correspondence and exchange of messages with John has a good deal in it from our shared time in Chicago, then little until the seventies during his time at Harvard and mine in Canada. We both were professors and had worked at developing original programs, and most of our communications were in some way work-related although also personal. They included conversations by phone and many more on paper — his typically written by hand (pre-email, and often on the back or bottom of another letter) and conversational in style. His report as external examiner (copy to me) in 1973 for one of my graduate students reflects his capacity to also write in incisive formal mode. He came in person to my university for the doctoral orals that followed.

John was strenuously occupied in his work at Harvard but took time to respond in affirming and supportive ways to people elsewhere whom he cared about, especially in *their* crises. I experienced this first-hand, and it applied also (for example) in his relation with Carl. While often, and to many of us, so generous in his response, John could be sharply critical where he saw self-serving motives either in 'revisionists' or in 'adherents' who lacked sensitivity or allegiance to what was precious to him in 'our' approach. Sometimes his strong reaction to people or ideas would surprise me (his objection to metaphor is an example). Felt kinship with others has varied roots and, for John, shared history, clear similarity in direction or vital overlap in values, fed strongly into this feeling. Concern for excellence was a value that both contributed to the exceptional quality of his own professional writing and limited its volume.

In 1984 John retired from his regular professorship, and one result was that his flow of correspondence multiplied. Already it had been building up between us, around my own transition out of full-time academia and on to the proposal to form an independent network, Centre for Studies in Human Relations ('Ceshur' — first discussed with John and a handful of others, in the Summer of 1981). John was a 'natural' to be part of this initiative, and was formally affiliated as an International Fellow of Ceshur from the beginning. In a long letter of October 1984, he commented on Ceshur-related matters in his affirming way, referred to the new book with Levant and to his and my current writing, and said that he had 'been doing very well without the demands and rigors of my job at Harvard', where 'I still teach one course per year and will finish some students' dissertations with them — if they hurry'. He also mentioned a yen to travel, possibly as far as Australia — a thought that he mentioned more than once but which, I am afraid, was never consummated.

A number of John's papers are gems, as the reader will see from this book. The one on schizophrenia, to me, remains the best single article on its topic coming from client/person-centred work, and is almost as fresh and relevant as when he produced it. His writing — on transference and on secrecy, for example — often is provocative and nearly always is evocative. He worked very hard on his highly original papers, none more so than the last on 'empathy in psychotherapy'. He wrote to me while struggling with that one, saying that the 'format' was a problem, he had 'too many ideas, not enough motivation' and had 'stopped trying' (October 26, 1994). Nevertheless, three months later, he posted me 'a disk with draft of my empathy paper' (February 25, 1995) — which my computer could not handle. In his next message on the topic he was suffering loss of confidence and feeling that 'my [his] empathy paper is kind of goofy' (March 10, 1995). Two weeks later a version came, which still needed reformatting, and I think that time ran out for any useful feedback from me. Looking at it now, he did not change his draft much, except the last part. As usual, his approach and thought is highly original, and vitally interesting historical anecdotes are woven in. I for one feel informed, 'stretched' and stimulated even at points of disagreement.

This book has a double significance. It brings together in accessible form a large sample of John's creative and engaging thought and is thus a valuable new resource. Second, it is a further recognition of a distinctive and high quality contribution to the movement in ideas and practice that John Shlien dedicated his career to. He himself was more involved in the tillage of ideas than in their marketing and I am very pleased that, by Pete Sanders' inspiration and work, this book will now enhance the visibility of these ideas.

RONALD F. LEVANT
Dean and Professor, Center for Psychological Studies, Nova Southeastern University, Ft. Lauderdale, Florida, USA.

I am so glad that Pete Sanders has taken on the task of editing this volume of John Shlien's writings, because it will make these gems more accessible to future generations of students and scholars.

I have had the honor of knowing John for over three decades. He was my principle mentor in graduate school at Harvard University, in an unusual interdisciplinary program that focused on applications and implications of clinical psychology for public policy, called 'Clinical Psychology and Public Practice' (CP[3] for short). I began working with John in the summer before the program started, in a project that led to the creation of an innovative therapeutic day-school (the Robert W. White School) for the treatment of lower socioeconomic, ethnic-minority adolescents who were adjudicated as delinquents. During this era, the Commonwealth of Massachusetts was deinstutionalizing the reformatories and establishing community-based placements for these children, some of whom had been institutionalized for many years (Levant, 1974; Shlien and Levant, 1974).

From the very beginning, I found John to be a remarkable man who listened in ways that I had never before observed nor experienced. His effect on hardened delinquent children was phenomenal. And I, as well, felt truly understood for the first time in my life when talking with him. John had been a student of Carl Rogers at the University of Chicago, and after Rogers left for the schizophrenia project at Mendota State Hospital in Wisconsin, John moved up the ranks and became Chair of the Interdepartmental Committee on Clinical Psychology and Director of Clinical Training. He came to Harvard in the late 1960s. John and I maintained a friendship and colleagueship until his death, and co-edited a book on client-centered therapy and the person-centered approach (Levant and Shlien, 1984).

Reading these collected writings has brought back many memories. One of them concerns a course John taught on psychotherapy, in which he conducted once-a-week psychotherapy with a client while a group of students sat in the room to observe. This had the effect of great immediacy, as emotions were generated in the students as we watched the subtle interplay unfold, and wondered how we might have responded were we the therapist. The follow-up discussions, which took place immediately after the sessions, were fascinating, bringing forth a wide range of perspectives, and illuminating puzzling interactions. For example, in one early session, in which the client had a hard time getting started, John (in what looked like a very un-client-centered gesture) reached over with his foot to nudge the client's foot. In the follow-up discussion, we learned that John sensed that, from the client's perspective, this situation appeared quite threatening, and as a result he was feeling isolated and afraid. John thought that a playful gesture might help lighten the client's mood and express caring and connection.

John was not only a good listener. He also had many thoughts of his own, including some quite strong views, which he had no hesitancy in sharing. John did not suffer fools gladly, and if he thought you were wrong, or, even more important, self-deceiving, he would tell you. This was not particularly easy to hear as a graduate student, but it was almost always beneficial. John also inspired tremendous admiration and affection in those around him, so that (embarrassing as it is to admit) I actively sought John's approval, was elated when I got it, and deeply disappointed when I did not.

John's writings were also inspiring. For decades, I have carried in my mind his anecdotes, and used them in my own teaching. There are many, but one in particular stands out, which appears in the conclusion to 'Phenomenology and Personality' (Shlien, 1963/1970, and Chapter 11, this volume). This story illustrates so very well the importance of seeing things from the client's perspective. Parents of a young boy were worried about their son who, among other symptoms, was lonely, shy and withdrawn, yet they were embarrassed about these problems and reluctant to make them public. So they invited a college classmate, who had become a psychologist, for a weekend visit. At dinner the mother mentioned their concerns and the father suggested that the boy might be observed at play on the following day. The guest now knew the reason for this invitation and accepted the mission. The next day he watched the boy play alone as neighborhood children played loudly in the background. He frowned, kicked the grass, scuffing his white shoes, and looked at the stain. Then he stretched out to watch an earthworm, picked up a sharp stone chip and proceeded to cut the worm in half. By now the psychologist was forming fairly negative impressions about the boy: 'Seems isolated and angry, perhaps over-aggressive, or sadistic, should be watched carefully when playing with other children, not have knives or pets' (p. 124). Then the psychologist noticed that the boy was talking to himself. Straining to catch the words as the boy finished separating the worm, the boy's frown disappeared and he said 'There. Now you have a friend' (p. 124, in Hart and Tomlinson, 1970, also p. 169 this volume).

One is never sure how much of one's approach is learned from mentors and how much is self-designed. I got some measure of this last October when presenting a workshop in which I showed a video of my therapy work. During the discussion, one member of the audience asked: 'Did you by any chance train with one of Carl Rogers' students?' Later I learned that the questioner had himself trained with one of John's contemporaries, Bill Kell, and recognized himself in my approach.

Carl Rogers was terribly important to John. When Carl died in the mid-1980s, I recall that John was quite mournful, and told me he wasn't ready for Carl to die. I spoke with John on the phone, when, as it turned out, he was dying from his illness. He was quite angry with his physicians, saying that they didn't know what they were talking about, and was about to leave Cambridge for Big Sur. I was so unprepared for the idea that John might be dying that I did not have the courage to discuss this with him in what turned out to be our last conversation. I wish I could have said: 'John I am not ready for you to die!'

REFERENCES

Hart, J.T. & Tomlinson, T.M. (Eds.) (1970). *New directions in client-centered therapy*. Boston: Houghton Mifflin.

Levant, R.F. (1974). The planning, development and administration of a therapeutic school for adolescents (The Robert W. White School). *Dissertation Abstracts International, 34*, 5684-B, (University Microfilms No. 74–11, 324).

Levant, R.F. & Shlien, J.M. (Eds.) (1984). *Client-centered therapy and the person-centered approach: New directions in theory, research and practice*. New York: Praeger. Paperback edition, Greenwood Press, 1987.

Shlien, J.M. (1963). Phenomenology and personality. In J.M. Wepman & R.W. Heine (Eds.) *Concepts of Personality*. Chicago: Aldine, pp. 291–330. Reprinted in J.T. Hart & T.M. Tomlinson, *New directions in client-centered therapy*. Boston: Houghton Mifflin, pp. 95–128.

Shlien, J.M. & Levant, R.F. (1974). The Robert W. White School. *Harvard Graduate School of Education Association Bulletin, 19*, 12–18.

DAVE MEARNS
Professor of Counselling, University of Strathclyde, Scotland.

My first contact with John Shlien was over his highly professional production, with Ronald Levant, of the 1984 book *Client-Centered Therapy and the Person-Centered Approach*. This was a significant publication for me because it marked my return from 11 years in the wilderness of educational research after an initial immersion in client-centred psychotherapy in the early 1970s. As Pete Sanders says in his introduction to the present volume, that 1984 book is full of gems, like Shlien's own chapters: 'Secrets and the Psychology of Secrecy' and 'A Countertheory of Transference'. However, such was the state of the approach in the USA by 1984, combined with the European pricing policy of the publisher (£50 for a book, in 1984!) that the book was not so much 'released' as 'escaped' with only a few hundred copies sold.

My first, and only, meeting with John was in 1987 at the 'Forum' held in La Jolla shortly after Carl's death. I found him to be an amusingly enigmatic figure who attracted me as one of the 'old guard' who stood for the same kind of academic values as myself. John was somewhat 'misfitted' at a Forum in California. He did not appear to have learned the 'rules' of the large group meeting. In fact, I think he knew the normative process rather well and was not at all discomforted by his dissonance with it. At one point he was challenged by a participant who declared that he had been a student of John's many years previously. The former student recounted a particular essay of his that John had graded. The climax to the challenge was the student's public declaration that he had got the essay back with scores of 'critical red marks' on it and that this, surely, was not very person-centred. John's response was: 'But it was a bad essay!' The former student metaphorically crawled into his corner.

The present book contains 16 papers, including, as well as the 1984 chapters, his epic 1961 paper 'A client-centered approach to schizophrenia: first approximation'. It was strange for me to read this paper after a gap of 30 years. It includes extracts from John's work with the client, 'Michael K.' and his humble observation that he might have listened to his teacher's (Rogers) advice and been more congruent in relation to this client.

In his introduction to the book, Pete Sanders refers to the ideas which have been laid down by John Shlien, in wait for others to discover them. One striking example of this is in the 1957 paper, 'Basic concepts in group psychotherapy: a client-centered point of view'. I had never read this paper before and shared the thesis of the early pages that it was difficult for such an individually-orientated theory to work out who was the client in group therapy. Then a single sentence both answered the question and potentially grounded a future pedagogy for person-centred group therapy: 'There is one goal for the group and its individual members — that is *the experience of freedom*'.

In many of the papers, including 'Can therapy make you happy?', 'Embarrassment anxiety: a literalist theory', and 'Empathy in psychotherapy: vital mechanism? Yes. Therapist's conceit? All too often. By itself enough? No', there is a wealth of fascinating comment about the early development of the approach, the difficulties encountered and interesting insights into its originator including his (Rogers') embarrassment at the external and internal criticism of the technique of 'reflection'.

Pete Sanders is right that John Shlien was highly generative of ideas. As well as that creativity, he also had the considerable intelligence to manipulate these ideas. Yet, I felt a slight sadness on reading this manuscript because I wonder if John Shlien lacked the collegial support needed to take these ideas, like the deconstruction of psychoanalysis, further.

ALBERTO ZUCCONI
Clinical Psychologist and Co-founder of the Instituto Dell'Approccio Centrato sulla Persona, Italy

John, the rainbow man: that is what came right away into my mind when trying to describe him. What sort of person was he? People differed in their opinion of him but I'll try to relate to you how I experienced him over the last 25 years.

The first time I met John was when Carl Rogers asked me to speak on a panel chaired by Carl that included John, Nat Raskin, Goff Barrett-Lennard and Gay Swenson, at the American Psychological Association Conference in Los Angeles. At the time he appeared to me as an important Harvard professor, impeccable in his dress, not a hair out of place and very articulate. I was a little intimidated by him, but he helped by promptly extending his hand with a friendly smile and a wink.

That was the beginning of a long and fruitful personal and professional relationship. John frequently participated in our European training programs for psychotherapists. I had the opportunity to see and appreciate all his multifaceted personality: he was a deeply caring person, shy, humorous, provocative, stubborn and very, very bright.

On the answering machine at his Big Sur home he had orchestrated the funniest and most creative answer-phone message I have ever heard: there was John singing a jazz song and then in the best mock-showbiz style, John kicked in with: 'TAKE IT AWAY HELEN!' at which point the message switched into a very mellow jazz piano piece. Images of his wife Helen sitting at the piano flowed through my mind. I also recall, with the same hilarity, the time John sent me and Irene an email invitation to lunch in Big Sur which concluded with: 'Helen will serve . . .'

He was ceaseless in his efforts to promote a revival of Client-Centered Therapy, and sought to protect it from those he felt were putting the label of the Person-Centered Approach onto whatever superficial and poorly-articulated work they were producing.

John was also very generous financially. He once offered me a large piece of land next to his house in Big Sur in order to create a PCA student center. Since my lawyer could not arrange the paperwork in time for the donation, he gave it, for the same purpose, to Richard Farson, one of his most loved colleagues from their time at the University of Chicago.

He had a sharp mind, was witty and full of insights. He had the courage to share all of himself, including his sharp corners and quick mood changes. He also openly manifested his dissent.

This proved too problematic for some, for at times I saw some of his colleagues frustrated with him to the point of not wishing to be on the staff of a training program on the same dates as he. Our students' expectations were also confounded — at times they were quite surprised that a 'Rogerian' could be so blunt. However, those who were willing to fully engage with him would eventually be rewarded with an exciting, stimulating, enriching, honest, challenging relationship which was at no time boring,

John, maybe you were not easy at times, but you were always great. I am glad I met you and I miss you . . . we all miss you here.

Thank you, John.

Editor's Introduction

HOW AND WHY I CAME TO EDIT THIS BOOK

Editing this book has been a labour of love.

Whenever I read a paper, chapter or book, I want to know something about the writer. Not who they are in the sense of academic qualifications or professional status, but a sense of them as a person — what makes them laugh, cry or get angry. It's not an exclusively person-centred thing; nowadays we are likely to call it 'connection', but it used to be just old-fashioned getting to know someone. That's my reason for writing this (and why you might want to read it). It's the short story of how John Shlien and I got to know each other and why I have agonised over preparing this book for the last year.

I first came into contact with John Shlien's work whilst I was a student on the Post Graduate Diploma in Counselling at the University of Aston in 1974. I remember struggling with John's contributions to *New Directions in Client-Centered Therapy* (Hart and Tomlinson, 1970). Ten years later, as a lecturer in counselling in Wigan, I bought a copy of *Client-Centered Therapy and the Person-Centered Approach: New Directions in Theory, Research and Practice* (Levant and Shlien, 1984) for the staffroom library.

Parenthetically you should know that even though I was course leader for a person-centred training programme, I was not centrally involved in the development of the Person-Centred Approach (PCA) in Britain. I was not part of the usual networks and had never met, nor been in the same room as, Carl Rogers. In fact, the prospect of actually *meeting* anyone who had written a chapter in a client-centred or person-centred publication (except the seemingly ever-available and ever-supportive Brian Thorne) was unimaginably remote.

I metaphorically devoured the book. It was so vibrant, spoke of an approach with so much vigour and life; the contributions were so intelligent, astute, *interesting* and a couple even made me laugh. The introduction, written by the editors, Shlien and Levant made the hairs stand up on the back of my neck. It still does — several of John's writings simultaneously make the hairs stand up on the back of my neck, bring me to the edge of tears and laughter and make me want to cheer or punch the air and shout 'yes!' Not many papers on psychotherapy can do that.

When trying to describe the qualities in John's writing that do this to me, I get a little stuck for words. Tony Merry (2002) wrote, 'His writing was both authoritative and lyrical. He breathed life into ideas and set them loose into the world of psychology, where many of them wait patiently to be discovered' (p. 1). John Shlien could be poetic, witty, angry and romantic in one sentence. And at the same time he could be right. In the intervening years, I became a fan, no less, and an avid collector of his work. This was no mean feat in Britain at the time, since contemporary Client-Centred Therapy (CCT)/PCA publications were like gold dust — I could have made a fortune selling bootleg photocopies of 'A Countertheory of Transference' (the volume it was in went out of print almost the moment it hit the bookstores and has been next to impossible to obtain ever since).

John Shlien was not a prolific writer — Goff Barrett-Lennard suggested to me that it was because John was such a perfectionist. This volume is slim in comparison to those of many of his contemporaries. He had, however, the ability to occasionally come up with something daring, coruscating, controversial. And, I think, his readers realised that he enjoyed the moment. You will be able to judge for yourself.

It was with much trepidation that I approached my first meeting with John in a hotel in London — I was invited along to be introduced to him by Irene Fairhurst. It was 1998. Inside, I was every tongue-tied fan who was about to meet their hero(ine). John was on vacation in London and we had arranged to meet so that he could give me some papers on time-limited Client-Centred Therapy he had written many years ago .[1] He had the reputation of not suffering fools gladly.

[1.] John's Ph.D. was on time-limited counselling and although the prospect of John Shlien writing on time-limited therapy might seem mouth-watering, it has proved too difficult to edit John's research into something appropriate for the twenty-first century. I have tracked down half-a-dozen or so pieces all written in the late 1950s, including a co-written chapter, but in the intervening years the meaning of 'time-limited' has changed dramatically. In the 1930s Otto Rank and his student Jesse Taft broke from the rigid Freudian understanding of 'time' and John Shlien was one who picked up the baton, emphasising, (i) client choice (rather than therapist advice or theoretical dogma) in the matter of how long therapy should last, and equally as revolutionary, (ii) the quality of time rather than the quantity of time was most important, i.e., a small amount of good therapy is more valuable than a large amount of poor therapy. Those looking at time in this new way were keen to point out that *time* does not heal, it is a *process* that heals.

Over a series of experiments, John Shlien discovered that therapy lasting 20 sessions (time-limited in the 1950s!) was equally effective as therapy with an unlimited number of sessions. Gains made in therapy held (actually slightly improved) over a six-month follow-up period after the end of therapy. (See Shlien, 1957; Lewis, Rogers and Shlien, 1959.)

I was not feeling confident. However, Irene was her usual brilliant self and so I relaxed. We had lunch and talked about research, Client-Centred Therapy and rumours of its demise, and what made a good gin and tonic. I had finally met one of my heroes.

Over the next two years John and I corresponded by email at least weekly. We had already had occasional email correspondence in which I had suggested that we publish a collection of his work. After our meeting, however, started a game of cat-and-mouse that we were still playing when he died. Except that by the time we last met in November 2001, it was more like Tom and Jerry. By then I had seen John play the same game with other people who wanted something from him. It was almost a test of endurance, resolve, interest, or love maybe. Anyway I wouldn't let go, kept coming back for more and so did he.

The problem was that John simply wasn't *satisfied* with anything that he had written. He considered all of his writing to be flawed 'work in progress'. How, then, could he agree to the publication of it in anything that hinted that it might represent his 'final word' on anything? Had he been younger or in better health he might either have shown me the door or rewritten some of his papers to account for his more up-to-date ideas. On this point, let me explain that when I visited him for five days in November 2001 to discuss this collection, and another publishing project, the majority of the time was spent in enthusiastic discussion on points of theory. With great purpose, John thrust upon me quotes from Freud and his own latest notes on the unconscious, together with exhortations that I and others complete his project of dismantling the unnecessary edifice of psychoanalytic theory. He wanted to update his countertheory of transference and write more on his idea of neurological innocence. With a smile and a twinkle in his eye he explained that he would start tomorrow.

WHY THIS BOOK IS A 'WORK IN PROGRESS' AND WHAT I MEAN BY 'INVITATIONS TO THINK'

In the preparations for this book, John opened up his personal archives to me. He expressed deep regret that after Carl Rogers' death he had thrown away boxes of valuable papers and correspondence which he realised might now have great historical significance. Our rifling through his filing cabinets, during which I would rescue documents from his junk pile, was frequently punctuated by him saying, with a sad sigh, 'If you think that's interesting, you should have seen what I threw away'.

In the quote I used above from his Editorial, Tony Merry says that many of John's ideas 'wait patiently to be rediscovered' (2002, p. 1). This book is an opportunity for us all to discover something new. During this search for notes, papers and correspondence, we discovered unpublished articles, discussion papers, presentations and notes, a few of which quite simply enthralled me. They were not 'fit for publication' in the traditional sense, but they were such vibrant expositions of a 'work in progress' that I wondered how I might include them in this book. Most were circulated as papers for discussion or prepared for verbal presentation. Either way, such writing has a special place in the development of academic ideas in that it is not meant to be read in the same way that a book is read. Often such pieces are ice-breakers, or fire-starters (forgive the figurative clash) and it is a question of not minding the quality but feeling the width. Some conceal undiscovered gems, others are kicks up the backside. You must be assured that I am not apologising for anything here, just explaining that some of the work included in this book would usually never see the light of day in the publishing sense. They are 'sketches'; unrefined, almost rude, invitations for the reader to think, discuss and maybe, if so taken, to pick up the baton.

The whole field (if indeed it is only one field) of relationships, mental health and the human condition is a work in progress, but most of the people I know do not think they should be the ones to make a contribution. Wrong. Either we believe that what is most personal is most universal, or we surrender to the 'expert' interpretation of our lives and dreams. So I have included the hitherto unpublished work in this volume to invite you (and myself) to join the discussion. And what a discussion! From the basic elements of life in 'Birth Certificate', through the thoughts on motivation in 'To Feel Alive', to another tilt at the roots of mental unease in 'Secrets and the Psychology of Secrecy', we are invited to think about, talk to each other, and refine our ideas on, what it is to be human.

A DECLARATION OF PRINCIPLES

In a couple of papers and notes John refers to his 'declaration of principles'. My short acquaintance with John led me to see him as a person for whom principles (and the struggle to live by them) were central to his life. His principles were the foundations of his professional thinking and practice, touchstones against which he judged his own work — and that of others. We all have such creeds, some of us have accepted them from religious texts, others of us have had them burned into us by life and still others of us have forged them ourselves through experience. But unlike John Shlien, few of us write them down. This is both brave and foolhardy, for here he has given us a rod with which to beat him if he fails to reach the mark. I am pleased to report, then, that the right to fail figures prominently in one of his principles.

I include them here, not so that those so inclined can judge him, but so that we can get another impression of John Shlien the man. They are also a further invitation to discussion. And finally they help create a context for this body of work. The reader will see these principles showing through the chapters one way or another — sometimes clearly stated (see below), other times providing the driving power behind a point. They might seem mysterious, or impenetrable right now, but my hope is that they will take on colour and life as you read this book. Principles one to five appear in Chapter 16 of this volume and Principle 7 appears in Chapter 6, and the Merleau-Ponty (1956) quote he got the idea from is in Chapter 11 on page 152. Principle 6 was a hand-written (double underlined) insertion in lecture-notes containing the remaining principles and is referred to in Chapter 16. It refers to the tendency to use the term 'person-centred' to refer to anything that vaguely puts an individual at the centre of a process. John has no quarrel with people developing new, innovative or unique methods as long as they don't pinch the term 'person-centred' saying,

> What I hope is that they will do what they want to do, and *call it what it is.*
> It is simply not acceptable to pour new wine into old bottles, especially since it is the *labels* that are the sought after objects. (p. 218–19, this volume)

I don't know what readers will make of these principles at this stage (and I think it would be a mistake for me to try to explain or interpret them any more than I have done already). I do have a clear idea of what they mean to me. At the very least they are an invitation for me, and you, to subject our own principles to scrutiny. John Shlien's principles, and the amplifications are, in his own words:

> 1. All theory is autobiographical.
> 2. No theory is universal. If it claims to be, it exaggerates, and has a totalitarian tendency, because the client is unique, has the right to fail as well as succeed and is the *main factor* in success.
> 3. In the history of ideas, everything is personal.
> 4. The main human problem is: how to lead an honorable life.
> 5. My objectives are clarity and cleanliness.
> 6. Do what you want. *Call it what it is.*
> 7. Everyone knows everything. This is not a theory of knowledge, it is that you, I, we, know everything about ourselves. There may be defenses, denials, cover-ups, secrets, faults and interferences and overloads in memory, but we know . . . we know. We are the ultimate source.

HOW THIS BOOK IS ORGANISED

You have already had the opportunity to read the forewords of Goff Barrett-Lennard, Ronald Levant, Dave Mearns and Alberto Zucconi. Each person influenced by John Shlien and each a person of influence on others in their turn. It was my intention that this should be published during John's life, and in addition,

I would have liked him to have read these appreciations.

The organisation of the book is entirely my own doing — I have only a dim notion of whether John would have approved. I may have invented themes that John never intended, or put things together in ways that would cause him offence, maybe some of his close colleagues will let me know.

This introduction (and acknowledgements) is followed immediately by biographical details which John sent to me when asked for 100 words on himself for inclusion in another book. This is to cater for Tony Merry's suggestion that readers might like to meet 'John Shlien the man'. My own feeling is that John Shlien the man is unmistakably clear and present in all of his writing, but this may add an extra dimension for those who never met him in person. Then the book proper starts with a 'story' titled 'Birth Certificate' which has appeared here and there over the years.

I have divided the rest of the work into four sections each representing a theme in John's work: Psychological Health; A Literalist Approach; Applications; and The Position of Client-Centered Therapy. With the exception of Section 2, each section contains some previously published material and some unpublished material. Some sections are organised to show a development of ideas (maybe the chapters are in chronological order, but not necessarily), other chapters are not linked at all other than by the general topic of the section. I have tried to give some better indication of this in the introductions to each section. Again, I have to cross my fingers that I have got this more right than wrong. At our last meeting John and I discussed many things, but none have been of much use to me in the final, detailed preparation of this volume.

For example, through conversations and correspondence, and in conjunction with reading his work, it became clearer to me how much John was influenced by existentialist writings. He certainly admired existentialist writers such as Merleau-Ponty and Sartre (calling the latter a 'genius' and basing his (Shlien's) theory of psychosis on the Sartrean notion of 'bad faith'). He took this further in his work on embarrassment anxiety and in his 'principle' that human mental health in the 20th/21st century pivots on the problem of how to lead an honourable life. I did not get the opportunity to explore these avenues with him any further, but now have to make do with extrapolation, which is really educated guesswork.

The book was to have concluded with the transcript of a brief interview I did with John. Although we agreed that I could include this, we didn't complete that part of the project since John only agreed to be interviewed on the basis that he would also interview me. His health was failing faster than I realised and he never did get to interview me.

I received many generous offers of help from John's friends and colleagues when preparing this book. He obviously had a great (if variable) impact upon those that met him — the phrase 'love him or hate him' comes to mind. As an example of the many unsolicited tributes to John that were sent to me, I have included, as an appendix, the articulate 'Memorial Minute on the Life and Work of John M. Shlien, Ph.D.', by William R. Rogers, Michael J. Nakkula and Chester M. Pierce. Neill Watson, an ex-student of John's, forwarded it to me explaining that Bill Rogers, a client-centred therapist, was supervised by John at the University of Chicago Counseling Center, and was John's colleague and friend at Harvard. The Memorial Minute was shared with the Faculty of Education on May 1, 2003 and published in the *Harvard University Gazette* on May 15, 2003.

A FINAL NOTE

If you have read this far you will get a feel for my personal involvement in this book. I hope I have done John Shlien and his work justice for three reasons. First, I want to get it right for John. Second, it is important to get it right for 'us', that is the community of client-centred and person-centred practitioners worldwide. It is important that our ideas are thought of as substantial and respectable, and I want to make that more possible, not less possible, with this book. Finally I want to get it right for me. I certainly don't want my presentation of John's work to be sycophantic or become an out-and-out homage to him — he would have chastised me in no uncertain terms had he suspected that. I was fascinated to read in Ronald Levant's foreword (p. iv) how he sought John's approval and I know myself well enough to realise how much I would have wanted his approval for my effort in putting together this collection, had he lived to see it.

Pete Sanders
Llangarron, May 2003

REFERENCES

Hart, J.T. & Tomlinson, T.M. (1970). *New Directions in Client-Centered Therapy.* Boston: Houghton Mifflin.

Levant, R.F. & Shlien, J.M. (1984). *Client-Centered Therapy and The Person-Centered Approach: New Directions in Theory, Research and Practice.* New York: Praeger.

Lewis, M.K., Rogers, C.R. & Shlien, J.M. (1959). Time-Limited, Client-Centered Psychotherapy: Two Cases. In Burton, A. (Ed.) *Case Studies in Counseling and Psychotherapy,* pp. 309–52.

Merleau-Ponty, M. (1956). What is phenomenology? *Cross Currents, 6,* 59–70.

Merry, T. (2002). Editorial. *Person-Centred Practice, 10* (1), pp. 1–3.

Shlien, J.M. (1957). Time-Limited Psychotherapy: An Experimental Investigation of Practical Values and Theoretical Implications. *Journal of Counseling Psychology, 4* (4), pp. 318–22.

ACKNOWLEDGEMENTS

There are several people without whose contributions, this book would never have seen the light of day. Most of these contributions are invisible to the reader. What has struck me in the preparation of the material is just how many people wanted to see this published and were prepared to put themselves out to help in various ways. Most important of all is my friend and colleague Tony Merry. Not only has he looked at drafts, helped with the structure, the selection of work, made reassuring noises at crucial moments and bought me drinks in the pub, but he also helped convince John that this project was a good idea. And on the latter point, I also have to thank Barbara Brodley, Jerold Bozarth and Ned Gaylin for the gentle pressure they applied at crucial times. Barbara also reviewed the manuscript for me. Sandy Green has given me invaluable assistance with the administration of the book and proofreading, and she gave me essential support and feedback on the quality of the whole project.

The copyrights for some of the chapters in this book are held by individuals and institutions who have been exceedingly generous in granting permission to reprint gratis: thanks go to The American Psychological Association, Joseph Hart, the Harvard Graduate School of Education, Ronald F. Levant and Peter Lang Publishers. However, I have been unable to trace the current copyright holders for the material appearing in Chapters 2 and 11, despite some effort. If any reader has information that might help in this matter, please contact the publishers.

I would like to thank Ronald F. Levant, Dave Mearns, Goff Barrett-Lennard and Alberto Zucconi for writing forewords in the middle of their busy lives. I want particularly to thank Goff for his gentle and reassuring support from thousands of miles away. He straightened out some historical details for me and was one of my touchstones to determine whether I had gone too far in my interpretation of John's work. Soon everyone who worked at the Chicago Counseling Center with Carl Rogers will be gone, an era will have passed and we will have no one to turn to to check myth against memory.

Finally I am grateful to Helen Shlien for her hospitality and continued gracious enthusiasm and patience, and Laura Shlien for her help after John's death.

A NOTE ON SPELLING

It has been next to impossible to implement a consistent policy regarding British/ American spellings. It is not appropriate to alter John Shlien's original writings, and as the book progressed my introductions and interpolations in my own voice as editor started to look odd with British spellings. Readers will have to be flexible!

Prologue

BIRTH CERTIFICATE

One of the great experiences of my life is to watch the opening, unfolding, of a poppy.

I do this every year. Today, it happened for the first time this spring. Takes an hour or two.

My wife called me when she saw it on the hillside. I ran up, not to miss it, but it had 29 minutes still to go.

The poppy is hidden inside a green cone, which is its 'cap'. As the poppy swells, it (water) forces the cone to slide upward. The poppy is a folded spiral, so the cap turns slightly, slowly twisting upward.

It didn't seem to make a full revolution. As the cone rises, the color of the poppy shows in a moist, fascinating, tender blaze at its base. It makes you want to see more.

Near the end, there is a strong temptation to 'play Doctor', to assist in this birth. The poppy really doesn't need me. It has its own strength, in its own time, and only my vanity, and impatience, pushes me to act. But there is some kind of prohibition for the witness. Let this thing unfold!

It has an exquisite design, whether through adaptation or/and creation! Further, some research on egg-born creatures shows that the infant needs to crack the shell itself, from inside, if it is to have its full strength. So know the temptation, yes, but why tamper? Who needs it? (I do, but not that much, having seen the whole thing many times.)

Finally, the cap drops off, the wind blows it away, and the gorgeous flower opens to full view. I don't know what else it is doing, to/for itself or its world, but it has done a thing of beauty for me.

I told a little boy about it. He wanted to know how the plant got its muscles. I tried to explain chemical transfer (sodium/calcium?) in the membrane, but failed.

Anyone know?

I remembered Titchener's saying that empathy 'stretched the muscles of his mind . . .' It seems to me that the 'mind' has no more muscles than the plant, and that the idea of muscle is a metaphor imposed upon the plant/mind/engine/whatever, to 'explain', in terms of our own physical experience, another phenomenon which has its own phenomenology.

Maybe you think I am talking about psychotherapy, or something like that.

No — just about a poppy.

You could look it up.

John Shlien

John M. Shlien
1918–2002

A SELF-PEN-PORTRAIT BY JOHN SHLIEN

I was born in 1918, the year World War I ended with an epidemic of influenza which killed fifty million humans on this planet — eighteen million in the USA, including my father, of whom I have no memory. This left me in the almost undivided attention of my wonderful mother, as the only child in a large family of doting uncles and aunts, two of whom were creative, unhappy, neurotics. This was part of my education.

I learned to read at age three. At age four, I was reading to the neighborhood children (and more adult material to myself). To a large degree, I am self taught. That does not mean well educated. My school career was erratic. Sometimes promoted too soon, sometimes refusing school entirely, expelled for misbehavior, etc. My ambitions were along the lines of jazz musician, race driver, brain surgeon, engineer/inventor. None achieved.

At the beginning of WWII, I was inducted into the army, and had the good luck to make a perfect score on the AGCT (Army General Classification Test).[1] Since there was no college training to justify this, I was forced to take the test twice again, under observation by the military police. This brought me to the attention of the officer in command of the testing operations, who put me on the staff administering and scoring those tests. Since I asked to be in the cavalry, and was told that it was being converted from horses to tanks, I suggested staying in the testing field. Thus, was sent to the newly formed Air Force Research Units,

---

[1.] The purpose of the AGCT was to serve as a measure of 'general learning ability' that could be used to assign new recruits to jobs. [Ed.]

where pilots were selected by still more tests.

When the war ended, I went to the University of Chicago, where Veterans were tested for placement in the college. Knowing so well the scoring systems for multiple choice, etc., and after quick studies in the Museum of Science, and college texts, I passed out of the college (still uneducated) and went directly to graduate school, intending to work in cultural anthropology. On this account, I met Carl Rogers, whose ideas I intended to examine from the standpoint of 'the sociology of knowledge'. That required some close acquaintance with the theory and practice, i.e., taking some of his courses. The rest, as they say, is history.

The first degree or diploma or credential I ever received in my life was the Ph.D. Later, Harvard University gave me an Honorary A.M., following an old rule (since discarded) that only Harvard men could teach Harvard men. At this point, it might be said of me:

'He is a Ph.D. from the University of Chicago, where he served in every rank from instructor to full professor, suffering thwarted ambitions to be a jazz musician, a brain surgeon and a racing driver all the while. In 1967, he was invited to Harvard as Professor and Chair of a new program (of his own invention), an interdepartmental/cross faculty administrative nightmare (Medical School, Divinity School, Psychology and Social Relations, and the Graduate School of Education). Title: Clinical Psychology and Public Practice. Wonderful idea. Difficult to fulfill. At first succeeded, then failed, phased out after a dozen years, when he retired.

What he loves best: small children and big dogs.'

Section 1

Psychological Health

EDITOR'S INTRODUCTION

On his appointment to the University of Chicago, Carl Rogers created an atmosphere in which everyone, graduate students and faculty, could share ideas. That atmosphere of informal sharing was later formalised by Jack Butler as a system of discussion papers. Rough drafts would be circulated as a 'University of Chicago Counseling Center Discussion Paper'. There are many priceless treasures buried in the metal boxes which contain an almost complete set of these papers from around 1954 through to the 1970s.[1] Some of the key concepts in Client-Centred Therapy were first aired in the discussion papers; the majority, however, cannot have caused enough of a stir to warrant further development.

The first three papers in this section started out as University of Chicago Counseling Center Discussion Papers and they bring to life the subtitle of this book: *Invitations to think about client-centered therapy and the person-centered approach.* We can read, think and join in the discussions stimulated by these papers since the subjects are as apposite to psychology and the helping professions today as they were then.

The first paper 'To Feel Alive' seems to have passed by largely unnoticed circa

---

[1.] The discussion papers are currently kept jointly by the Person-Centered Archive held by Alberto Segrera at the Universidad Iberoamericana, Mexico and the Chicago Counseling Center.

1964, although it was the subject of correspondence between Rogers and Shlien when Rogers was at the Western Behavioural Sciences Institute, in which Carl encouraged John to refine and extend his ideas, saying '. . . the idea deserves a more careful working out. I found it to be more meaningful than most of the stuff on motivation' (Rogers, 1964). Although some of the ideas in this paper surface as echoes in other of John's writings, unfortunately he never did develop this into anything other than 'A thought on motivation'. It is one of the most stimulating papers I have read for years — as a psychology undergraduate I was most dissatisfied when my personal experience did not fit the theories of motivation, whether behavioural drive-theory or Freudian theory. John's ideas in this paper make more sense to me. Above all, I find these ideas resonate with my everyday experience; it doesn't take a great leap of my imagination to apply these seeds of ideas to so-called 'self-harm', suicide and a range of other reactions to human distress.

The front cover of a 'University of Chicago Counseling Center Discussion Paper' circa 1956. The inside front cover bears the text:

COUNSELING CENTER DISCUSSION PAPERS ARE CIRCULATED PRIVATELY TO STIMULATE DISCUSSION AND HAVE THE TENTATIVE CHARACTER OF INFORMAL CONVERSATIONS.

TO PROTECT THE TENTATIVE CHARACTER OF THE DISCUSSION PAPERS, THEY SHOULD NOT BE SUBJECT TO CRITICAL APPRAISAL OR COMMENT IN PUBLICATIONS WITHOUT CLEARANCE FROM THE AUTHOR. HOWEVER, ACKNOWLEDGEMENT BY A WRITER THAT HE [SIC] HAS HAD ACCESS TO DISCUSSION PAPERS IS PERMISSIBLE.

In Chapter 2, 'A Criterion of Psychological Health', John proposes that the ability to listen is not only a condition for successful therapy, but also a criterion of psychological health. It marked the beginnings of his interest in empathy which culminated in his contribution to *Empathy Reconsidered: New directions in psychotherapy* (Bohart and Greenberg, 1997) reprinted as Chapter 12 of this volume.

As the fledgling Client-Centred Therapy quickly established itself, all those associated with Rogers at the University of Chicago worked hard to advance its influence in diverse professional areas. Throughout his life John enjoyed making music and was enthusiastic about the visual arts, painting, photography and sculpture. He valued creativity and was himself creative.

Chapter 3, 'Creativity and Psychological Health', again originally a University of Chicago Counseling Center Discussion Paper (1956), moved forward on two fronts: first it introduced the world of management at work to psychology with a positive, reflective, client-centred flavour. Even though Thomas Gordon had contributed a chapter on 'Group-Centered Leadership and Administration' to Rogers' *Client-Centered Therapy* in 1951, this was still relatively new territory. Second, it is holistic: it considers creativity, not as an abstract human trait, but linked to psychological health; an essential element in an integrated healthy organism.

Academic psychology at the time was more interested in the trait of creativity in the context of a creative person, meaning a person with special talent, a virtuoso musician or artist. Psychologists may also have been interested in the relationship between creativity, genius and madness.

John Shlien was not interested in the creativity of the few, with the rest of us as spectators. Rather he proposed that in order to be fulfilled as persons we must all discover and nurture our personal creativity, and furthermore that that would improve the quality of our lives including getting more satisfaction from the work that we do. It was as a direct result of reading this paper that Ned Gaylin wrote his paper 'On creativeness and psychological well-being' (Wexler and Rice, 1974; Gaylin, 2001).

In 1961 John Shlien wrote a chapter for Arthur Burton's (1961) *Psychotherapy of the Psychoses* which was subsequently abridged and reprinted in Rogers and Stevens, (1967) *Person to Person*. It includes case material and a theory of psychosis which John referred to, tongue in cheek, as a 'work of genius'. He would quickly add that the genius in question is Jean-Paul Sartre — John's theory of human distress leading to complete breakdown being based on Sartre's notions of 'bad faith' (Sartre, 1943/1958). This original 1961 work appears unabridged as Chapter 4.

The theme of internal clarity and honesty, the keeping of good faith with oneself, is continued in Chapter 5 as he explores the effects of secrecy on psychological health and the therapeutic process. He also continues his careful delineation of the differences between Client-Centred Therapy and other therapeutic approaches.

Chapter 6 was written to be spoken, but never tidied up for publication (as was, for example, Chapter 9) and I find it helps me to imagine I am in the audience. I am unapologetic in including a paper that John told me once was 'dumb'. This, then, is not a 'crafted' paper, where the author has rewritten passages to get just the right nuance, the logical progression of ideas, the best flow. But dumb it is not. In addition to adding a couple of small points of clarification and references, I have edited this writing in a number of places just to smooth out the flow of the text — I hope I am not being patronising either to you, the reader, or to John.

The title of the paper is self-explanatory and it does just what the title suggests — it invites us to consider this awkward question, hiding behind which is an even more awkward one: 'What is therapy for?' Although the paper was presented in 1989, this question will always be contemporary wherever and whenever therapy is practised in some form or other. In his exploration of what therapy is for, he suggests that if 'happiness' is an end with no regard to the means, then we should all take pills or potions — a 'solution' resorted to and advocated by many, from those in the pharmaceutical industry to the suppliers in your local night-club. Here is yet another manifestation of John Shlien's enduring conviction that means and ends are indivisible.

I think the paper deserves to be included for no other reason than it contains two of my favourite killer-quotes: the first is ' . . . the most important personal objective in modern civilization is: *how to lead an honorable life*' (a piece of the evidence that John was an existentialist-in-waiting, see p. xiv). The second is a dark prediction: 'In a world where fun has become a commodity . . . Psychotherapy could suffer the worst possible fate. It could become part of the entertainment industry!' There are several such gems in here. My great concern is that John Shlien's warning has already come true in our Western Euro-American culture.

This first section lays one foundation-stone of John Shlien's work. Specifically the link between psychological health and honesty with oneself at all levels from the organismic to the superficial — and conversely how self-deception leads to systemic ill-health. These ideas are not new. Shlien credits Sartre, but doesn't make the, in my view, obvious link between the Sartrean idea of bad faith (with oneself) with the Rogerian formulation of '(in)congruence' (as delineated in Rogers, 1951, pp. 481–533), or Seeman's notion of 'integration' (Seeman, 1983). It is possible that he thought the link was obvious enough. On re-reading this work, however, I cannot help thinking that this clear coupling between existential philosophy and client-centred theory has received insufficient attention and awaits development.

REFERENCES

Bohart, A.C. & Greenberg, L.S. (Eds.) (1997). *Empathy Reconsidered: New directions in psychotherapy.* Washington DC: APA.

Burton, A. (Ed.) (1961). *Psychotherapy of the Psychoses.* New York: Basic Books.

Gaylin, N.L. (2001). *Family, Self and Psychotherapy: A person-centred perspective.* Ross-on-Wye: PCCS Books.

Rogers, C.R. (1951). *Client-Centered Therapy.* Boston: Houghton Mifflin.

Rogers, C.R. (1964). Letter to John Shlien dated August 12.

Rogers, C.R. & Stevens, B. (1967). *Person to Person.* Walnut Creek, CA: Real People Press.

Sartre, J-P. (1943/1958). *Being and Nothingness.* First published in English by Methuen (1958).

Seeman, J. (1983). *Personality Integration: Studies and reflections.* New York: Human Sciences Press.

Wexler, D.A. & Rice, L.N. (Eds.) (1974). *Innovations in Client-Centered Therapy.* New York: Wiley.

CHAPTER 1

To Feel Alive

A thought on motivation

TO FEEL ALIVE

A previous article (on Schizophrenia)[1] contained a brief section on intimacy and responsiveness as sources of 'reaffirmation of being'. In it was an attempt to explain an aberrant behavior on the basis of a common motive — 'the quest for such affirmation is so desperate in a person who has forebodings of his disappearing, or loss of self, that it best explains the sadist, who tries to force, through pain, the responsiveness he needs to bolster his falling sense of selfhood. His urgency makes victims of those from whom he would rather receive love, but he dares not risk rejection since he must have response just to sustain being at all.'

In trying to understand behaviors, the motivational question has become 'responsiveness for what?' To phrase it in somewhat existential terms of 'being' comes close to the point, but masks it. So does the terminology of 'self' and 'selfhood', which creates a theoretical superstructure of great power, but one which casts things at a level of abstraction which is so entirely psychological as to overlook the biological base. Years ago, discussing the 'social self', William James described the horror he would experience if he were to enter a room full of people who ignored him completely, 'cut him dead', showed no response whatever to his touch, his voice, etc. In his vivid description, he concludes that he would consider that the most fiendish punishment possible from which the cruellest bodily tortures would be a relief.

This chapter was written in the early sixties and originally distributed as a University of Chicago Counseling Center Discussion Paper.

[1.] The 'previous article' referred to here was another Counseling Center Discussion Paper, the ideas in which eventually were published as 'A Client-Centered Approach to Schizophrenia: First Approximation' as Chapter 11 in *Psychotherapy of the Psychoses* edited by Arthur Burton. This is reproduced in full with kind permission of the publishers as Chapter 4 in this volume.

Carl Rogers has entered the question 'who needs motives?' and reduced the range to that single purpose which he sees as underlying and explaining all others, i.e., self-actualization.[2] Here too the emphasis is upon the psychological elaboration of the 'self', and all motives reduce to its growth, enhancement and maintenance.

There is, however, a somewhat different way of looking at the problem which appears to me to give a still more fundamental explanation to wide varieties of behavior. The basic motive of behavior is to enable the behaver to *feel alive*. This is perhaps implied, certainly not contradicted, by theories of existential 'being', of self-actualization, of theories of growth and excitement, but it may increase our understanding to explicitly recognise that the organism seeks to confirm its own *sense of aliveness*, by evoking responses which will stimulate its sensory apparatus in such a way as to fill and refill the fundamental need to know that it is a nervous, sensing organism capable of *re*action.

It is my guess that this is a 'learned' motive, in that the organism is not born with this motive in operation, but the 'wired-in' capacity must develop through experience. As an infant develops its ability to differentiate between itself and the rest of the world, feels bruises, warmth, cold, hard, soft, even gas pains, and soon sees attitudes represented by smiles, frowns, harsh sounds, etc., this infant becomes aware of the primary capacity to feel. ('I feel therefore I am' preceded 'cognito', etc.) Through sensory input it knows that it is alive, and when the signals of experiencing diminish, it is threatened; when they stop, it is functionally dead. Therefore, the one steady purpose is to assure not only that one can stimulate a response, but that even more essential, one can respond to the responsiveness, i.e., *feel alive*.

There is, of course, much uncertainty in theories of motivation. Opinion ranges from 'no motivation, only behavior' to 'for each behavior a specific need'. Although some motivational analysis is much overdone, two tendencies seem to distinguish two types. There is the investigative type who wants to ask 'why?' of behavior, and there is the observational-synthesizing type who wants to know 'how?' the mechanisms of behavior operate. To my mind, 'why?' is a journalistic-political type of question, 'how?' is more scientific. The way in which the question 'why?' is approached by different orientations of therapy seems to distinguish between the psychoanalytic and the more existential therapies. The former seems dedicated to historical-analytic searches for a complex of motives, the latter dedicated to more instant recognition of the rush of experience, with only a few

---

[2] In the correspondence referred to in my introduction to this section (p. 6), Rogers draws to Shlien's attention that in his most recent work he (Rogers) deliberately refers to 'the actualizing tendency' rather than 'actualization'. Rogers writes: 'This is not accidental. I realize that it is the organismic tendency toward fulfilment which is important, not just the actualization itself' (Rogers, 1964). [Ed.]

simple purposive motives. I would side with Rogers in the general effort to reduce motivation to some simple basic set, not to eliminate motives but to try to understand as much behavior as possible in the same context. If motivation can be sufficiently settled so that it does not offer a constant distraction, behaviors themselves can be more seriously attended to.

It is not a startling new revelation, this theory that the basic motive is '*to feel alive*'. Not only is it more or less implied in other theories, but it is enunciated informally every time someone takes a deep breath of fresh air and says 'It's good to be alive'. The theory needs, however, to be made more explicit as a theory, and to be raised to the level of its true worth, whatever that may be. (Probably the theory needs a name in order to become a credible identity.) Ultimately, this theory will have to be validated by phenomenological studies. Meanwhile, what kind of explanatory power has it? What kinds of observations lead to, or support it? (Let us assume that the strength of the motive is, like other universal characteristics, distributed through a range of individual differences.)

The sadist in the first example tortured another person, in theory, to force a response of love, or something approximating love to him (obedience, unveiling of secrets, intimacy of some sort). This effort was interpreted as seeking response from another to bolster his own sense of self by proving that he, the sadist, was capable of evoking that quality of responsiveness in another. But a deeper level of interpretation is that the sadist is trying to fulfill his need to bring about a response or responses to which he can respond, so that he knows he is alive.

A cat may be interpreted as sadistic when it 'plays' with a mouse. For all we know, there is no sense of cruelty whatever in the cat. It could be that he simply follows an instinct to cripple but not kill, thus keeping his meat fresh but immobile for a longer time. But beyond just nourishment to stay organically alive, suppose that the cat also needs continued stimulation from an external source of a kind which exercises the cat's peculiar neuromuscular system and so assures the animal that it is *functionally* alive. If we observe the play or early activity of the kitten (often assumed to be a preparation for mouse-hunting), we can see that the later mouse-hunting and its perhaps incidental killing is much along the same lines that the kitten's *early* experience would dictate. The cat is behaving in a way which confirms to a cat that it is alive. The longer the victim lives, the more it fulfills the need of the cat to know that it can cause effects and feel reactive to those effects, thus feel its own aliveness. (The 'big cats' — lions — are observed in their natural environments to kill quickly, often breaking the back or neck with a first blow. This might indicate a primary hunger need, or a sufficiency of excitation through the stalking process itself, or might mean that the more powerful and natural an animal, the less it needs to depend on invented or extended stimulation. In human counterpart, the audiences for plays, shows, poetry readings, TV westerns, etc. are more likely to be those whose lives are emptier, who do not produce or encounter drama or excitement in their day-to-day activities.)

There are said to be masochists: people who find pleasure only, or mainly, in pain, and who wish to be treated painfully by others. One interpretation is that they seek punishment. I have seen clients who inflict pain upon themselves. One cut, pinched, and burned herself on occasion, sometimes drawing blood. It was tangible proof, through the feeling of pain, when depression offered no hope of pleasure, that she was *alive*. If it was punishment, it was punishment for not having the courage or capacity to find pleasurable ways of fulfilling the stimulus hunger. Punishment for not being able to feel alive.

The same sort of explanation applies to risk-taking as applies to pain-seeking. The death wish is often invoked in regard to racing drivers, etc. It is not death they seek, but death (from lack of excitement) which they wish to escape. They are, in fact, exhibiting a 'life wish' instead, at the very point where the 'death wish' is interpreted. It is life by exhilaration rather than death by boredom which the adventurer seeks — [Arthur] Schopenhauer says the evils of life, which man can escape only in nirvana, are pain and boredom.

So far, the discussion has hinged upon pain and danger.[3] That is an artifact of the argument. It is not that pain is primary, on the contrary, *pleasure* is the real 'reality principle'. When it fails, pain is a good substitute — second best — but better than no input at all. And since pleasure is often hard to receive, pain is all the more frequent and its meanings need to be understood. Pleasure is primary, and its reward is the main reality principle. Constant pleasure is not possible, thus pain has some positive psychological value in filling the need to feel alive. For that matter, when physical circumstances are so fortunate as to make lives mainly pleasurable, it appears that people will seek to create various conditions of psychological hardship for themselves. Otherwise, they suffer from ennui, become effete, die of boredom, disintegrate in *la dolce vita*.

Creativity may easily be understood in terms of the motive to feel alive. One builds, exerts energy, perceives the results, feels *alive*. Creativity is easy to appreciate, because it produces things and is good for us, but destruction is threatening, and therefore not easy to understand or appreciate. It is often called 'senseless' destruction. From the standpoint of the motive to feel alive, however, it is understandable in the same terms as is creativity. Except that it most often serves only the purposes of the destroyer. The boy who turns in a false alarm to see the fire engines race, the child who knocks over the pile of blocks he has painstakingly set up, or stirs up an ant hill, is behaving for his own ends, though at the expense of others, in order to cause effects which he can sense as the necessary signals of his own aliveness. Often, we notice, the most carefully built and attractive structures

---

3. In a handwritten note, John had inserted: 'The pain referred to here is periodic pain — no one seeks the steady pain of arthritis or cancer'. [Ed.]

seem to be singled out for destruction (beauty attracts malevolence). The more perfect the object destroyed, the greater the sensation in the destroyer. But it is not destruction for destruction's sake, nor because perfection is hated, but because perfection is valued and its destruction arouses signals of aliveness in the destroyer. Watch a boy break a pane of glass; if you can free yourself of value judgments about the destruction of property, etc., you may see the possibilities of excitement: risk-taking, tingling sound, shattering visual patterns. An act which has, for the individual, creative aspects. He feels more alive as a result of it.

The 'expansion of consciousness' through use of so-called 'recreational' drugs fits this theory of motivation. The user seeks to feel more alive. The electric and other convulsive therapies, if they have any value, might depend on the ability to arouse heightened awareness of feeling alive, through an exaggerated stress reaction if nothing else. Stimulus deprivation may be as frightening as it is precisely because it diminishes the signals of aliveness and approaches functional death. Stimulus hunger, the exploratory drive, the need to be loved, to be needed, self-realisation, the problem of 'aimlessness' in psychopathology, the meaning of the 'law of effort', perhaps the need for dreaming during sleep; all of these can be explained in terms of the motive 'need to feel alive'.

Sexual behavior seems to hinge a good deal on this motive, since it is thought to involve curiosity, cruelty, and pleasure components at least. Masturbation, and an important meaning of the orgasm as a reassuring signal, also fit the theory. So does the post-orgasmic emptiness sometimes reported in the literature. In the area of interpersonal relations in sex, this motive can make many behaviors comprehensible.

Questions come to mind: Why does a boy want the dog to chase the ball? Why do spectators rise and cheer to see the horses race? Why do generals want to see armies move? In all cases the act may be somewhat an end in itself, but fundamentally relates to the value of the event in making the perceiver feel a sense of his own reactive aliveness.

These are some notes toward a theory (of motivation). It has been simmering for some time, starting with the section on isolation and response in the schizophrenia chapter[4] aided by thoughts and conversation of colleagues, Fiske and Maddi, Butler and Rice, and first set forth in a recent seminar with Bakan. In a sketchy outline it is presented here for criticism and comment. Perhaps it is what everybody knows, or perhaps it is not very important. I have dropped the idea many times, and it keeps coming back to me with some force. It seems to be a genuine motive, it may be one which is learned in an observable way, and one which gives alternative explanations for many behaviors, especially ones classed

---

[4.] I take it that John is referring here to the chapter in Burton (1961) reprinted as Chapter 4 in this volume. [Ed.]

as pathological. Those we think of as healthy happen to partake already of this sense of aliveness quite naturally. Those whose ability to partake is impaired will go to different, possibly unacceptable lengths (to themselves and others) to feel alive. Granted that this is roughly drafted, poorly worded, lacking definition, I still would like to offer it for reaction to the sense of it.

REFERENCES

Burton, A. (1961). *Psychotherapy of the Psychoses*. New York: Basic Books.
Rogers, C.R. (1964). Letter written to John Shlien dated August 12.

CHAPTER 2

A Criterion of Psychological Health

During a recent panel discussion,[1] Lundin made the point that while all therapies claim some success, criteria of success vary in such a way as to make these claims both questionable and incomparable. We had witnessed the demonstration of a variety of techniques invented or modified by some very competent group therapists whose vitality was evident in their work. I suggested that *the health of the therapist is transmitted to the client*, and that this may account, in part, for the 'some success' of all therapies. By the health of the therapist, I meant his aliveness, his alertness, his openness, and freshness in using whatever techniques he has chosen to represent his originality and sensitivity. I would like to develop the meaning of this therapeutic behavior in such a way as to set a criterion of psychological health applicable to any person or form of therapy.

The criterion is simple to name. It is *the ability to listen*. Though simple to name, it is not easy to do. This means to listen to another person, to be able to understand and if desired to reproduce the essential thoughts and feelings he expresses, without being impeded by the reverberations in oneself. Such listening can be operationally defined, and measured in graded performance.

It has been taken for granted that the *therapist* should have this ability to listen, and it is generally thought that the therapist should be in a psychologically healthy state.[2] The function of listening provided by the therapist is thought to

Originally a University of Chicago Counseling Discussion Paper (1956). First published in *Group Psychotherapy*, Volume IX, No.2, August 1956. Special thanks to two staff colleagues, E. Gendlin and G. Barrett-Lennard, for their helpful comments. [JMS.] I have been unable to trace the current copyright holders. [Ed.]

[1.] At the February 1956 meeting of the Midwest Society for Group Psychotherapy and Psychodrama. Discussants besides this writer were Drs. J. Masserman, Chairman, R. Driekurs, W. Lundin, F. Perls, Mr. Ben Wright.

[2.] This is not to demand that the therapist be in perfect health. There are those who believe that the therapist must bear some wounds himself in order to 'empathically' understand. Still he should at least be free enough of his *own* pain to give his attention to the client.

be an opportunity for the client to be heard, to air his problems, to be understood. It surely is that, but it is also a demonstration of health by the therapist. In the act of listening, the therapist presents his vitality and awareness and readiness to meet new experience. It is his own health which enables him to listen. Then, if psychological health is contagious (somewhat as physical disease), listening accomplishes two therapeutic efforts at once. Is psychological health contagious? When positive attitudes such as relaxation, security, confidence, joy, friendliness, are perceived in another person with whom one is in close contact for an hour or more, does the perceiver feel some of those attitudes within himself as a result?[3] That he does is one assertion of this paper.

As an example: a client is tense, anguished, scattered. The therapist is relaxed, integrated, unwavering in his sympathetic understanding, but still relaxed. Besides listening, he presents the aspect of steady, secure attention in the face of the client's pain. How would a client feel about that? As one person put it, 'I realize how much his listening and understanding mean to me. Then I become aware of *his ability to do that.*' The client recognizes the health of the therapist, beyond his skill.

How is it 'transmitted' and, more important, how does it help? The mechanism of transmission is unknown. Therefore, the observation of the phenomenon is uncertain, and we are forced into conjecture and analogy. 'Contagious' simply means that health is 'catching' but does not seriously postulate psychological germ theory. The idea of models, and learning, imitation, or introjection, comes easily to mind. That may be, and much of what we value we have gained this way. But I am suggesting that health is 'sensed' in the way warmth is felt. It is not learned, and one does not have to learn to feel better for it. Perhaps appreciation of health is built into the organism as is appreciation of 'warmth'?

The other assertion is that listening, carefully defined, should be taken as a fully-fledged behavioral criterion of health. If it represents health and security for the therapist, why should it not be a measure of those qualities in the client? Perhaps we are divided in our feeling about what listening means. We may think of the listener as passive or submissive or ignorant. We tend to think of listening as a commonplace — what everyone does or can do all the time. (Actually, it is so rare that it has to be institutionalized, and paid for as psychotherapy.) Also, listening runs counter to what some observers consider to be our cultural characteristics of success. The need to 'sell yourself'[4] stresses the value of capturing attention and persuading — of talking rather than listening. But clinically speaking, we have valued listening, too. Comprehension is taken as one of the main signs of intelligence. The inability to listen, to comprehend, to follow instructions, to

---

[3.] More often we note that some people depress us, that we would like to avoid them.

[4.] See also, for instance, G. Gorer, *The American People*. New York: Norton, 1948.

communicate, has been considered cause for reproachful judgment ranging from stupidity to insanity. The person who 'can't understand a word I say' is likely to be hospitalized. When, as a patient, he shows signs of hearing by responding in such a way that he seems to have listened, the therapist is likely to say that he has 'made contact' — and to take this as an indication of improvement.

From both experimental evidence and common experience, it is clear that anxiety, pain, fatigue — all conditions of *ill health* — make for a restricted perception. Rather than listening comprehendingly, the insecure person is likely to talk too much.

Self-understanding has long been considered a measure of mental health. This surely does not mean, though, that to be absorbed in listening to oneself is an ultimate ideal. It would seem healthier to be free, having the ability to hear oneself readily, to listen to another. In these terms, a successful case of therapy would be described thus: a disturbed person (X) is listened to by a person (Y) who is (at least momentarily) healthier; in the process of being heard, X begins to listen more deeply and fully to himself; eventually X is able to extend his listening beyond himself to others.

All of the above aims at the conclusion that the better one's health, the more fully one can listen. Is this conclusion reversible in the sense that learning to listen (genuinely, not assuming a posture) may be productive of health? If so, it would help to explain why the practice of therapy is 'auto-therapeutic', as many therapists find it. It would also suggest that group therapy provides an especially advantageous opportunity to listen, to learn to listen, and thus to experience a state of health.[5]

In the past, mental health has been a 'residual' concept — the absence of disease. We need to do more than describe improvement in terms of, say, 'anxiety reduction'. We need to say what the person can *do* as health is achieved. As the emphasis on pathology lessens, there have been a few recent efforts toward positive conceptualizations of mental health. Notable among these are Carl Rogers' 'Fully Functioning Person', A. Maslow's 'Self-Realizing Persons', and W. Henry's current work with the theory of 'Affective Complexity'. Offered here as a contribution to the developing *positive* conceptualization of health is the idea that listening is more than a means to the end of communication.[6] This one dimension of therapy, listening, can be a cause, an effect, a representation, a criterion, and possibly a means of achieving mental health.

In brief, it has been suggested that listening is a therapeutic method which is also an expression of psychological health. Three conclusions stem from this: (1) The client gains health through contact with this expression of it. (2) An effective

---

[5.] Perhaps in the same way that exercise develops muscles.
[6.] Rogers, C. R. (1952). Communication: Its blocking and facilitation. *Etc.*, Vol. IX, No. 2.

psychotherapist must be one who invents or selects a method of expressing some of his originality or creativity[7] so that he can present himself to the client as a vitally interested, alert person and that means listening. (3) Listening can be a fully-fledged criterion of the success of therapy, definable, measurable, and useful to any orientation.

[7.] Of course, not just to be different. That happens, too. But the therapist who simply takes over a traditional method without eventually, in effect, reinventing it for himself will find it time-worn in the most dulling sense.

CHAPTER 3

Creativity and Psychological Health

I

Lately, creativity has become respectable. It used to be viewed with scorn or suspicion, as if it meant impractical and unmanly things — arts, crafts, cooking with herbs, the crazy inventor, mad scientist, odd types in the village. Now it is seen as desirable and a very practical quality. An outstanding engineering school offers courses in 'creative thinking'; several universities have set up projects to study it; industry shows a keen interest in it.[1] Now the artist and the creative person does not need the help of a wealthy patron. He is widely admired and highly paid; he may well be a patron himself, supporting libraries, scholarships, and the like.

Why has the climate changed so? Perhaps because, as David Riesman [US sociologist, 1909–2002, Ed.] and others point out, we are shifting, in our economy and ideology, from scarcity to abundance. This means more leisure time, some of which is used to seek out and develop new ideas. The technological base is growing so fast that we could now have nearly any invention we might conceive. Ideas are almost all that are needed. (Westinghouse recently advertised its corps of 12,000 scientists: 'At your service. What would you like for them to do for you?') Automation, increased consumption, expanded production, the rapid rate of change and obsolescence, mass communication, and the desire for an ever higher standard of living — these combine to enlarge the demand for new designs and products. Creativity will play a bigger role, and have wider meaning, than ever before.

Given as a talk given at Fall Personnel Conference of the American Management Association, September 1956, New York City.

[1] When Dr. Morris Stein of this University [Chicago, Ed.] opened his study of creativity among research chemists, many more companies than he could accept were eager to participate.

In industry, it is likely that applied creativity will have to spread from the top. First, this is in general the only level at which conditions presently exist for the development, recognition, and reward of creative action. Second, talent for executive levels seems hardest to supply, so it must be enhanced in quality. Third, and most important, top management levels set the tone of action for those below them. Creative output depends heavily on the atmosphere that only a creative executive can establish.

We need, then, to know much more about creativity — who has it? How can it be developed? We can start the discussion with a distinction between two kinds of work; *creation* and *production*. Both are useful. An individual may combine them in varying degrees so that they need not be mutually exclusive, though in practice they often are. Perhaps this is why the so-called 'practical man' scorns the so-called 'creative man' as a 'dreamer', for there is a sharp difference at some points. We tend to forget, though, that nothing is so practical, in a completely utilitarian sense, as a good dream.

Most useful work is *production*. It is improved by being accelerated. It can only lead to more of the same. It is mainly routine. It is learned, as one 'learns a job'. *Creation,* on the other hand, involves novelty and originality. It is not learned; it is invented. It is improved by expansion. It leads to new things, other than itself. This last distinction — that creation leads to other activity while production does not — offers a measure of the degree of creativity in a given invention, and a more useful measure, perhaps, than the apparent complexity of the invention or act. The wheel, for example, is simple (though some cultures still have not thought of it) but it leads to gears, vehicles, motive power, and many other consequences beyond itself. The eight-tone musical scale is less complex than the general relativity theory, or the electronic computer, but, like them, it opens whole worlds of variation and new invention. *The important measure is in the consequence, in terms of further creativity, rather than the complexity of the original invention.*

This same measure might be applied to the creativeness of management. The most effective leadership would be that which facilitates the greatest creative output in subsidiary branches, rather than the one having the most complex control and accountability system. One good idea in the way of policy or atmosphere could lead to innumerable concrete developments in a plant, office or laboratory.

II

For what it is worth, I have offered a distinction between creative and productive work. Here are some of the many possible characteristics which may identify a creative person. Intelligence alone — memory, analytic reasoning, etc. — is of great value and solves production problems, but does not, by itself, constitute the creative approach. The following characteristics are in theoretical terms, though they can be put in measurable terms, and with variations some are being used in current selection research. Let me stress, incidentally, that selection is not the sole, and perhaps not even the primary, problem. You may be able to find devices by which you can recognize people currently in a creative frame of mind. This does not guarantee that they will stay that way, or imply that the 'others' lack creative potential. The main problem may be that of *development*. For the moment, though, here are some descriptive indices of creative behavior, attributes or modes of thought.

1. The creative person exercises choice, taste, discernment. He is not sorting through possibilities with the vague hope that 'something will turn up'. He operates on a hunch, or a hypothesis, which gives him a determined aim. The unique result he achieves might have been reached mechanically by combining all known elements in all possible ways, but that would produce an almost infinite number of useless combinations. The creative act, however, is efficient, precisely because it is *not* mechanical. Even if he stumbles on a 'lucky accident', the creative searcher knows that this fits the direction of his aim.

2. Related to this is a quality so close to the essence of creativity that it is hard to reduce it to any other terms. Besides being nonmechanical, the creative act does not depend on 'retrospective logic' — the kind we ordinarily use. In his book *The Creative Mind*[2] Henri Bergson gives this example. 'Let us take the color orange. As we know red and yellow, we can consider orange red in one sense, yellow in another. But suppose that, orange being what it is, neither red nor yellow had yet appeared in the world. Would orange still be composed of these two colors?' Retrospective logic leads us to say that a created reality in the present can be reduced to the elements that *might* have been compounded to make it in the past. Perhaps this is true, analytically it might seem so, but that is not the logic used in the moment of creation. At that moment, directed by a hunch that it exists, orange is experienced as a simple sensation, not a combination of red and yellow. It is independent of what on later inspection appears to have been the component parts. Except for this forward aim, the effort might as well have been mechanical. One would mix colors on a color wheel until orange appeared, and if it were recognized as what one sought, it would be seen to be the result of combining red and yellow. But that would not be creative. Further, it would seem, on review, that red and yellow had been *inherent* in orange when it was first experienced as a simple sensation. *Now,* you think this is so, but you are looking

---

[2.] Bergson, H. (1946). *The Creative Mind.* New York: Philosophical Library. [Ed.]

backwards, after the fact, while I am trying to explain that creation looks forward. If this were not true, there could be no invention, only discovery. *That* may seem so, too, after the fact. But it is before the fact that matters. In order to *find* the fact, the logic of that moment bears the belief that novelty can truly emerge, like the quantum leap in physics, where the result cannot be predicted, though it can be understood after a combination of elements at certain energy levels takes place. The attitude this logic engenders means that the inventor acts as if he believes something really new could emerge.

3. The creative mode of thought exceeds obvious boundaries of a problem. This requires a sense of freedom, which enables the person to range imaginatively around the problem. Creative thinking has been defined as 'the ability to destroy old gestalts in favor of new ones'. Intelligence can supply alternatives. Creativity makes room for them. A simple illustration is the parlor puzzle in which the task is to draw four straight connected lines through nine dots without retracing. The only solution lies in 'going outside the field' by breaking the apparent rectangle.

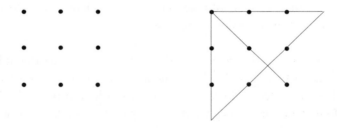

4. Another quality is illustrated by the problem posed when six matchsticks are placed on a desk. The task is to form them into four equilateral triangles, each side the length of a matchstick. On a two-dimensional plane this is impossible. Standing the tripod upright, the base makes the fourth triangle. The quality illustrated here is that of *adding another dimension to the problem*. In this example, solution comes automatically as the third dimension is added. Other kinds of problems have many dimensions, and there is the further matter of *thinking in terms of* the added dimensions. In spatial problems, the addition of a third dimension seems simple, yet it took centuries for perspective to show up in human art work. Einstein added a fourth dimension, which few grasp, and in terms of which still fewer think. Adding a dimension is no small thing.

5. The creative adult is likely to have a history of creative experience to report. This is partly because special talents such as music, imagery, some intelligence factors, develop fully within the first several years of life. They may have been

expressed and recognized. More important, the creative person who has had this recognition is likely to see himself as someone who can meet new problems, find out things, do something original. This confidence makes a great difference — so much that given two people of equal ability, the one who has such a view of himself is much more likely to turn out original work first.

6. Although he has confidence in his ability, he also has an attitude of respect for the problem, such that he admits the limits of his conscious power in forcing the problem to solution. At some point ('incubation'), he treats the problem 'as if it had a life of its own', which will, in its time and in its relation to his subliminal or autonomous thought processes, come to solution. He may work like a beaver, but there comes a point at which he will 'sleep on it'. Edison called genius '90 per cent perspiration and 10 per cent inspiration', but this last fraction *is* a part. Answers often come as moments of sudden, unexpected illumination — 'Eureka' — the chemist boarding the bus sees the image of the benzene rings; the mathematician wakes out of a sound sleep and writes a formula he has sought for months. Respect for the problem, coupled with respect for themselves as thinkers who chose the problem but cannot force the solution, is characteristic of the creative attitude.

7. The creative person is willing to be different. This does not mean strident or rebellious eccentricity. It means that at some point he is willing to stand alone, in order to keep faith with himself. As Brewster Chisellin[3] puts it, 'The faithful formalist has no chance of creating anything'. The imitator, who may be comfortable or even flattering to work with, simply cannot invent. The inventor cannot simply imitate.

8. Finally, the creative person is likely to possess 'a liberal imagination' — an ability to hold two contradictory views in mind at the same time. This might mean simultaneously considering two frames of reference, his own and another's; it might mean knowingly and accurately having 'mixed feelings' such as love and hate, or respect and contempt, toward a single object or person; it might mean balancing conflicting theories before setting up crucial experiments. Is light explained by wave or corpuscular theory? Does gravity pull or push? (It pushes!)

III

Earlier, a distinction was made between two kinds of work — creation and production. In the last few minutes, I have tried to give you a sample of the

---

3. I have been unable to trace any reference for this, Ed.

variety of attributes by which the creative person might be recognized. Here is another distinction. This one is between two kinds of human motivation. Maslow terms them *deficiency motives* and *growth motives*. The deficiency motive is a need which must be filled for self-preservation and maintenance of health — for example, need for food, water, vitamins, social prestige, self-esteem. Without these satisfactions, whether physical or psychological, man is an animal in pain. In order to avoid this pain, men do productive work. They earn a living. Most work is of this nature, and from this motive. In a scarcity culture, this is bound to be so. Starving men struggle for a primitive diet of whatever will keep them alive. But when deficiency needs are fully met, a second set of motives come into play — growth motives, and from these come creative work. In a culture of abundance, well-fed men develop appetite beyond hunger, and invent a complicated cuisine, and schemes of balanced nutrition. Whenever subsistence is guaranteed, and security guaranteed, people begin to venture into new areas of experience. Why should they do this? Why doesn't comfort simply lead to idleness? (And there are some who think it does.[4]) *It is because there is a drive for new experience.* The healthier the person, the stronger this drive will be, and the more the growth motives will influence behavior.

This is a point of some significance. One often hears a statement to the effect: 'Some of the most creative people I know are the most neurotic', as if creativity and neurosis were causally related. Although this idea is less in vogue now,[5] theories of compensation and sublimation have left their mark and there are some who advise the artist to cultivate his neurosis, or believe that the orator who stuttered became a great orator *because* he stuttered. But I believe that where creativity and neurosis are connected, the creativity develops in spite of the neurosis, not because of it.

There is also a notion that deprivation leads to creativity. We hear this in the romantic myth of the artist in the garret. 'You have to suffer before you can

---

[4.] Terms like 'idle rich' and 'contented cows', for instance, imply the dangers of comfort. This is 'bathtub psychology', i.e., 'if you give 'em bathtubs, they'll only put coal in them'. It is true that new comfort may lead to relaxation approaching lethargy, but eventually it leads to the development of energy which then *seeks* expression. In fact the action we value because it appears as a response to stress is based on energy built during rest, so that comfort is *always* the basis of action. Without wanting to be an apologist for either wealth or stupidity, I would point out that there are 'idle poor' more depressed than motivated by poverty, and that the bitterest malcontent of a cow is not brighter or more inventive than a contented one — she simply can't give any milk. Comfort is misused as 'slothfulness' only by those who are not sure they can really count on it.

[5.] This question is brilliantly debated by two of America's best literary critics — Edmund Wilson in *The Wound and The Bow* [University Books, 1961, Ed.], and Lionel Trilling's essay 'Art and Neurosis' in his book *The Liberal Imagination*. [Doubleday Anchor, 1953, Ed.]

create.' So, some would-be artists dwell in garrets, live on French bread and red wine, and wait, but not much happens except that their teeth decay. On the other hand, the pyramids and the Taj Mahal were designed in palaces, and much of western science was developed by upper-class Englishmen.

There is also a belief that pressure will force creative effort. 'Necessity is the mother of invention.' If this means that people create because of external pressures, it is an error. Soldiers under fire dig good trenches, galley slaves can be whipped into greater effort at the oars, but except for fairy tales, where straw is spun into gold cloth overnight, one never hears of a great creation being accomplished to avoid severe punishment, or even death. People can only create because of growth motives which are inside the person, not because of externally imposed needs. When a jumper clears a hurdle, he does it, believe it or not, because he has the leap inside him waiting to get out, wanting to be expressed. Does that sound queer? Consider the alternative. Is it the hurdle that makes him jump? That could not be, or anyone could be made to jump any hurdle by presentation of the apparent stimulus. The hurdle is a measure or a challenge, but the jumper could jump whether the hurdle were there or not, and often does just that. Because we usually see this jump in relation to the measure of it — the fence or whatever — we wrongly think of the obstacle *as the motive*. But creation comes only from resources of health which free internal growth motives. This is stated with clarity and conviction by Carl Rogers (1961)[6]:

> The mainspring of creativity appears to be the same tendency which we discover so deeply as the curative force in psychotherapy — man's tendency to actualize himself, to become his potentialities . . . (pp. 350–1)
>
> . . . the individual creates primarily because it is satisfying to him, because this behavior is felt to be self-actualizing . . . (p. 352)

IV

Thus far, I have tried to characterize creative work by some distinguishing features. And to argue that health is prerequisite for the growth motives which lead to creativity. It is psychological health I have in mind and here I would like to turn to a discussion of psychological counseling as a way of achieving this health.

The state of knowledge about psychological health is primitive, but it is

---

6. Although this chapter was written circa 1956, the quote by Rogers used here was not published until 1961. In the preface to Chapter 19 of *On Becoming a Person* Rogers wrote, 'In December 1952 a Conference on Creativity . . . led me to produce some rough notes . . . later expanded into the following paper' (p. 347). The quote included in the text must have been in Rogers' notes available to John Shlien in 1956. Thanks to Kathy Moon for this detective work [Ed.].

lately being redefined in positive terms. This needs to be done because health is more than the absence of disease. When a man is 'back on his feet', the crippling pain is gone, and he can walk. But is this health? No, health has to do with being able to run, jump, and do other things hard to specify. Likewise, a positive description of peace would mean far more than just 'the end of war'. It is relatively easy to describe the concrete fact of sickness, malfunction, inability, or death. It is much harder to define the seemingly abstract ideal of a healthy life.[7] Yet what we need is knowledge about attributes of healthy and competent people, in order to have positive goals. Learning to define health in terms of what is to be achieved rather than what is to be avoided will have a special benefit for the field of counseling and psychotherapy and for its industrial applications. Such learning will take the curse off psychotherapy as something 'shameful' for 'sick people only'. For one thing, we will realize that we are all more or less sick and healthy at different times, and that, over time, there is no distinct category of the 'sick person'. More important, we will realize this: that if the skills developed in psychological counseling can release the constructive capacities of malfunctioning people so that they become healthier, this same help should be available to healthy people who are less than *fully* functioning. If we ever turn towards positive goals of health, we will care less about where the person begins, and more about how to achieve the desired endpoint of the positive goals.

One aspect of psychological health is self-esteem. It is generally thought of as a condition underlying the state of autonomy that leads to productive or creative behavior. Here I would like to turn to some research on counseling in relation to this one aspect of health. There is no time here to go into details about counseling and what it is or how it is done. But I would like to say that there is nothing arcane or mysterious about it. Counseling is an effort to provide in relatively pure form some health-giving conditions which are found to some degree in many parts of life — wherever good human relations provide psychological safety, understanding, honesty and warmth. If this were not so, if these conditions were not to be experienced in many places, we would all be in a bad state indeed. That professionally trained counselors can successfully counsel is an established fact. But further, Dr. Thomas Gordon recently told me of his success in a west coast industrial plant where counseling has been applied to the whole organization, and not for the most part by professional counselors but by the executive members

---

7. Not just psychology but all of social science has been stuck with focus on pathology, malfunction, disorganization. Besides the reason given above, there are three less compelling ones. First, disease is a 'problem'; health does not demand attention in that way. Second, the malfunctioning person is available for study, localized in hospital or prison; the free and healthy person is no man's subject. Third, the social scientist often exhibits a somewhat morbid curiosity. Thus, the literature abounds with studies of prostitution, delinquency, neurosis, social conflict, etc.

of the plant themselves, after some training. This in itself is an exciting, valuable experiment.

The results and ideas I want to present to you are illustrated on the chart. This research has to do with the growth of self-esteem as measured by a device called the self-ideal correlation. This measure, and several others, are reported in detail in *Psychotherapy and Personality Change* edited by Rogers and Dymond (Rogers and Dymond, 1954) — a book honored with last year's [1955, Ed.] award by the American Personnel and Guidance Association. Self-esteem has already been mentioned as basic in the concept of psychological health. Here we can see how self-esteem is affected by counseling, and consider what meanings it may have. The numbers at the left are the measures of self-esteem with the effective range running from just below zero to perhaps .80 to .90. Across the bottom are indicated the number of counseling interviews, from zero to 50. All the lines shown are averages — group means for about 20 people. The two broken lines at the top and bottom of the 'actual' section are control groups given the test, but receiving *no* counseling, then retested at a later time.

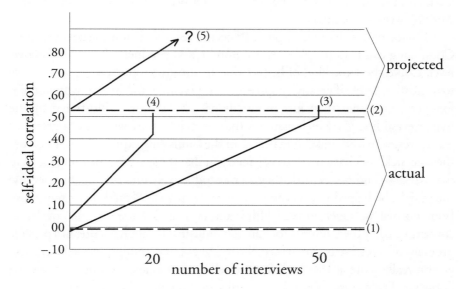

Line number (1) shows the average score of a group needing counseling. These people were tested when they applied for help, asked to wait 60 days, retested. The average score is zero (-.01 to be exact), both at the time of the first testing and second testing. This group mean does not change without counseling. The people in the group can be called 'nonproductive' in the sense that they present this kind of problem: unable to study, if they are students; unable to manage their families, if they are housewives; unable to hold a job, if they are workers, etc.

Line (2) shows a group of people who do *not* ask for therapy. They are so-called 'normal' controls. So far as we know, they can be called 'productive', i.e., are able to study, work, live in moderate social comfort. Neither do *they* change over time on the average when tested and retested. They score an average .53, later an average .54. And these two groups (1) and (2) (which differ from each other to a degree [that is statistically] significant beyond the .01 level) empirically define the direction of movement we would hope for as a result of successful counseling.

Line (3) shows the change in a group designated by other measures as successful. There we see that when they are tested a few months after about 50 hours of counseling took place, they have achieved an average score of .55, almost identical with that of the 'normal controls'. Line (4) shows a later group which applied for counseling and was limited to a maximum of 20 hours of interviews. This group showed the same kind of change, moving to .52 when tested a few months after their counseling had ended.

Successful counseling clearly helps, so far as this measure indicates, to start a process through which people move from a 'non-productive' to a 'productive' level, and this movement can be achieved after only 20 hours — roughly half a working week — of interviews.

On top of this chart I have put a 'Projected' section, to raise the next question. Counseling can help people to move from a 'non-productive' to a 'productive' level. Could the same kind of help enable an already productive group to move to a 'creative' level? If creativity springs from psychological health, why not aim for creativity rather than just productivity? This notion is illustrated by the hypothetical line (5) which assumes that we might start with, say, a group of executives, who undertake to make use of the counseling experience, not because they are 'sick' — I have tried to convince you that there is little meaning for us in that word — and not because they aren't productively functioning, but because they might be helped to become more creative as well. Would this group move from 'normal' to 'supernormal'? This is a next research question, one now being contemplated by the University of Chicago Industrial Relations Center in a possible program of executive maintenance. We might ask first, though, 'does the creative person really score at that high level of self-esteem as assumed here?' We don't know yet. From some of the theory earlier in this paper, they should.

And why didn't those who started at zero move up near the top of the chart, near the assumed 'creative' level, if counseling is capable of promoting such movement? For one answer, a few individuals did move that far, though the group average did not. For another, I believe it may be a matter of different goals, and of different resources at the start. Perhaps those who are not productive start with the goal of *becoming* productive, and may stop when they reach that goal. This, and many other questions, we will have to answer in the future. The index of self-esteem shown here may not even be an appropriate measure for this research.

But the important idea is that counseling *is* the appropriate tool.

I do believe that in the future, in the next ten years perhaps, there will be methods of selecting and developing creative people. Rather than summarize, I would like to conclude with a personal suggestion. If these methods do become available, and you are a manager who wants to find or develop a creative work-force, perhaps you should be a creative person yourself. I do not say that in a taunting or challenging way, but because it may be necessary. You will have to provide an atmosphere to facilitate the work of those you manage. That in itself is a creative act. Without it creative people will not stay with you, or will disappoint you. And if you feel uncreative yourself, your own psychological security is likely to be threatened by the activities of creative people working for you. So besides being interested in creative people, it may be a wise first step to be interested in *being* one.

REFERENCES

Rogers, C.R. (1961). *On Becoming a Person.* Boston: Houghton Mifflin.

Rogers, C.R. & Dymond, R.F. (1954). *Psychotherapy and Personality Change.* Chicago: University of Chicago Press.

CHAPTER 4

A Client-Centered Approach to Schizophrenia

First approximation

The truth shall make ye free — but first it shall make ye miserable.
Proverb

In the complex and challenging field of psychotherapy with the psychoses, client-centered therapy is a relatively new entry. The orientation now known as 'client-centered' and formerly by the less accurate term 'nondirective' is itself less than two decades old. Unlike most clinical or therapeutic developments, it has grown up in an academic setting, where its rate of growth and degree of influence has increased enormously in the past several years. Where it was once considered a radical view, it is now accepted as a partial technique and a general attitude by many orientations, and much of the power and originality evident 20 years ago is obscured. Its influence has spread into the guidance and counseling fields, education, religion, sociology, and social work, as well as industrial and clinical psychology; but it has only recently begun to develop in the field of psychiatry. Carl Rogers, central figure in the development of this orientation, is a psychologist; his main experience, and that of his students, has been outside of medical settings. This has limited our contact with the frankly psychotic, who often may need, or be seen as needing, hospitalization. Thus most of the theory and practice has been applied with patients who would be called neurotic. Rogers once held, in fact, that this form of therapy was not applicable to psychotics.

The situation is changing. Therapists have developed in depth and capacity.

From *Psychotherapy of the Psychoses,* edited by Arthur Burton. Copyright © 1961 by Arthur Burton. Reprinted by permission of Basic Books, a member of Perseus Books, L.L.C. Prepared under a grant from the Ford Foundation (Psychotherapy Research Program) to the Counseling Center, University of Chicago. I am indebted to many for critical and encouraging discussion of this chapter, especially Drs. Eugene Gendlin, Jacob Getzels, Ann Holloway, Richard Jenney, Carl Rogers, Morris Stein, Alice Wagstaff, Mrs. Helene Sarett, Miss Julie Klorman, and Mr. Bruce Cushna.

As more deeply disturbed clients have been seen and helped, further reaches of maladjustment have been explored. Some of these more deeply disturbed clients had been treated elsewhere by physiological or psychotherapeutic means which failed. Some were seen 'inadvertently', beginning, for instance, as moderately anxious maladjusted cases[1] which developed much more severe manifestations as defenses peeled off. Also, client-centered therapists have been called upon to demonstrate in VA [Veterans' Administration, Ed.] and state hospitals whatever contributions they might make in work with 'psychotics'. (This is a word which we do not yet use with conviction or comfort. It is wrong enough to call a person with diabetes — an established disease entity — 'a diabetic'. That is far from being all he is. He has diabetes; but when his sugar-insulin balance is normal, so is he, in that dimension. Psychosis may simply represent a mode of *fluctuating* adjustment to a realm of experience within everyone, so that while the existence of 'a psychotic *state*' is undeniable by definition, the term 'a psychotic' is very questionable.) One more influence in this trend deserves mention. A growing number of psychiatrists have taken an active interest in client-centered therapy, usually having invented its rudiments independently, often thinking it most appropriate for their own self-directed personal therapy and wanting to learn more of its spirit and formal elaborations. One overall mark of this trend is the appointment, a few years ago, of Dr. Rogers as joint professor of psychology and psychiatry at the University of Wisconsin.

The main outcome of this trend is that at present we are engaged in the earnest study of treatment of schizophrenia. Although we cannot speak from extensive experience, intensive experience abounds wherever there is therapeutic contact with the schizophrenic condition. It seems certain that this phase of work will bring about modifications of theory and practice, where they are not confirmed, for no one can face the full individual and social impact of psychotic encounters without a 'shaking of the foundations'.

As Freud said, 'Much is won if we succeed in transforming hysterical misery into common unhappiness'. In this chapter we seek to understand the schizophrenic psychosis in more literal terms as an extreme form of an all-too-common unhappiness: self-deceit. What follows is (1) theoretical discussion of the nature of psychosis; (2) a general statement of our therapeutic principles, and (3) a case to illustrate the theory and the therapy.

---

[1] There is always a risk that therapy will expose deeper levels of disturbance. The topic of diagnosis seems relevant here; it is a probability statement of such risk, but will be dealt with later.

PSYCHOSIS

SOME FUNDAMENTAL QUESTIONS

Within this discussion of psychosis, many basic questions need to be asked. The answers will be incomplete and personal, representing no 'official' position because there is none, and having no claim to scientific certainty via research. Still, questions of this order must be asked: What is psychosis? The psychotic experience? How can psychotherapy help? What is psychotherapy? Are there psychological laws of behavior that apply to this strange, bizarre, confusing world of the deeply disturbed person?

In this area, the words themselves are vague and insecure and our ignorance so great that we tend in desperation to assume meaning where none exists. Let us recognize that the true nature of psychosis is a mystery. (And the nature of the most prevalent convulsive treatment, electroshock, is called 'a mystery within a mystery' by the most authoritative book on the subject (Hoch and Kalinowsky, 1946, p. 242)). One of our problems, then, is how to deal with a subject consisting of experience which at its worst is indescribable from the inside and incomprehensible from the outside, and this without using words which are themselves confounding. 'Psychosis,' for instance, has an authoritative, antiseptic sound, but its real sterility lies mainly in its lack of clear meaning. It simply replaces 'madness' — now a literary term — and 'insanity', which represents a dated legal concept. Falling into pseudoscientific conventions of language will not help. At the present stage of knowledge the questions are well enough represented by asking simply: What does it mean to 'lose one's mind'? How can a 'lost mind' be recovered?[2]

[2.] For that matter, how is the mind developed in the first place? It is our assumption throughout this chapter that 'mind' develops and exists beyond brain, and following from this, the assumption of social psychological origin of much mental disturbance. It sounds simple, but there is by no means wholehearted agreement in the field on this issue. Current work on molecular structure and the chemistry of schizophrenia, for instance, challenges psychological assumptions. It is possible, of course, that biochemical methods of treatment will develop actual cures for psychotic states, thus outmoding psychotherapy. No less a therapist than Freud thought so in regard to schizophrenia. Also fashionable are experiments with drugs which induce pseudopsychotic states, which suggest to some that if such states can be caused by chemical means, they can also be cured by chemical means, and further that the mechanism of disturbance is fundamentally biochemical.

Undeniably there is always a biochemical basis for behavior of the human organism. But this does not rule out psychological influence, in either the sickening or the healing process. It is certain that anxiety can cause diarrhea. Chemical mechanism? Surely. And a virus or a laxative might cause the same apparent result, but that would not alter the fact that anxiety, a psychological state, can and does cause diarrhoea (as surely as a . . . /cont.

That which we call 'a psychosis' is not a disease. It is a learned behavior,[3] exaggerated to a point of no return, i.e., where control is lost and the exaggeration 'takes on a life of its own' temporarily. Because this exaggeration is so overwhelming, so much beyond our ordinary capacity to assimilate, it appears to us that we are no longer dealing with, for instance, ordinary suspicion, but something *quite* different — 'paranoia'. Then it appears that psychosis is not of the same order, not on the same continuum, as 'normal' or 'neurotic' behavior. But as psychotic behavior becomes more common it is seen as a form of maladjustment similar in kind to lesser degrees of maladjustment, though so much greater in quantity that it seems different in *quality* too. There is one sense, unfortunately, in which it *is* different. A boulder balanced on the edge of a precipice can be pressed ounce by measured ounce toward rolling off. Each ounce is just like the last, but when the quantity of pressure totals to the 'breaking point', the quality of the *consequences* changes radically. No longer will the relief or counterpressure of one ounce recover the balance. Even if the boulder is not smashed in the fall, an enormous effort is required to restore the original position. It is because of this effort (which so few can make, and so many need) that it is necessary to prevent the 'psychotic situation' in life. The 'psychotic situation' is a precondition to the psychotic state, which may or may not follow.

PSYCHOTIC STRESS

What is the 'psychotic situation'? To put it briefly, it is that of *having an impossible life to live.* Here is an example of a prototype of impossibility which is not itself psychotic, and may for that reason give a clearer illustration of the meaning of 'an impossible life'. A normal young woman had a recurring dream.[4] In it she dwelled

---

/cont . . . nonchemical stare may cause someone ten feet away to blush). Nor would it mean, more obviously but no more truly, that even though the eventual chemistry mechanism and result are the same, two different causes (laxative and anxiety) are therefore the same. Nor would it mean that an antidote for diarrhea is a specific treatment for *either* anxiety or a virus, or that a specific for one is of any use for the other. Similarly, a chemically induced psychotic state may not be a true psychosis even though it has the same appearances in terms of hallucinations and like effects. A chemical antidote for the pseudopsychosis is not necessarily effective for a true psychosis, even though a chemical mechanism exists in either case. Psychological influence is not eradicated by the artificial imitation of its effects. Even though 'tranquilizers' will tranquilize, so will a blow on the head, and neither one is equivalent to, or can deny the existence of, 'peace of mind'.

3. 'Oh, what a tangled web we weave, When first we practise to deceive!' Shakespeare.

4. This is only an illustration, not intended to imply that psychosis is a waking dream, though that idea is not new, nor necessarily wrong. It may be that the psychotic 'unreality' which approximates a dream will yet be best influenced by manipulation of . . . /cont.

in a green, filmy, gurgling underwater world, meeting and working with mermaid-like people, her vision wavering and distorted by the current. In discussion she connected this dream, easily and certainly, with an actual experience in which she and a companion had been swimming across a river. The current was too strong for them, and they could not swim to the beach they had set out for. Instead, they were swept to a slippery and steep place on the bank. The companion managed to pull himself up on some of the rocks, and tried to help the young woman crawl out of the water too. It was too slippery and they were too tired. Their fingers were slimy, as were the rocks, and they lost their handclasp. The young woman slid back into the water, fought, gasped, screamed, got her lungs full of water, perhaps fainted from exhaustion, *knew* she was drowning, and sank. People on the bank heard the screams, formed a human chain, pulled her from the water unconscious, and revived her. What had happened? In a word, she drowned. She lost her life. She experienced death as certainly as one can. It is also true that she was revived and was still alive. In her consciousness there were two thoroughly contradictory conceptions: life and death.

Experience, especially an intense one, demands some sense of completion *if* the person is to have a healthy life. The intense experience cannot be brusquely denied to awareness. This young woman was now in the seemingly peculiar position of having two contradictory lives to lead. She died, and she could not put the consciousness of this together immediately with the other fact that she was living. For a while it was necessary for her to have some expression of the life after death, since death was her intense experience and she was still alive, experiencing being. Eventually some process of integration allowed her to know herself as simply, unquestionably alive, someone who drowned but lived through it. Then she could live as a single self, in relation to this issue at least. But for the time it illustrates in a nonpsychotic way the meaning 'having to live an impossible life'. A significant thing is this: she was able to recall, without shame, her impossible life. It was impossible simply because one cannot easily assimilate the experience of being both alive and dead at the same time. But the impossible life in the psychosis is one which may be built on *many* experiences, and they are permeated with the deepest humiliation. They can hardly be recalled without shame. They are impossible in that one cannot bear to live those experiences, yet must in order to be a complete person.

This comes close to the core of the matter — when there is an impossible life, which involves unbearably painful humiliation, a defense (later called self-

------

/cont . . . the sleep centers of brain areas which control dreaming. Much research is under way in this field. One researcher finds that waking a person just before measured EEGs indicate the beginning of a dream state will produce hallucinations, as do other forms of sensory deprivation. The dream is *like* a psychosis in that it is one way in which this person could live her impossible life.

deception) develops to deny part of consciousness in such a way that isolation follows, and it is this which leads to a psychotic state (later called self-negation). The 'impossible life' does not alone precipitate a break with reality, and a lucky thing that is, since contradictions and irreconcilable opposites are within and around us from childhood on. These contradictions are always reflected in individual reactions, some of which are psychotic, some not. I am acquainted with a Negro 'passing' for white. It is precarious, and his choice stems from and carries with it considerable feelings of humiliation and discomfort; yet he has not and is not likely to become psychotic as a result because his choice is deliberate and voluntary. He deals as a white man with other Negroes, knowing perfectly well that he too is a Negro as well as white, and he does so with a calculated cynicism which denies nothing.[5]

A more widespread example is the person who is uncertain of sexual identity, not knowing whether male or female is his or her real status. (The more fortunate of these are contented homosexuals.) This complexity, when severe, is more likely to lead to defenses which have a psychotic consequence. Indeed, considerable clinical literature, chiefly psychoanalytic, asserts that paranoid types of schizophrenia always suffer from inadequate sexual identity. Not only is there shame or humiliation attached to this kind of confusion; it is also an *isolating* uncertainty. If it should become, as it often does, the basis for deprivation of any and all sexual contact (excluding masturbation) it is doubly dangerous because sex is of the greatest importance, beyond its intense physical satisfaction, as an antidote — perhaps the best antidote — for the threatening sense of disappearance of self which an isolate experiences. How else can he achieve such intimacy and responsiveness, both of which are prime sources for the reaffirmation of his own being? (I believe that the quest for such affirmation is so desperate in a person who has forebodings of his own disappearing, or loss of self, that it best explains the sadist, who tries to force through pain the responsiveness he needs to bolster his failing sense of selfhood. His urgency makes victims of those from whom he would rather receive love, but he dares not risk rejection since he must have response just to sustain being at all.)

But it is not simply in hidden or esoteric ways that the impossible life is experienced. I asked a 19-year-old, remarkably healthy swimming champion where or how he had learned to swim. Of course he had been coached in various strokes, but he had been taught just to stay afloat by his 'daddy' (a term widely

---

5. 'The Negro has the simplest of alternatives: live a life of constant humility or ever threatening danger,' says Norman Mailer in his penetrating essay, 'The "White Negro"', *Dissent*, summer, 1957. But again, the point is that simple alternatives are not prepsychotic stress. It is the required complex of both, not the choice of either/or, which creates the impossible life.

used in the South, reflecting affection, authority, and close family affiliation). How had he been taught?

> *Well, my daddy threw me over the side of a rowboat. When I started to sink, he said to stand up if I couldn't swim — it wasn't over my head. Yeah, but I didn't know that. Man, I was just a little boy, 'bout five years old. I spluttered and thrashed, and I stayed up for — must have been two or three minutes. Every time I got near the oar he held out to me, he'd draw it back. Man, I hate to even think of it.*
> *Must have been an awful struggle.*
> *Yeah, but I don't even remember it.*

For two years this boy had nightmares; he lived in a complex relation to his father, composed of love and respect on the one hand and hatred and fear on the other. He still has occasional nightmares, and when his fond 'daddy' wakes him up by 'roughhousing', he has been 'glassy-eyed' and semihallucinating for as long as 15 minutes — 'So my daddy stopped waking me up that way.' A part of his experience has never been completed, except in troubled sleep, for he and his father are the 'best of buddies'. An 'impossible' but not uncommon sort of experience, and though a little less raw, made of the same stuff we are accustomed to see in case histories of hospitalized psychotics! 'Two years of nearly incessant rape and obscene sexuality initiated by her grandfather, who was also a "fire and brimstone" preacher who demanded very prim moralistic behavior of her.'

One might ask here, who was psychotic? The grandfather? The father who throws his son into the water? The society which pits black against white? (And to some extent pits male against female?) *That depends on the extent to which conscience and defensiveness operate within each individual.* The cynical brute is not in the hospital. He may have other psychological maladjustments, but the hospitals are filled with those most sensitive to oppression and injustice, the would-be moral ones. Artaud, in his essay on Van Gogh, says, 'A lunatic is a man who has preferred to become what is socially understood as mad rather than forfeit a certain superior idea of honor'. And this seems not far from the truth. The calculating exploiter may not be in the hospital, but the granddaughter mentioned above is there, and she says, in her acute psychotic states, 'It never happened'. She cannot live all of her experience. Conscience forbids. At best, one self must be denied to awareness, or distortedly perceived.[6] That is a chronic state of maladjustment.

[6.] How can there be a 'true' or an 'original' self *and* a distortedly perceived self? How can there be a denied and a denying experience in the same experiencer, or a known which is its own knower, or *anything* more than one self in one person, really? Metaphysics aside, client-centered theory is a clinical-perceptual theory, and turns to the same kinds of questions in more tangible modes of perception. If one looks through two monocular tubes, separating the vision of each eye, and looks at one color with one eye, . . . /cont.

THE PSYCHOTIC STATE

At worst, the denying self, the self as knower, *also begins to disappear.* At this point a schizophrenic psychosis becomes acute. (And this is really the only point at which I feel sure there is such a thing as a psychotic state.) Denial of part of experience is chosen in self-defense, but the nature of deception is such that the process becomes autonomous.

Then the disturbed person cannot stop it if he wants to. He is 'beside himself', out of control. He will doubt his own existence, even try to bash his head against the wall to prove, by pain, his own being. He may not recognize what to us seems 'real' — his body, his history, his social image. Normally the self is a realm with powerful known boundaries. That which is 'not me' is excluded. Interestingly enough, the normal person will refuse to accept as part of himself what was clearly so before being separated from himself — will not, for instance, willingly drink from a glass saliva which was a moment ago in his mouth, or blood which was in his veins. (Though he will often quickly suck a wound at first, as if to hold onto himself.) But in a psychotic state he will swallow his blood, his urine, perhaps his feces, as if, when not knowing who he is and fearing that he is not at all, he tries in desperation to reincorporate that which he was. The boundaries are gone. He does not know where he begins, ends, or even if he is. Once experienced, this is indescribably frightening, and the acute state leaves him deeply shaken and unsure of himself. Now *he* knows what psychosis is, even though we do not.

Complete loss of self — of all selves — is the ultimate dread faced in the acute psychotic state. The person we call neurotic has an intricate but firm connection with a false self. (In clinical folklore, there is a saying: 'A good neurosis is the best insurance against a psychosis'.) The acutely psychotic one has no self. His is the essence of fear. Compared with this 'experience of nothingness' all other fears — of starvation, ridicule, impotence, castration, or whatever — seem trivial. Even more than existentialist 'not-being', the 'experience of nothingness' is a confused paradox in its very expression. One cannot doubt it, having been in its presence, but I cannot explain its paradoxical quality better than to relate the words of a hospitalized patient. In trying to describe part of his hallucination, he

---

/cont . . . a different color with the other eye, one will see first one color, then the other, with quick shifts of the rival eyes and some advantage for the dominant eye. Or with certain colors, one may get a blend giving a binocular yellow, for instance. Or, two separate eyes looking at separate patterns such as crosses and circles may fuse them in a binocular visual field. How can two eyes managed by one nervous system in a single skull see things separately, alternating or fusing them? If there is a mechanism for this, there can also be one which enables the personal self to view the world or the experiential self as now one reality, now another, or as a blended confusion. (My thanks to a colleague, Professor Austin Riesen, for personal communication on this problem.)

put his face in his hands and quaked, 'I seen this — this — this *shapeless shape* near me'. Shapeless shape is illogical, but that is just the point. This man retains or comes back to concepts, such as shape, and they are all he had when he became detached from the world he has known. Where he now goes, the psychotic reality does not fit even such a broad concept as shape. The mind he had, and was losing, was not equipped to comprehend a world so foreign to experience. In the same way, even 'experiencing' itself could not apply, since it was equipment to sense 'something'. Now it is jolted into primitive terror when it senses 'nothing', which the concept of 'being' cannot encompass.[7] This is one way in which psychosis is viciously circular. I have asserted that crucial emotional experience must be completed, i.e., integrated, to assure health, and instead we have now the experiencing of that shapeless shape, nothingness, which we are not conceptually prepared to understand, much less integrate. It forms another 'impossible life', and the cycle begins again. What is worse, it involves further humiliation, which leads to further defensive denial of the 'impossible' psychotic experience. ('It never happened.') Two colleagues have described to me their reaction to a hallucinogenic drug. Both were deeply shaken, both terrified by the sense of 'not being', and significantly, both wanted above all to have human contact with a person or persons who *must not leave.* But the relevance of this is mainly to point out that it was far less difficult to pull out of this artificial episode, since there is little felt humiliation. Following the genuine psychotic episode the effect is usually further humiliation and loss of self-esteem ('People will think I'm crazy'). And finally, the result is withdrawal by others and from others. Isolation is increased. Thus a psychosis tends to repeat the three elements which led to it: the 'impossible life', the attendant humiliation and denial, and consequent isolation ending in self-negation.

The crux of this line of thought is in the way in which defensive denial ends in undoing rather than becoming — ends in the complete loss of self. Isolation is a mid-point in explanation. There is increasing evidence demonstrating that a major effect of isolation is the hallucination we so readily associate with the psychotic state. Hebb and others have experimentally deprived human subjects of external sensory stimulation, blocking eyes, ears, muffling fingers, sometimes suspending the body in neutral buoyancy and steady temperature, etc. When outside stimuli are blocked, the void is quickly experienced, with discomfort, and then filled with 'ghosts', sounds, colors, 'waking dreams', and a wide range of images (Heron, 1957). For days after the experiment ended, the subjects (college students) were fearful of the return of ghosts and other imaginary phenomena.

[7.] With others, we share the view that the phenomenological reality is that which the individual perceives; but I believe that the intense state of psychosis is not the psychotic's 'reality'. At that point he has none, except nothing.

This effect of isolation is not new, of course. It has been observed by aviators (Lindbergh reported it in his solo flight across the Atlantic), submarine crew members, prisoners in solitary confinement, etc. Nor are such effects caused only by absence of sensory stimuli; they can also be caused by monotony or too much of one thing. Any substance — water as well as alcohol — is toxic or intoxicating in excess. Any stimulus in excess — constant noise as well as constant silence — produces the effect of isolation, as it excludes all other sensation. The human nervous system needs variety, and has a definite 'stimulus hunger'. (It is well established, for example, that animals will work to stimulate portions of the brain by electric shock (Olds and Milner, 1954). This, rather than destruction of 'associative memory pathways', may be the useful function of shock therapy, if it can be justified at all.) Isolation is the next to final step in the development of the acute psychosis.

SELF-DECEPTION AND SELF-NEGATION

The remaining questions relate to the development and 'loss' of the mind. Particularly crucial is the way in which defensive denial leads to isolation.

We tend to think of human intelligence, once formed, as an individual capacity. That is mind: our hopes that man will be rational rest upon it. From the standpoint of psychotherapy, it matters a great deal whether mind is 'given' or 'gotten'; i.e., biological or social. The ideas of G. H. Mead (1934) are the foundation of a social psychology which has provided basic assumptions for several schools of psychotherapy.[8] Mead says,

> It is absurd to look at the mind simply from the standpoint of the individual human organism, for although it has its focus there, it is essentially a social phenomenon . . . The processes of experience which the human brain makes possible are made possible only for a group of interacting individuals; only for individual organisms which are members of a society; not for individual organisms in isolation from other individual organisms.

The mind emerges through a process of communication. This involves social interaction on the basis of what Mead calls 'significant symbols' (usually words). A significant symbol is one that is 'reflexive', i.e., when it is used it *presupposes another* person, anticipates his response, involves on the user's part some sense of how that other will feel. The bully, for instance, differs from the lion, which roars at the whole jungle, in that the bully participates somewhat in the fright of his victim. He is not trying to frighten himself — quite the opposite (for he is a

---

[8.] H. S. Sullivan is one who explicitly acknowledged this influence.

coward too). But he does. He senses the meaning of his threat and reacts to it, 'taking the role of the other'. The lion only gestures. The human communicates, and communication means taking into account the other. *Acknowledging the other is essential to the existence of mind,* from beginning to end.

What follows here hinges upon that very point — the existence of the other as a necessary condition for the psychological existence of oneself. That exterior distinction is *paralleled* by an interior but similar duality within each individual consciousness, *where being involves a possibility of not-being.* This view draws upon the social psychology of Sartre, which advances Mead's foundations to a new level. Before offering an interpretation of Sartre's ideas, let me offer the clinical opinion that the psychosis begins with (or stems from) a 'lie'.[9] This may at first sound like moralizing. Then it may seem immoral, because the lie is seen as the salvation, or at least a resort, of sanity. The mind, which we have been considering as emerged from social experience, is the instrument by which reality is apprehended, and it is founded upon the knowledge of (if not the commitment to) truth. For all the qualifications we can make about 'truth', that is what we mean when we speak of 'reality contact', for instance (to be without which fairly designates the psychotic state). We think of the lie as treacherous to others, but it is even more treacherous to the liar himself if he falls into self-deceit: he will either be foiled by his consciousness of the truth, or he will find that there is 'no one there' within himself to whom he can lie. Self-deception cannot succeed for long. It will either fail or destroy the self of the deceiver.

It is the nature of human consciousness to be able to doubt and this includes doubting one's own existence. Children old enough to comprehend the concept of death have also been heard to ask, 'How do we know we're really here?' This capacity to doubt is necessary to the capacity to think, and also to believe, with any real conviction. Lose doubt and you lose belief. (The psychotic says of his delusions, 'There is no doubt about it,' but obversely, 'I can't believe any of it.') To be able to doubt is to be able to negate, and to doubt oneself is self-negation — not a desirable end to actualize but a required possibility for belief in being. Self-negation as an actuality, not just a possibility, can derive from self-deception.

Self-deception is not a lie, in the first place. A lie is in conjunction with the truth; self-deception has lost it. Sartre points out, in his careful analysis:

> The essence of the lie implies in fact that the liar is actually in complete possession of the truth which he is hiding. A man does not lie about that which he is ignorant of; he does not lie when he spreads an error of which he is himself the dupe; he does not lie when he is mistaken. The

---

[9.] No single lie, probably, but a series, or perhaps a habit, at first successful. Usually we speak clinically of defenses, distortions, etc., because *lie* carries more threat of reproach. Here the plain word *lie* is used to simplify a complex argument.

ideal description of a lie would be a cynical consciousness, affirming truth
within himself, denying it in his words . . . (Sartre, 1958)

The liar, for one thing, is in possession of the truth. He sees both sides. He
intends to deceive, and does not hide his intention from himself. (Later we see
that the self-deceiver intends the self-deceit, but he must hide his intention
from himself or he could not even attempt to carry it out.) But we are talking
now about what Sartre calls the *ideal* lie and this, he says, seldom holds for
long. It 'happens often enough that the liar is more or less the victim of it, that
he half persuades himself of it'. There's the rub, there's the treachery of it. The
lie ('I could not have done that', 'It never happened', etc.) begun in self-defense
slips into self-deception.[10] But as long as it is still a lie, it does this; it affirms
one's consciousness, as something hidden from the other! It presupposes the
other! 'It presupposes my existence, the existence of the *other,* my existence *for*
the other, and the existence of the other *for* me' (italics Sartre's). Clearly, the lie
fulfils the requisites of communication and social identity which Mead described
as fundamental to the emergence and maintenance of the mind and the self;
even though it is a falsehood, it relates to the truth and acknowledges two
separate communicants.

[10.] A famous scene in Tolstoy's *War and Peace* will remind you of the ease with which a lie
can slip into self-deception. It can even do so in a group, where it seems so appealing, so
protective, that individuals find social reinforcement for their self-deception. Nonetheless,
even the social consensus is not the truth. It has its effects as self-deception.
After an undeserved victory, Russian officers are reporting to Prince Bagration:
*The general, whose regiment had been inspected at Braunau, submitted to the prince that as
soon as the engagement began, he had fallen back to the copse, mustered the men who were
cutting wood, and letting them pass by him, had made a bayonet charge with two battalions
and repulsed the French.*
*'As soon as I saw, your Excellency, that the first battalion was thrown into confusion, I stood
in the road and thought, "I'll let them get through and then open fire on them"; and that's
what I did.'*
*The general had so longed to do this, he had so regretted not having succeeded in doing it,
that it seemed to him now that this was just what had happened. Indeed might it not actually
have been so? Who could make out in such confusion what did and what did not happen?*
Other officers are easily drawn in:
*'I saw here, your Excellency, the attack of the Pavlograd hussars,' Zherkov put in, looking
uneasily about him. He had not seen the hussars at all that day, but had only heard about
them from an infantry officer.*
'They broke up two squares, your Excellency.'
*When Zherkov began to speak, several officers smiled, as they always did, expecting a joke
from him. But as they perceived that what he was saying redounded to the glory of our arms
and of the day, they assumed a serious expression, although many were very well aware that
what Zherkov was saying was a lie utterly without foundation.*

As the lie slips into self-deception, this fundamental duality of identities is lost. There is no longer a separateness of deceived and deceiver. Self-deception implies the undifferentiated unity of a single consciousness (not to be mistaken for healthy integrity). It is something one is doing to oneself, yet one cannot. One's consciousness cannot intend, yet hide its intention, nor lie unless it simultaneously knows the truth from which it wants to depart. The very attempt to enter into self-deception will destroy the possibility of a successful lie (defense). If the one who lies is the same as the one to whom the lie is told, then he must know, in his capacity as deceiver, the truth which is hidden from him as the one deceived. Must know it well in order to conceal it, but this requires a duality which has been lost, so he can neither know certainly nor conceal cynically, nor affirm his being by negation of the 'other'. He ends with only self-negation, which is isolation with all the dangers that entails. One final, somewhat intricate step is this: he denies the one thing he still is — a being in self-deception. It is the nature of existence to be *and* not be what one is. To be courageous, for instance, one must in some sense be a coward also, otherwise one is only 'fearless' — (i.e., unaware of danger, unfeeling of fear). Whatever one is, to be meaningful one must also not be. But self-deception is not being what one is, for one is running away from that; neither is it being what one is not, because the deception cannot succeed.[11] So there is *nothing* — no truth, no cynical lie, no belief, no sustaining other, no being oneself or otherwise. Self-deception is the end of sanity, because it leads to self-negation, which is the end of being. That is the final loss of self and the ultimate anxiety. The mind develops through a process of differentiation between self and other and is sustained by a duality in one's own consciousness. It is lost when the boundaries are erased by self-deception.

Psychotherapy offers one road back through the intervention of another consciousness — a person who may re-establish both contact and separate identity; and to whom the lost one can at least lie. The psychotherapist ordinarily hopes to see the client or patient divest himself of all but the clearest perceptions of reality, and throughout, to speak the truth without reservation (whether by the 'fundamental rule of free association', trust and confidence, or whatever). That is

---

[11.] In an article which will be relevant later in the chapter, Tausk points out the way in which an infant believes that others know his thoughts, and that a child is surprised when he first learns, quite early, that he can lie, and lie successfully. (That he did have a bowel movement, that he did not take a cookie, etc.) The successful lie puts an end to the infantile stage of 'omniscience of thought' and helps to establish ego boundaries. Tausk posits stages in which (1) the outer world does not exist separately; (2) it exists but there is omniscience of thought, joining and controlling the ego with all else; (3) the external world is separate and can be deceived. Thus the lie helps to establish ego boundaries. (Viktor Tausk, 'The Influencing Machine', in R. Fliess (Ed.), *The Psychoanalytic Reader.* New York: Inter-nat. Univ. Press, 1948.)

an ultimate ideal — a combination of freedom and courage which is the healthiest of human conditions. The therapist working with the psychotic can be grateful when the patient can genuinely 'lie' again. He has at least restored secrecy, privacy, a separate identity, though shame and conflict will trouble him again.

Of course this is not the final goal of therapy. Self-affirmation through negation is not the end, but the beginning. And there are other means of helping, which include anything that will overcome isolation; or will facilitate complete experiencing of the 'impossible life' (i.e., to live with the truth) without unbearable humiliation; or will imply duality and differentiation. There is no virtue in the lie. There is a purpose in understanding it, and its relation to the truth at one pole and to self-deception at the opposite pole; that is, to throw some light on the dynamism of a 'defense mechanism' as it leads to self-destruction and essential loss of being — a dimension which will help us to understand the open face of health, the half-hidden face of normalcy, the mask of neurosis, and the hollow stare of psychosis, in relation to one another.

PERSONALITY AND PSYCHOTHERAPY

A GENERAL STATEMENT

Turning to client-centered therapy, this section will briefly review some salient features of our general position. Why 'client' instead of 'patient'? The negative distinction now seems somewhat picayune and, in hospital work, more embarrassing than useful; but it was intended to avoid the doctor-patient relation, with its implication of 'sickness' requiring 'treatment'[12] from someone who 'understands the patient better than he understands himself'. A possible reason is that we really want to think of that person as a person — someone unique with dignity and capacity, worthy of our unreserved respect. If we must have a word for it, 'client' seems more expressive of that. Why client-'centered'? This matters much more. Again, the negative purpose is only to distinguish between this and 'therapist-centered', 'theory-centered', 'society-centered', etc. There are such things. The positive meaning is immense. It expresses the major goal of the therapist: to understand and accept the perception and feelings of the client, to share the client's view of reality rather than to impose his own (Rogers, 1951).

It follows then that we rely heavily upon the *growth capacity* of the individual. The therapist is an active and significant person, but he cannot heal — he can only

---

[12.] Like the psychoanalyst Szasz, I much prefer the word *influence* to *treatment,* but we all continue to use the latter. See T. Szasz, The Case of Prisoner 'K', in A. Burton (Ed.), *Case Studies in Counseling and Psychotherapy* (Englewood Cliffs, N.J.: Prentice-Hall, 1959).

help to create conditions in which the natural regenerative powers take effect. As for *motive,* the drive toward self-actualization is a primary one; every human being would rather be better than worse, and strives toward the enhancement of self even though the strivings may often be thwarted and regressive. These assumptions about motive and capacity combine into a general *ethic,* which can simply be called self-determination. Client-centered therapy is founded on the conviction that man should be free, and to this end makes freedom a major means in the therapeutic experience. This is not, as some think (e.g. Harper, 1959), a reflection of political attitudes which supposedly prevail in America. It is a personal psychological conviction that the man who is most free will be most healthy. Freedom means the widest scope of choice and openness to experience, therefore the greatest probability of an adaptive response. For the individual, it seems that the urge to freedom is an urge to health, and precedes, rather than reflects, a political order.

SOME FUNDAMENTAL PROPOSITIONS

The conduct of therapy is based on propositions developed from a perceptual 'field theory' mode of psychological thought. These are detailed elsewhere by Rogers (op. cit., Chapter 12). Many have been experimentally tested. A small but essential portion will be outlined here, and these are so fundamental that we ask ourselves, of necessity, 'If this is not true, what is?'

1. Each person is unique. No one else can ever completely know his experience. Some of his experience is consciously symbolized. Some is at lower levels of awareness, beyond the scope of his attention. Beyond joint perceptions of shared experience, the closest approach we have to another's private world is to try to look through his eyes, understand through his interpretations.

2. Behavior is a consequence of perception. The organism reacts to reality as he perceives it. 'Objective evidence' notwithstanding, he who thinks the room hot opens the window; who thinks it cold turns up the heat; sees a red light, stops; sees it green, goes; sees an object as good, eats it; the same object as refuse, avoids it. Whatever 'it' really is by consensus, physical measurement, or philosophical proof — the way in which 'it' is perceived determines behavior toward it. Because perceptions can change, behavior can change. To promote a *stable* alteration in behavior, it is necessary to facilitate a change in perception.

3. Threat is followed by defense. Defense may take many forms, but it is the general and inevitable category of reaction to danger.

4. Defense narrows and rigidifies perception. Rigid perception blocks change in behavior. Attacking the defense system is likely to complicate it, causing more of the psychological economy to be devoted to defensiveness, inhibiting change.

5. A portion of the total field of perception becomes differentiated as the self (called here the 'self-concept'). The self-concept is an intervening perception which

affects outer percepts and determines their values. The self-concept may be one of weakness or of strength, may be of worth or contemptible; lucky or unlucky; lovable or hateful, to name a few dimensions. If one feels thoroughly adequate, no job is too difficult to try; if thoroughly inadequate, no job is easy enough. If strong, one may see a boulder as something to throw into the treads of an armored tank; if weak, the same boulder to hide behind. Experience is evaluated as friendly or dangerous, interesting or boring, possible or impossible, etc., *according to the self-concept* of the experiencer.

6. As experiences occur, they are related to the self-structure, and depending on it, each experience will be (a) symbolized accurately, perceived consciously, and organized into the self-structure; (b) ignored, because it has no significance to the self; or (c) denied or distortedly symbolized because it is threatening to the self.

In short, the self-concept stands between the stimulus and the response. Since self-concept is itself a perception, it can change, so that psychotherapy is possible — not guaranteed, but possible.

TECHNIQUE

In the framework of these rough statements, the main technique of client-centered therapy may be understood. That technique is 'reflection' — particularly reflection of feeling rather than content. At most points in communication where others would interpret, probe, advise, encourage, we reflect. This is the implementation of the attitudes and the propositions expressed above. Reflection can be, in the hands of an imitative novice, a dull, wooden mockery. On paper, it often looks particularly so.[13] Yet it can also be a profound, intimate, empathically understanding response, requiring great skill and sensitivity and intense involvement.[14]

Technique is certainly subordinate to relationship (though it contributes to

---

[13.] I have in mind an example which, if printed, would look like a passive repetition of the patient's statement. Yet to hear it spoken conveys a wealth of feeling and clear assurance of communication. Any interested professional person may obtain this excellent example, on tape recording, of Carl Rogers during an hour with a hospitalized schizophrenic patient. This recording, called 'Loretta', contains separate interviews by Drs. Richard Felder and Albert Ellis with the same patient. It may be obtained from the American Academy of Psychotherapists, 30 Fifth Avenue, New York, N.Y.

[14.] It has always been galling to me to hear client-centered therapy, because of its techniques, referred to as passive or superficial. It is often quite the opposite, though dazzling interpretations and other intriguing esoterics are missing. An Australian colleague with whom I once discussed a particularly deep commitment I felt in a case said, 'It's a life for a life.' Nothing ever rang more true. This is especially so with psychotics, and I have wondered, as have many other therapists, how many times in my life I will be willing and able to make as deep an investment as seems needed.

it, and is therefore not to be slighted). Currently the emphasis is much more upon relationships out of which new techniques may develop. In his first public paper on schizophrenics,[15] Rogers ignores technique to discuss the conditions — the atmosphere and the relationship — necessary for therapy:

Congruence as a Condition of Therapy
The first condition is that the therapist, within this relationship, is internally congruent, or integrated. By this I mean that he is unified in being exactly what he *is* in the relationship. From a more theoretical point of view, it means that his actual experience of himself and the relationship is accurately matched by his awareness of himself and the relationship. Such a condition is the opposite of presenting a façade, a defensive front, to the patient or client. If the therapist is experiencing one thing in the relationship, but is endeavoring to be something else, then the condition I am attempting to define is not met. On the other hand if he is transparently himself, if he is able to be 'that which he truly is', as Kierkegaard says, then this condition is met.

I have gradually come to believe that this is the most basic condition of all psychotherapy, and extends to being aspects of ourselves which we regard as non-therapeutic. Thus a therapist experiences a disturbing fear of the deeply suppressed violence which he senses in a psychotic client. Assuming this fear is a persistent one, it is part of my hypothesis that it is more therapeutic for him openly to *be* that fear, even expressing it to the client, than to present a calm and unruffled front in the relationship. To be transparent to the client, to have nothing of one's experience in the relationship which is hidden — that is, I believe, basic to effective psychotherapy.

As I examine my own experience I believe that this holds for working with any individual, but it is especially important in working with the deeply disturbed person, who is so extremely and often accurately sensitive to precisely what is going on in the relationship. Brody, in the 1950 symposium on psychotherapy with schizophrenics, pointed out the sensitivity of the schizophrenic to the unverbalized or partially conscious feelings of the therapist. All therapists have, I am sure, observed this, and the resolution of the difficulty which I am suggesting is that the therapist transparently *be* those feelings. When they are in the open, they cannot interfere with therapy.

What I am saying means that the therapist, by being openly and freely himself, is ready for, and is offering the possibility of, an existential

---

[15.] Paper given at a symposium on psychotherapy with schizophrenics, at Southeast Louisiana State Hospital, Mandeville, Louisiana, February 20–1, 1958.

encounter between two real persons. The schizophrenic, to be sure, can only rarely and fleetingly and fearfully avail himself of such an encounter, but it is these moments, I believe, which are therapeutic.

Empathic Understanding

A second necessary condition of psychotherapy, as I see it, is the experiencing by the therapist of an accurate and empathic understanding of the client. This means that he senses and comprehends the client's immediate awareness of his own private world. It involves sensing the cognitive, perceptual, and affective components of the client's experiential field, as they exist in the client. Where the therapist is adequately sensitive, it means not only recognizing those aspects of experience which the client has already been able to verbalize, but also those unsymbolized aspects of his experience which have somehow been comprehended through subtle non-verbal clues by the delicate psychological radar of the therapist. The skillful therapist senses the client's world — no matter now hallucinated or bizarre or deluded or chaotic — as if it were his own, but without ever losing the 'as if' quality.

I would like especially to note that in dealing with the schizophrenic the therapist, at his best, empathizes with the client's world as it is at that moment and the meanings it has for the client at that moment, whether it is wildly bizarre delusion, a moment of essentially rational self-control, or a chaotic disorganization. It may seem strange to some that I make no distinction as to what the therapist responds to, save that it be whatever aspect of experience is immediately present. This seems to be a sufficiently important matter that I should like to digress to discuss the basis of that point of view, though I shall return again to the topic of empathy.

The Nature of Schizophrenia in Relation to Psychotherapy

I have discussed elsewhere the significant place of the self-concept or self-gestalt — the way the individual perceives himself — in the psychological economy of the individual. *The self is the referent which supplies the 'feedback' by which the organism regulates behavior.* It is the criterion as to what is threatening to the individual since only those experiences are threatening which are inconsistent with the self-concept. Those experiences which do threaten, which are inconsistent with the self, are denied to awareness or distorted in awareness, since to symbolize them accurately in awareness would involve a disruption of, a contradiction in, the self-gestalt.

Now in the normal or neurotic individual, and in the paranoid individual as well, the self is intact, and is defended against disruption, either by simple or sometimes by enormously elaborate defenses. The schizophrenic individual, however, (other than the paranoid) is in my judgment one who has never developed or been permitted to develop a clearly differentiated, strong internally organized self-configuration. In the face of some deeply threatening feelings or circumstances, or with a mounting accumulation of such threats, a wave of previously denied experiences which are incongruent with this weak self sweeps over the individual's awareness. The self-concept is so disrupted that its function as a guide for behavior is surrendered. This is the way I would describe the moment of the psychotic break. Feelings previously denied to awareness are now predominant or regnant, and behavior is consistent with their content. This is the acute stage of the psychosis.[16]

Following the break, confusion and disorganization may reign, or the previously denied or repressed feelings may retain their regnancy, or a badly disrupted self protected by some new pattern of defense may be regnant, or these different conditions may alternate irregularly. If the person is ever again to be whole, all of these real elements of experience must be accepted into a reorganized and more inclusive self-concept which accurately represents more of the total experience of the organism.

Empathic Understanding (continued)

If I have been able to communicate my theoretical views in this brief digression, it will now be clear why, for the therapist, it is immaterial which aspect of the client's personality is momentarily regnant. If he can relate to that aspect with a sensitive empathy and a complete acceptance (of which more later) then this understanding acceptance will enable the client to accept it within himself, and thus eventually to become more of a whole person. Therapy involves the acceptance by the client of the 'awful' feelings he has denied to awareness, or the terrifying experience of being chaotic and out of control, and of the elements in his previous self. If he can accept all these as being a part of himself, he will gradually assimilate them into a new self-gestalt which includes more of what he is.[17]

Hence the therapist's sensitive understanding is equally effective with every changing facet which is communicated by the client. Whether he is empathizing with a fantastically strange dream-like expression of a feeling previously denied, or with a self frightened by a sense of its own vulnerability and striving desperately to keep control, or with the chaos

---

[16.] An advanced, but not the acute, state as I conceive of it. [J.M.S.]

[17.] It is evident that I am here sharply in disagreement with the psychoanalytic view as voiced by Redlich when he says 'the therapeutic aim must be directed at re-repression rather than at lifting repression'. [Rogers' note.]

produced by a confused regnancy, he is supplying a basic condition of the therapeutic process.

Unconditional Positive Regard

A third condition which is hypothesized as necessary to the establishment of an effective therapeutic relationship is described by the term unconditional positive regard. Let me speak first of positive regard. This means that the therapist is experiencing a warm acceptance of the client, a caring. His feelings are adient — toward the client, rather than abient — away from the client. The word 'love' can be used to describe this attitude, providing it is understood as a nonpossessive caring for the client as a separate person, and not a love which primarily gratifies the therapist's own needs.

It is hypothesized that to be most effective this positive regard should be *unconditional*. This means that there are no conditions of acceptance, no feeling of 'I like you only *if* you are thus and so'. It means that the therapist prizes the negative, defensive, regressive, asocial, mature, positive expressions. He values the client as a total person, and hence values each expression of any facet of that person. I believe that Frieda Fromm-Reichman has frequently shown, in her work with her patients, a very high degree of unconditional positive regard. On the other hand I have listened to recordings of other therapists whose attitude seems to be 'I like you, but I feel much more liking and acceptance when you are being rational and "normal" than when you are being bizarre and regressive'. I would hypothesize that these therapists would be less effective.

The Experiencing of these Conditions by the Client

The fourth essential of a therapeutic relationship is that the client experiences, to a minimal degree, the congruence or transparency of the therapist, his empathic understanding, and his unconditional positive regard. These conditions do not exist for the client and hence do not exist effectively, unless they are experienced by him. Here again it is undoubtedly more difficult to achieve this in the schizophrenic individual, than with the neurotic or normal. How can the therapist's caring be communicated to a withdrawn and suspicious individual? Some therapists have communicated it by gentle physical contact, some by violent argument, in which the schizophrenic is dealt with as an equal, some by the tone of voice.

It seems to me that much of the experimentation in psychotherapy with psychotics comes at this point. If the therapist experiences within himself the conditions of therapy: if he feels 'I care: I can sense your experience from your point of view; and what I am and feel in this relationship is completely open to you'; then he will use a variety of personal ways to communicate these attitudes to the client. He will not always be successful, of course. But where the client does experience some degree of these attitudes in the relationship, then the final condition of therapy exists, and the process of therapeutic change will, it is hypothesized, get under way.

OTHER CHARACTERISTICS

There is in client-centered therapy an overall characteristic — an inclination toward the most literal of explanations. There is a deliberate shunning of the arcane, the esoteric (and, some say, the erotic). Empiricism and 'commonsense' conjecture typify the research and theory. These lean on and are expressed in terms of learning theory, perception, social psychology, interaction analysis (Butler, 1952; Porter, 1950; Snygg and Combs, 1959). This characteristic leads to positions which diverge from traditional clinical opinion on many issues. It is possible only to skim over such issues here. Attitudes toward transference, for instance, range from considering it a fiction which protects the therapist from the consequences of his real behavior and effect to viewing it as early stereotypic behavior which will be extinguished in the natural course of events if it is not cultivated. Symbolic analysis plays little role, partly because it is usually content-specific and covered by response to emotion. (I believe the so-called archaic symbols are significant, chiefly because they are cleaner communicants; like new words in a foreign language, they shake loose the multiple complexities of conventional meanings, and say just the elementary things each person means them to say.) The unconscious does not currently figure in client-centered literature. It is considered a reductionistic assumption about phenomena better understood in terms of attention and 'levels of awareness'.

An ahistorical bias has always been plain among us, and this is one of the currents which moves us to an appreciation of some of the existential writings (Sartre, 1953; Binswanger, 1956). Diagnosis is a moot point too, though our departures are not as radical as they once were. We have written elsewhere our views questioning its validity and usefulness (Shlien, 1959). Jung has made a masterful statement with which we agree (Jung, 1954). For the moment, a statement of Menninger's is one to which I can thoroughly subscribe and which seems especially appropriate in regard to the case you are about to read:

> The word 'schizophrenia' becomes a damning designation. To have it once applied to a young man can be to ruin a career, despite all evidence of subsequent healthiness. A name implies a concept; and if this concept

is unsound, the diagnosis can ruin treatment; the very naming it can damage the patient whom we essay to help. Nathaniel Hawthorne in *The House of Seven Gables* told us what we psychiatrists should well know:

'The sick in mind . . . are rendered more darkly and hopelessly so by the manifold reflection of their disease, mirrored back from all quarters in the deportment of those about them; they are compelled to inhale the poison of their own breath, in infinite repetition.'

It is not that we decry classification as such; we recognize it as a useful scientific tool. But it is dangerous when it leads to reification of terms. (Menninger, 1958)

TREATMENT OF A CASE

ONE WHO 'NEEDED HELP BAD'

Few things are more difficult for a therapist than presenting 'a case'. It was a living, breathing, sometimes gasping, sweating experience. I seriously doubt that we can really picture each other's work this way. I know we cannot do it justice. Also, there is a natural reluctance to make public what was private, even though it is disguised. (I have always admired Freud's forbearance, waiting until 'Anna O.' was dead before writing about her.) How to present the material? The raw data are verbatim dialogues, but that would fill a book, a sometimes tedious book. Subtleties of gestures, unspoken thoughts, analyses, would fill a shelf. They play a part. Worse still, we are conditioned to look for journalistic answers — who did it, what was wrong, where are the points of insight and the hidden keys uncovered by the detective-therapist? It doesn't happen that way. Therapy is bigger — a whole atmosphere — and smaller — moments of internal experience — than can be conveyed by the synopses we can offer.

Michael K. was 28 years old when I first saw him. He had been committed by his family, and was sitting beside the examining psychiatrist at a 'diagnostic staff' in a state hospital. He said he 'needed help bad' and spoke of the 'machine on his head'. My reaction: sympathy, fascination, and challenge. I liked this boy. I wished I could help him. The timer rang indicating an allotted five minutes had passed (the hospital has 8,000 patients), and he was gently dismissed by the overworked psychiatrist. Diagnosis (no question): paranoid schizophrenia. Recommended treatment: electroshock.

Two weeks later, cardiograms and other records completed, his treatment was about to start. I had a vacancy in my schedule and asked that shock be canceled and he be assigned to psychotherapy. During sleepless nights in some of the tense nine months ahead, I often wished I had not gone to the hospital that day.

Michael served as a navy frogman during the Korean war; tough, but scared; was 'trigger-happy' on landing parties, shooting at the dark. After discharge he worked as a carpenter until auditory hallucinations became so distracting that power saws endangered him. His family put him in a private sanitarium. There he received electroshock for three weeks, insulin for seven. He once escaped by climbing over a seven-foot wall on a midwinter night. While there he was given 'truth serum', and on becoming conscious saw his father standing at the foot of the bed while the white-coated attendant wrote down answers to questions. He confessed to some childhood sexual incidents which caused him great shame. Discharged with no improvement he stayed at home. He visited a sick friend, who died the next day. Mike wondered if the cigarette he gave his sick friend had poisoned him. He went to a veterans' hospital for outpatient treatment. To the psychiatrist there he seemed 'outwardly friendly and co-operative, but unwilling to talk about himself because these were "personal" problems'. Mike had the typical attitude of his socio-economic class toward 'talkin' doctors'.

His mother, who later came to see me a few times, said that 'Mickey' had always been a good boy, loyal to his family, always told her the truth — 'would never lie to me' (!). She first noticed 'something wrong' after Korea. 'He began to wolf down his food when it was so hot it would burn.' During the next few years she was his confidante when he was confined to his house. She would listen to him for 'as long as I could stand it, then I'd have to leave the room. I tried to tell him not to talk about those things [whorehouses, etc.] — just to forget it.' She mentioned his need to have more relaxed relations with girls, nice girls, and her distaste was evident when she recalled a time she had cleaned him up with medicinal soap after a visit with other boys to a prostitute.

The father was a first-generation immigrant, a cabinet-maker, in poor health and irascible with his sons, though meek and polite with authorities. There were three sons in their twenties and one older married daughter.

Early phase

Mike came from his locked ward to see me at my request. I told him I would visit the hospital twice a week and would be there to talk with him as part of his treatment. He plunged into a description of the 'machine on his brain'.[18] He thought 'on', and it went on, broadcasting his thoughts over radio and television; he thought 'off' and the broadcast stopped, but his thoughts continued to repeat in his brain. 'Off' caused less shame than the broadcast, but more confusion and loss of sleep. He had 'nothing to hide — a clean record from Washington on

---

[18.] The influencing machine is described in its classical forms by Tausk, see footnote 11, p. 42.

down'. The thoughts changed in voice — maybe an old man, a woman, or a little boy. He had been to the FBI to complain. They had laughed, and he laughed as he told of it, but said it hurt him at the time. His mood shifted from friendly affable amusement at being a source of entertainment to feeling extremely angry and resentful at being exposed. For some of his thoughts were 'rotten', expressed in obscenities which 'shouldn't be broadcast — what if children are listening, for gosh' sake'.

It frightened him to think that nothing in his past could be hidden (he had indeed been grievously exposed at many points), but he reassured himself that he had done nothing wrong — 'a couple of *mistakes*, yes'.

'They' had screamed at him this morning that he 'has a fruity voice' and he'll 'have to suck dick' to get out of here. 'Telling me I'm a fairy — I'm a *man*. I been a man since I was nine.' Whether there was real homosexuality or not, Mike at least expressed a defiantly false sureness of his manliness, his independence and power to cope with the world.

In the next two weeks we began to talk to one another. Mike felt relieved. The voices subsided in volume, talking instead of screaming. He asserted complete innocence — except for a few mistakes, such as blaming the Masonic temple for his problems. He struggled to face himself. 'It's pretty hard for a guy to tell a doc what's really wrong with him.' As he moved closer to this effort, he moved farther away defensively. Now he bore no responsibility for his thoughts, much less their broadcast; everything was put into his mind. 'They can even shove images right into your head. Maybe it's Hollywood. Maybe it's the FBI.' Now his moods switched around to the theme, 'Why me?' reflecting his vacillating self-concept.

> 'I'm nobody. Why pick on me? I'm just an ordinary guy, a worker, I don't make any trouble or had much education — just an ordinary guy. [Brightly.] I'm the only one in the U.S. it's done to. It's something for me to find out for everybody. They tell me I'm a movie star. I'll go down in history. [Suddenly deflated.] I'll go down in history — yeah. I couldn't make a pimple on a movie star's ass.'
> I say, 'Mike, sometimes you feel worthless, and sometimes great, don't you?'
> 'Yeah — I dunno. I — what am I? I don't know. Just nobody, I guess.'

During the next weeks he began to challenge me: I was like everyone else, knew everything, would not tell him about it. He didn't want to hurt my feelings, but did not hide his anger and disgust. We were still friends.

He wondered what his 'mistake' really was. For he too was 'journalistically conditioned' — to find the guilty culprit, to track down the fatal flaw. Maybe it was picking up a blond girl in his car, thinking she was a movie actress, then spending weeks trying to find her again. Then he left the city, alone for the first time, feeling isolated. Some fragments of the interview of this period illustrate typical interaction:

MIKE: *I drove up past the Great Lakes Naval base — the electronics station there, and I thought — maybe that's where it's done. It all seemed so strange. I was all shook up. I felt so, so — ill at ease — so ill at ease. I got to a little town, got a room. Then I started to cry.*

THERAPIST: *I guess you mean you were trying to get away, and it wasn't making you feel any better — you still felt strange and scared.*

M: *Yeah — I felt so strange — I went — Can you please tell me where to find a Lutheran preacher? They told me, and I went to church and prayed, 'Jesus Christ, please help me now,' and I tried — I wanted to talk to someone — to ask 'em if it was all recorded, and that I didn't do it. And I said a lot of foolish things, blamed a lot of people.*

T: *Wanted someone to know. Someone to understand.*

M: Oh they all *know. You know, Doc — everyone knows, but no one will tell me. Maybe I'll have to pull the silver out of my teeth, but that won't help — my dad caught some of it, and he has false teeth. I've got a right to live a normal life, Doc. Why don't people understand? A man makes a mistake, you don't have to murder him, drive him out of my mind. [Strikes match ferociously.]*

T: *[Could respond to the admission of error and resentment of punishment but impressed by match.] Makes you* mad.

M: *Hell, yes. [Glares.] Then I heard these two guys at the plant say, 'We can't turn 'im off yet we got a sum of money invested in 'im.' Now, why don't they tell me what it's all about?*[19]

T: *Why won't some*body *level with you?*

M: *That's right. Why won't — I've had a hell of a time, Doc. I'd hate to see anybody go through this. Seemed like if I tried to explain this to somebody, they'd think I was nuts. Why won't someone believe me? They laughed, the FBI. I guess they got a charge out of it.*

T: *Makes you feel there's nobody on your side, nobody who sees it your way.*

M: *They don't seem to. I been to a lot of places. Doc Millman, I told him, and he said, 'I don't see no wires on you, Mike'. Yeah, don't see 'em — well, I don't know how it's done, it's electronic or what. Anyway, I know I'm personally not to blame, but they can't help me.*

T: *How about me, Mike?*

M: *I don't know about you. [Pause.] If you could go through it maybe a week, maybe a few days — but I'd hate to see anybody else go through this. But if you could, just for a couple of days — they can illusify your mind, like I seen [movie actress]*

[19.] Probably distortion; the men are in a woodworking machine plant and it takes only a little twist to misunderstand *them* (the machines) as *him*.

and she called me over, waved, like this, and she was so real, you could reach out, shake hands, dance, do anything you want —

T: So real, so vivid — it's an amazing and marvelous thing. I guess you're telling me maybe I ought to experience it too, but — [Mike looks startled] — what's the matter?

M: They just said, 'What a son of a bitch you turned out to be.' Screaming it at me. I never done anything. I never killed, raped, or crippled. People put thoughts in my mind. I'm all confused. Everybody must know I'm not a bad guy. [Begins to sob.]

T: Hurts so much.

M: If somebody was in my shoes, they couldn't tell nobody. I told my fiancée. She says, 'See a doctor.' I told the minister. He says, 'Mike, better see a doctor.' What's the use? I ain't got a chance. Not a chance in hell.

T: I guess you're feeling, 'I've tried, and nobody understands. Nobody shares with me — I'm just all alone with it'.

M: All alone, Doc, that's it. What's the use? [Pause.] Can I bum one of your cigarettes?

At the next session, Mike said he had received shock treatment that morning (to my dismay!) and had 'forgotten a lot of things'. He was meek, submissive, watchful for cues as to what his behavior should be, anxious to please, and showed temporary amnesia for recent events. The administration of shock was by accidental order, and was discontinued, but it was a breach of trust which affected our relation in ways I can never appraise.

MIDDLE PHASE

Mike was very morose. He thought his behavior had undermined his family's confidence in him. He felt very helpless now — caged, imprisoned, victimized — and said he got himself in this jam by blaming others (the Masonic temple, etc.). He remembered being given 'truth serum', strapped in bed and struggling not to tell the answers to questions put to him. It was on this occasion that his father heard him confess his childhood experience of fellatio, for one thing. When he was taken home from the sanitorium, he thought he ought to tell his mother about it, but she was 'not too pleased'. At about this time Mike began to develop and/or hint at long-standing feelings toward psychiatrists as the punishers, the probers, the exposers, the unhelpful villains in his experience.

Some of this developed in the next interview. Mike was talking about his observations of a woman patient at a dance.

M: I was trying to figure it out. Everything I thought, I saw her lips repeating. She was in the same sort of shape I'm in. She repeated every word that ran through my head. Then I thought — maybe it was the patients who were mentally ill, it might be good to use this machine on those people. It might help them. Now, it might be the psychiatrists who are doing this. Who else would want to know the function of the mind? I don't. It's a wearying thing to me. I'm pretty tired of it.

T: *Maybe this would help some other people, but it's not helping me — I'm tired of it.*

M: *Yeah. Well, I studied it, up in my mind, I thought about it. I was given truth serum, and I wondered how the inventor did it, and what I worried about was* whether the inventor is responsible.

T: *I don't understand that, Mike. What do you mean?*

M: *I read books on it, and studied on it. And maybe when I told about this during truth serum, maybe that's when they heard of it. I don't know if I had anything to do with it. I can't figure it out. It's too impossible. You can't see anything. All you can do is hear — and you can see hallucinations.*

He went on to speculate that he invented it, but they (the psychiatrists) perfected it, wanting to test his strength.

M: *Let 'em experiment with somebody else. The mind is a delicate thing. I'd hate to see anybody else go through this shit. It's not funny. I know I didn't invent this thing, and if I did, I'd like to burn it. It's like taking your fucking life away from you. I don't go around pulling switches and throwing the juice in people. [Probably a reference to shock therapy.] Now the guy at the foot of the bed — he wrote everything down, and maybe they got the idea from me. Whoever invented this fucking thing oughta be shot — then I'm thinking, oh oh, maybe I'm partly to blame for this.*

T: *Seems as if somebody else ought to be punished, but then you think, 'God, maybe I thought of this — I wish I hadn't.'*

M: *That's right. I think I kind of invented it but the psychiatrists perfected it.*

As Mike began to assume some responsibility (symbolically), he defensively moved farther away from ultimate blame and further into self-deception. He finished the interview in a rage at being deceived, the butt of jokes, dishonesty, experimentation.

In the ensuing week, he told the ward physician to 'please cut my brains out before I kill somebody'. This referred to me, for I had become the enemy of enemies. Nor was this simply transference. I do represent hospital, professional people who treat and mistreat, I *do* refuse to 'tell him all about it' (couldn't), I do frustrate, misunderstand, and disappoint. Mike became violent in the ward, for which he was sent to 'security' or given sedation. Often he refused to see me. When he would come, his 'oceanic rage' was more than I could bear with equanimity — I became afraid, and often wished I did not have to see him.

During this period, attendants sometimes waited outside the closed door.

Looking back, the most interesting thing is the advice given at this time. What Rogers says in this chapter, 'It is more therapeutic for him openly to *be* that fear, even expressing it to the client, than to present a calm and unruffled front', was probably written with me in mind. I regret that I did not test his hypothesis. Rather, I took the 'lion-tamer's' advice of the ward physician who said, 'Never let them know you're afraid.[20] It frightens them'. The clinical director, a wise and experienced therapist, felt that there were really safeguards in Mike, and that I need not be afraid, but if I was — 'You have to live with it while it lasts'. So I presented a calm front while I worked through my fears and Mike worked out his rage. The end of this period (which lasted three months) was marked by my suggesting that we walk outside on the grounds for the hour. We trusted each other to do this, and the most significant moments of therapy took place thereafter while sitting on a bench or on the grass.

LATER PHASE

Mike asked for and obtained a grounds pass — freedom to leave the ward. He was given permission for home visits.[21] His family said he was 'fine'. Does that mean he had solved the riddle of the influencing machine? Or that it was gone? Neither, completely. He was much less affected by it. For one thing, he recognized *some* of the images as recollections of his own past experience. This was an advance over acknowledging the possible invention of the machine — it acknowledged the content of his experience. Second, he began to deny, to his mother (and less to me) that he heard any voices. He took the view (a realistic one) that if he told us, it would delay his release from the hospital and that *if he did not tell us, we would not know.* His privacy was restored! He might say, with a grin, 'I don't want to talk about it', or soberly, 'I can live with it', or just 'No, not any more'. If his privacy was restored by human contact, what sort of contact was there in those hours on the lawn? Sometimes silence. Sometimes talk of the same sort already reported. Sometimes he began to cry softly, saying, 'They talk about needing love and affection. I know what *that* means. The only good thing I ever had [his engagement to a girl] taken away from me, broken up.' He blew his nose, dropped his handkerchief, and as he picked it up, glanced at me. He saw tears in my eyes. He offered me the handkerchief, then drew it back because he knew he had just wiped his nose on it and could feel the wetness on his hand. We both knew this, each knew the other knew it; we both understood the feel and the meaning of the handkerchief (the stickiness and texture, the sympathy of the offering and the

---

[20.] Really laughable, since no one was fooled, and we knew it.

[21.] These and all administrative decisions were made by the ward physician.

embarrassment of the withdrawal) and we acknowledged each other and the interplay of each one's significance to the other. It is not the tears, but the exquisite awareness of dual experience that restores consciousness of self. A self *being,* the self-concept can change.

Six months earlier, there had been an interchange like this:

M: Can I bum one, Doc?

T: Does it make you feel like a bum, Mike, to take my cigarettes?

M: Yeah. I — it's a way I feel. I hate to have to ask for anything. At home, when I'm not working, I hate to see Mom put the food on the table.

T: Hurts your pride?

M: I hate to feel like a bum. I guess I am a bum.

Having a grounds pass, Mike could buy his own cigarettes (but not carry matches), and he offered me one, or bought me a Coke, as often as I did him. These were important ways in which he restored his feeling of equality and self-respect. More often, he did not want to talk about himself, was sometimes surly, wanted to discontinue therapy, insisted he was ready to go home. No one felt he was 'cured', but he made it look good enough on the outside and was so much better on the inside that the hospital was not helping any longer. His parents took him home. He told them that legally they could, because they were the ones who 'signed him in'. At one time this was 'impossible' to him; his parents could *only* love and want him, *never* would commit him.

Where is Mike now? Happy ending? No — this is really a fragment, a fragment of therapy and of his life. Mike does not come to see me. Where he lives, 'A person has to be goofy to go to a psychiatrist'. After four months at home, he is working again at his carpenter's trade, trying to make a life for himself. He said on the telephone that he is 'pretty *good'.* His mother said, *'pretty* good.' Shall the curtain of privacy be drawn against the inquiry of science? I think so. My mind goes back to a scene on the lawn of the hospital. Mike said, 'I went to church yesterday, Doc, and I said a prayer that I could go home and this would never happen again. I said a little prayer for you, too — that you could help me and always be well yourself'. I was moved, and said, 'Thank you'. Right now, in my way, Mike, I say a little prayer for you. For all of us.

REFERENCES

Binswanger, L. (1956). Existential Analysis and Psychotherapy. In F. Fromm-Reichmann & J.L. Moreno (Eds.), *Progress in Psychotherapy Vol. I.* New York: Grune.

Butler, J.M. (1952). Interaction of Client and Therapist, *J. Abnorm. Soc. Psychol.*

Harper, R.A. (1959). *Psychoanalysis and Psychotherapy, 36 Systems.* Englewood Cliffs, N.J.: Prentice-Hall, pp. 83–4.

Heron, W. (1957). The Pathology of Boredom. *Scientific American, 196*, 52–6.

Hoch, P.H. & Kalinowsky, L.B. (1946). *Shock Treatments and Other Somatic Procedures in Psychiatry.* New York: Grune, p. 242.

Jung, C.G. (1954). The Practice of Psychotherapy, *Collected Works 16.* Bollingen Series 20, pp. 85–6.

Mead, G.H. (1934). *Mind, Self, and Society.* Chicago: Univ. Chicago Press.

Menninger, K. (1958). The Unitary Concept of Mental Illness. *Bull. Menn. Clinic, 22.*

Olds, J. & Milner, P. (1954). *J. Comp. Physiol. Psychol., 47*, 419.

Porter, E.H. Jr. (1950). *An Introduction to Therapeutic Counseling.* Boston: Houghton Mifflin.

Rogers, C.R. (1951). *Client-Centered Therapy.* Boston: Houghton Mifflin.

Sartre, J-P. (1953). *Existential Psychoanalysis.* New York: Philosophical Library.

Sartre, J-P. (1958). Self-Deception. In W. Kaufmann (Ed.), *Existentialism from Dostoevsky to Sartre.* New York: Meridian.

Shlien, J. (1959). In M. Lewis, C. Rogers, J. Shlien, Time-Limited, Client-Centered Psychotherapy: Two Cases, in A. Burton (ed.), *Case Studies in Counseling and Psychotherapy.* Englewood, NJ: Prentice-Hall.

Snygg, D. & Combs, A. (1959). *Individual Behavior.* New York: Harper.

CHAPTER 5

Secrets and the Psychology of Secrecy

All secrecy corrupts; semisecrecy corrupts absolutely.

This paraphrase of Lord Acton's famous dictum, 'All power corrupts; absolute power corrupts absolutely',[1] connects us at once with the idea that secrets and secrecy are related to power. Absolutely true. The paraphrase (from the British statesman R. H. S. Crossman) further tells us that there is danger and destruction inherent in secrecy. It is not the total falsehood but the half-truth that corrupts completely. The half-true lie captures all available energy for its disentangling. Things do not fit as a whole, but neither can the right and wrong parts be separated from the intentionally sticky wrappings. The mind-numbing outcome is 'learned ignorance'.

Crossman's paraphrase was developed after World War II, during a period of obsession with 'security' and 'intelligence' that extends to the present. Interestingly, those two words, 'security' and 'intelligence', tell us something about the alluring but false meanings of secrecy. Strong, honorable, and humane security and intelligence do not come from secrecy, but we are misled to think that they do, and we are weakened (corrupted) thereby. Documents are stamped 'Secret', 'Top Secret', 'Read and Destroy', so that merely 'Secret' is a mild classification. Moreover, everything is 'leaked', sometimes deliberately. Thus the atmosphere of semisecrecy, the worst.

First published in *Client-Centered Therapy and the Person-Centered Approach: New Directions in Theory, Research and Practice*, pp. 390–9. Edited by R. F. Levant and J. M. Shlien. © 1984 Praeger Publishers. Reproduced with permission of Greenwood Publishing Group Inc., Westport, CT.
Originally adapted from a paper presented at American Psychological Association Symposium, 'Client-Centered Therapy in the 1980s' (Shlien, 1981).
[1.] It may not be absolute power for that is seldom if ever achieved, but it is the striving for absolute power that we see so often corrupting so many.

In such an atmosphere, everything is suspect. That is one illustration of the difference between secrets and secrecy. When everything is suspect, most people seek safety in a conspiracy, for reasons they do not quite know or fully inquire into, and thereby become outsiders supporting a secret society — which, if it actually exists, may have some *secrets* (rituals, documents, symbols). Even if so, and if these secrets become known surreptitiously, the society is still surrounded by *secrecy*. That is the real source of its power. Secrets and secrecy are separate concepts, and our true intelligence is sapped by the search for the secrets, leaving us victim of and co-conspirator in secrecy. Meanwhile, there are countervailing forces pressing for public exposure of *all* information, but we do not know whether these are true libertarians ('open covenants, openly arrived at') or enemies from another unfriendly secret society. The cross-currents from this uncertainty further paralyze and imbed us in secrecy.

Much of our lifetime is geared to the production of excuses, defenses, masking images, to contend with our own and each other's unwanted realities or to create desired appearances that we wish might become realities. That is how we actually live. Then there is the other side of the ambivalence — how we (sometimes) want to live. In the psychic (and perhaps neurological) economy of the individual there is an urge for 'cleanliness', the wish for straight and clear passage without delay and confusion. If constant cleanliness is not the wish — because there is also an urge for disguise, adventure, and intricacy as an art form — people at least seek occasional 'purification' in forms of confession and psychotherapy. (Failing that, there are the deathbed confessions, those sad final clearance sales for which the owner paid the price and lived the worse for it.)

Secrets and secrecy have always been a force in the history and literature of psychotherapy. In fact, it seems that secrets have been the main currency in the commerce between therapist and patient since Freud developed the psychoanalytic method and described his early case studies, setting the tone for a long tradition. 'Dora' is an example. 'I believe that Dora only wanted to play "Secrets" with me, and to hint that she was on the verge of allowing her secret to be torn from her by the physician' (Freud, 1959, p. 94). In the same study he presents a description of symbolic behavior: 'a very entertaining episode', he calls it, when another patient opens and closes a little box she always carries, leading to the now predictable conclusion that it, 'like the reticule and jewel-case, was once again only a substitute for the shell of Venus, for female genitals' (p. 94). The clever detective, the amused and powerful physician, the disclosure of 'private parts' to the curious public, and the unmistakable fact that anxious neurotics do want both to hide and reveal — all these combine to make psychotherapy a study of secrets. Secrets appear to be the hidden treasure (buried, repressed), and the quest for the 'keys' — the techniques of uncovering — is the central objective of practice. How different it might be if practices could enable clients to feel safe enough to reveal more willingly what they quite well know.

The atmosphere of secrecy is enhanced by the pseudorespectful air of 'confidentiality', such as postponement of publication of personal material and the reasonable ethical concern that guarantees should attend personal revelations confided in good faith. That is, there should be secrecy about secrets. It is important to mention three points here. Keeping other people's secrets is not the same as keeping one's own, so confidentiality should not be mistaken for a secret. Second, the somewhat-abused and often-honored-in-the-breach concept of confidentiality tends to draw a curtain of deferential inhibition around the phenomenon of secrecy, leaving the focus on techniques of uncovering secrets. Third and most important, secrecy is a separate layer, over and above content, therefore not the same as secrets. Secrets may be negative, positive, or neutral in social value, but secrecy is *always* ominous.

To illustrate: a child goes for a walk with her mother and aunt. 'I heard the F-word at school today. What does it mean?' Mother to child: 'Nothing.' Mother to aunt, audibly but over the child's head: 'How can you tell a child a thing like that?'

The child has just learned that there are secrets, and there is also secrecy. About that latter she does not quite know, or what to ask. She will learn the meaning (content) of the secret, overcome that particular ignorance, but how will she ever completely 'unlearn' (overcome) secrecy and the sense of it? The secret has captured her attention. When she solves that, she thinks she has solved the whole — except for that half-sensed knowledge that there is always something still more forbidden in the world, in the air, like a cloud, almost nameless. Call it secrecy. Secrecy is the whisper in which the secret is told or hidden. This is how 'learned ignorance' comes into being.

A black student once told me, 'They [white parents] tell their children something about not playing with us, and I don't know what it is.'[2] He isn't supposed to know. Even the white parents aren't supposed to know, nor are their children. It just 'happens', and how it happens they hope will be forgotten because they did not intend an open instruction. That might have been questioned. Even if presented as a secret ('I'll tell you this, but don't tell'), it can, though with difficulty, be questioned. Secrecy, on the other hand, would have you believe that you thought of this yourself, even if ashamed, even if you can't account for or justify it.

---

[2] This could happen to any child of another local minority — Jewish, Catholic, Protestant, poor — in some way frightening or despised and arousing both a need for self-protection and shame at the injustice.

CLIENT-CENTERED APPROACH TO SECRETS

I first heard of Carl Rogers (during World War II) when a fellow soldier-psychologist characterized the Rogerian position as, 'Let the patient keep his secret until the pain of bearing it is greater than the shame of revealing it'. It was unfriendly, it was wrong, but it was the prevailing image of the cold-hearted 'brass-instrument' American psychologist turned to therapeutic endeavors. Such ruthless patience made the 'probe' seem relatively benign, and the symbolic analysis of dreams as the 'royal road to the unconscious' seemed a warm and sunny passage by comparison.

That statement ('Let the patient keep his secret until . . .') left me with a considerable prejudice against Carl Rogers. When we first met, I was interviewing him from the standpoint of the sociology of knowledge. He surprised me. He was not cold and implacable. Still, I was not a client, but an inquisitive and somewhat bumptious student, and might not be seeing him at his ruthless worst. Later, I came to know him well, have been a close observer of his work and a friend to him and his family for 30 years. I can say with certainty: *he is not very interested in secrets.* Interested in privacy, self-discovery, expressions of hidden feelings and thought, yes, but as for searching out secrets as key events or hidden traumatic episodes, no. The client will hardly have her secret 'torn from her'. Rogers does not play the game.

Here are some excerpts (around the thirty-fourth interview) from the well-known case of Mrs. Oak — a case filmed and reported in detail in Rogers and Dymond, *Psychotherapy and Personality Change:*

1C: And then, of course, I've come to . . . to see and to feel that over this . . . see, I've covered it up. (*Weeps.*) But . . . and . . . I've covered it up with so much *bitterness,* which in turn I had to cover up. (*Weeps.*) *That's* what I want to get rid of! I almost don't *care* if I hurt.

1T: (*Gently.*) You feel that here at the basis of it, as you experienced it, is a feeling of real tears for yourself. But that you *can't* show, mustn't show, so that's been covered by bitterness that you don't like, that you'd like to be rid of. You almost feel you'd rather absorb the hurt than to . . . than to feel the bitterness. (*Pause.*) And what you seem to be saying quite strongly is, 'I do *hurt,* and I've tried to cover it up.'

2C: I didn't *know* it.

2T: M-hm. Like a new discovery really.

3C: (*Speaking at the same time.*) *I never really did know. But it's . . . you know, it's almost a physical thing. It's . . . it's sort of as though I — I — I were looking within myself at all kinds of . . . nerve endings and*

> — *and bits of — of . . . things that have been sort of mashed.*
> (*Weeping.*) [emphasis added]

3T: As though some of the most delicate aspects of you — physically almost — have been crushed or hurt.

4C: Yes. And you know, I do get the feeling, oh, you poor thing. (*Pause.*)

4T: Just can't help but feel very deeply sorry for the person that is you.

(C. R. Rogers and R. E. Dymond, Eds., *Psychotherapy and Personality Change*, pp. 326–7. Chicago: University of Chicago Press, 1954. Copyright © 1954 by the University of Chicago Press. Reprinted by permission.)

This case was important to Rogers. He was fully invested in understanding this sometimes vague and poetic woman. He was anything but inattentive. For years after her therapy ended, I had many opportunities to talk with Mrs. Oak about her family, work, and pleasures, as a friend. (She is, sorry to say, no longer alive.) At the point (3C above, italicized for emphasis), she had been thinking, among several simultaneous thoughts, of a secret, an experience she had never wanted to tell anyone. It was about the awkward, painful, disillusioning first sexual experience and the rupture of her hymen. The shock and disappointment lasted for months. She knew it need not be so, had not been so for some other women ('It's just a little piece of skin'), but it had been for her.

Perhaps without much stretch of the imagination you can read it in her words, 'within myself at all kinds of . . . nerve endings and bits of . . . things that have been sort of mashed'. It is not that Rogers missed the delicacy, the almost physical quality of the hurt. Nor had the two of them failed to explore her sexual feelings. But he did not probe. He did not dart, alert for the secret.

Mrs. Oak laughed when she told me about it. It was no longer a 'secret'. Though she hadn't told anyone, though she easily could, she no longer feared to tell it. It was a matter of indifference. She said that she could have told Carl the explicit details — there was plenty of opportunity both in his response and later — but 'he heard me then as he heard me always, in terms of my feelings and my whole self'. In a most fascinating way, she felt that she *had* told it.[3] It was explicitly included in her mind, though not in her words, and his understanding seemed to

---

[3.] What is so fascinating? First, that understanding of the general seems to the client to include understanding of the particulars! Second, it is damned fortunate that is so, since we all have simultaneous thoughts in awareness, but only one voice to express them. That is a comment on the nature of consciousness, levels of awareness, problems of selection and retrieval — all of the greatest importance in themselves, and as related to secrecy, but beyond the scope of this chapter.

her to cover that. At any rate, if it was just a little piece of skin, then it was just a little bit of journalism lost, but at stake was a big broken dream. Life was supposed to have been beautiful. Did they then discuss broken dreams? To judge that, you must read the whole case. (Yes.) The practical point here is that Rogers was not waiting for and did not pursue typical secrets in typical ways.

LINES OF INQUIRY ON SECRETS AND SECRECY

Prompted by the significance of secrets and secrecy in this field, and the contrast in ways of dealing with such material, I have joined in an attempt to investigate the subject, which has become a matter of keen interest to scholars from many fields (Bok, 1982). What can be briefly mentioned in these pages does not have the status of proven facts, only of tentatively supported opinion.

From informants in dozens of interviews and from reflection upon the topic and its literature, there are many interesting leads for research under way. In material from psychotherapy, it appears that secrets, however dramatic or titillating, are reported *by the therapist* as (1) intimate disclosures; (2) tiny in their social significance; (3) about someone *else's* (the client's or patient's) demeanor. The secrets themselves are large to the withholder but make almost no difference to anyone else. (A hidden blemish, wicked thoughts of personal deeds or intentions.) The therapist is usually impressed by the content *only because of the difficulty the client has in exposing it*. Therapists are also impressed by their own status as receivers — that is, exceptionally trusted and trustworthy. The effect is to turn attention away from science and toward journalism. It leads the therapist to the role of 'investigative reporter'. The allure of tracking secrets keeps the focus on the other. Secret-collecting is almost entirely 'the psychology of other people', when the best source of knowledge is, in this topic especially, oneself. Obviously, the material does not lend itself readily to the researcher. That being its nature, inquiry is difficult. That difficulty should drive investigators to self-examination and disclosure rather than the torture of recalcitrant subjects.

It is well known that secrecy is judged by a double standard. Secrets and lies play a positive part in the development of ego boundaries or the sense of individuality during childhood.[4] Later in life these same behaviors may be socially corrosive and psychologically deadly. The ambivalence continues. While it may be healthy to live openly and honestly, it would, however, be dreadful — indeed,

---

[4.] Standard examples: 'I did not take the cookie', 'I did have a bowel movement', when neither is true. The discovery that a parent cannot with certainty know otherwise is a source of separate identity. The trouble is, it is confused with guilt, and we must wonder, is there not a better way to assure individual development of autonomy *and* integrity?

a condition of realized paranoia — to be totally transparent against one's will.

In our studies, lies do not clearly or necessarily at all qualify as secrets. Secrets have to do with shame. Privacy has to do with dignity. Lies may be used to cover secrets, but lies do not fit well with maintenance of privacy and the desired sense of dignity.

Secrets and lies have an odd relation to the truth. Secrets — when they have content — are phenomenologically true, and may never have been lied about, simply not revealed. Curiously, the audience for a revealed secret tends overwhelmingly to take it for the truth, simply because it had been hidden. The lie, however, starts with factually known truth, departs from that base, and is often then supported by a network of subsidiary lies so far from the original truth that the connection grows dim, and the most recent lies are for the sake of the just previous ones, rather than the departed truth (which may, by this time, be forgotten).

Secrets are mistakenly described as undiscovered facts of nature (the location of the lost Atlantis, etc.), but no, secrets are only human, They are the property of persons who do not want someone else to know something. The secret must have some value to the withholder. Secrets told anonymously have relatively little effect on the teller. To have full effect the secret should not fall on deaf or indifferent ears. The receivers of secrets have their own problems as containers, a subject of great complexity and of considerable interest to therapists.

Informants believe that they can recollect their first lie, and usually their first secret. They seldom feel sure that they can recall the points at which they learned the concept or sense of secrecy.

Secret-having tends at an early age to become a content-empty, abstract form. Children frequently manipulate others by claiming, 'I know something you don't know', when in fact all they know is that this is a source of power and attraction on an inclusion-exclusion basis. (This is, of course, the basis of the elementary 'secret society'.)

In the psychological economy, many secrets are kept as treasures, but the keeper pays the interest. Keeping secrets prevents change. This may be valuable if it is a good thing to hold the personality in place, even though very expensive to support.

On the other hand, revealing secrets has at least two powerful effects. One is the initiation of change. In therapy, it is of enormous importance, a *giant* step in moving out of a frozen pattern. *The act of revelation seems to be more significant than the content of the secret.*

The second effect of revealing is the investment of your personal power in the guardianship of the receiver. Depending somewhat upon the nature of your secret, one tends to think better of (to attribute goodwill and trustworthiness to) the recipient after than before telling the secret.

Often those who have told secrets feel empty and depressed, since secrets are exciting property. Finding secrets is as exciting as holding; therefore two or more parties often agree to share secrets by way of recompense.

Every informant knows or recognizes at once these three features of secret-giving and taking: (1) the power of the secret in bonding; (2) the dread of isolation; and (3) the artifice of making something valuable by making it rare. Each is of enormous significance, a chapter in itself.

Daydreams may be more important than night dreams. Certainly informants are more cautious and secretive about daydreams. Most feel more responsible for them, as if waking production of a fantasy is more deliberate, calculated, and therefore more revealing.

There are five main classes of people to whom secrets are told: (1) The Stranger — perhaps a chance meeting with someone not to be seen again; (2) The Confidante — a friend, priest, a hired or furnished professional; (3) The Loved One — a relationship of intimacy, probably reciprocal, in which they not only exchange secrets but create secrets; (4) The Captive — a harmless prisoner, unable to betray, could even be scheduled for death; (5) The Fellow — a recognized covert or 'closet' kinship, matching stigmata, dangerous but in the same danger. The psychotherapists who see these five categories believe that they are involved in at least three, sometimes all, at various stages.

So far, this is largely about secrets. The psychology of secrecy is about that next layer, secrecy. No one tells us how it is brought about, and we are not to expose its existence, though no one told us that, either. That is what the psychology of secrecy must be about. In terms of modern systems theory, it is *recursive*. The task for a psychology of secrecy is to describe the phenomenon, and to explain (1) the *motives* that keep secrecy alive, and (2) the *purposes* it serves, both well and poorly.

One of those purposes is to preserve the reciprocal infliction of mixed pain and pleasure called 'the tyranny of the neurosis'. There are some, and I am one, who think that the tyranny of neuroses is the most powerful thing on earth. You have seen it many times. It starts with some content, and a mutual agreement not to acknowledge that content. You might think this an 'agreement to disagree', but no, it is an 'agreement to agree'! That may seem unnecessary, but no, they must have the agreement to agree because (1) it is secret, and (2) they know that there are also reasons why they should *not* agree (see Chapter 8, pp. 101–2, this volume, for example). Then follows a forever-expanding collaboration of reverberating deceit and self-deceit which in fact *both parties know* well but dare not admit to themselves or each other.

For example, a woman gradually entices her adolescent son to turn with her against his shy and inoffensive father, who later kills himself. No, this one: a professor, out of jealously, dislike, or possessiveness, ruins a brilliant, effeminate student. Then, out of some guilt and much fear of criticism, he rescues the student. The student knows that he should hate the professor, but cannot afford to, and is also grateful, as he is supposed to be. The professor knows he is hated and should be, but the gratitude, real and pretended, is a balance he seeks. They need each other. They invent intricate and, to observers, preposterous affectations, defenses of each other (to just short of the point of real clearance). Soon they are quite dependent upon one another. They play off third parties, who are also aware but pretend not to be. They bind one another in renewed ways until they become both slave and master to each other. Each makes the other pay heavily by further elevating, then humiliating. Both know the process all too well. Both are so ashamed of it and gratified by some aspects that they cannot bear to acknowledge it, much less make public confession of their *semisecret* relationship, and now the process (of secrecy) takes control.

From this process, as always happens in the analysis of secrecy, a new and this time a socially significant secret emerges. In this instance, the secret is: slavery is not dead. It may be outlawed in the social system, but it is alive and unwell in the individuals. The masking 'agreement to agree' constitutes a culture in which this neurosis can develop. Some people want to be masters. Others are willing to be slaves, at least temporarily, knowing dimly or more clearly that they may later enslave their erstwhile masters and again at least temporarily reverse the roles. Or the roles become intermingled in what some call *complementary neuroses*, which then produce the tyranny from which escape is no more likely than revolution.

That is the danger in the game of secrets. If it would only stay that game; but it becomes secrecy, and very much needs a psychology.

REFERENCES

Bok, S. (1982). *On the ethics of concealment and revelation.* New York: Pantheon.

Freud, S. (1959). *Collected papers* (Vol. 3). New York: Basic Books.

Rogers, C.R. & Dymond, R.E. (Eds.) (1954). *Psychotherapy and Personality Change,* pp. 326–7. Chicago: University of Chicago Press.

Shlien, J.M. (1981). The psychology of secrecy and another generation of best-kept secrets. In C.R.Rogers (Chair), *Client-Centered Therapy in the 1980s.* Symposium presented at the Annual Meeting of the American Psychological Association, Los Angeles.

CHAPTER 6

Macht Therapie Glucklich?
Can Therapy Make You Happy?

*The Chinese, while trying to increase longevity through
the use of alchemy, accidentally invented gunpowder.*

This is a surprisingly difficult question. At first, it was hard to take it seriously.
The idea seems so benevolent, so cheerful. Then it became quite serious, even
dangerous. I am afraid to be the messenger who brings the bad news.

My opinions may not be right or true — certainly not for other people,
other cultures, other times. From the program [of the Congress, Ed.], it became
clear that others will also address this question. I hope to learn from your opinions.

Repeatedly, as I ask myself 'What is the answer?', I think, 'What is the
question?' Also, why this question, and not others? If you had asked, 'Does therapy
bring sweet dreams?' I could answer with considerable confidence, 'No — it
brings more lucid dreams.'

Happiness, however, is something else — it is an old philosophical question.
It does need to be reviewed. The world changes, new possibilities emerge. 'Human
rights' have become a universal concern, as never before. Perhaps they include
happiness, as never before.

We often hear it said of successful clients, 'He/she seems to be a much happier
person.' That sounds true, but also incomplete and therefore superficial. It does
not necessarily extend from adjective, 'happier', into noun, 'happiness'. It raises a
question; is happiness the description of a constant and permanent condition?

The world around us hardly justifies living in such a state. Happiness would
mean a kind of indifference to the unhappiness of others; self-deceit, or withdrawal
— or even perversely, enjoyment of the unhappiness of others. On the other
hand, there is the possibility that happiness is contagious, so that it would be to

Keynote Address presented to the Congress of the Gesellschaft fur Wissenschaftliche
Gesprachspsychotherapie, Cologne, on February 20, 1989.

the benefit of others. Then the question 'macht therapie glucklich?' refers to the world at large. Does therapy introduce a factor of happiness into the world-at-large? I am inclined to think so, but it is a very small contribution, so far.

Is happiness a 'natural' condition, only waiting (like the growth motive) to be released? I do not think so. It is no more natural than other feelings. Most adults think that happiness is more a condition of childhood than adult life. In fact, happiness appears to be a concept more related to the past or to the future than one to be found in present existence. It is more an abstract idealization, the Garden of Eden, or the eventual Paradise Restored. I would not rule it out as a possibility any more than I would rule out the idea of eternal youth. But life everlasting and life painless is not to be. *Growth would not permit it*. First, growth itself is painful as well as joyous.

Second, each step forward leads closer to the end of life. Happiness as an *objective* of life is a question in itself. For life, and for therapy, I believe the poetic line, 'A man's reach must exceed his grasp, else what's a heaven for?', because I believe in dynamic growth rather than any achieved final state.

Perhaps people enter therapy because they are unhappy, leading us, and them, to imagine that 'happiness' is at the other end. Wrong. *Health*, instead, is at the other end (especially in more positive terms than the 'absence of pain or illness'). Happiness is a poor misconceived substitute for health.

One might say, 'health for what?' Oddly, we do not ask, 'happiness for what?' We think of it as without further purpose. That is only a mirage, or illusion.

I was recently called for a case supervision of a couple, in which the same event seemed to bring happiness for two different people. These two had been, separately, in various forms of therapy for several years. They discovered a strong and passionate affinity. After their first sexual adventure, she asked hopefully, 'Are you happy?' He, with his arm still around her, said, 'Yes. Are you happy?' They seem to have found happiness together. However, she is happy because she is able to give pleasure. He, because he can take pleasure. This may not be happiness after all. It is more like what is called 'a complementary neurosis'. Each was relieved of some doubt and anxiety about themselves. They were happy, but not healthy.

This brings up the question about therapy: what kind? Also what quality? The quality, of course, matters very much. It is useless to make judgments about the value of any form unless it is the best of its kind. We can read about what therapy, theoretically, is supposed to do. Very few therapies do all they are supposed to, fully or ideally, because very few therapists, with their vast differences in ability, experience, and understanding of the theory, can demonstrate the theory in practice. (That is one of the reasons for the research finding that the more experienced and capable therapists of *different* orientations are more alike than the less experienced and less capable therapists of the *same* orientation.)

Knowing that there are large differences in quality, we still have the important question about what *kind* of therapy relates to what meaning of 'happiness'. In the case illustration of the temporarily happy couple, a behavior modification practitioner might think that relief of anxiety was sufficient, regardless of meanings. Behavior modification is *pragmatic*. What works is enough. Symptom relief is enough. The world in general is ready to settle for this.

I would say that the attitude of psychoanalysis is stoicism. That is, happiness is the ability to endure life, the vicissitudes of life — and still be able to love and to work (and recently, some psychoanalytic modernists have added, 'to play').

From my experience in observing 'gestalt therapy' (which has nothing to do with gestalt psychology of Kohler, Wertheimer and others) and my personal knowledge of Fritz Perls, I would say that Gestalt therapy has a sort of Epicurean philosophy in relation to happiness. (Not the more refined and cultivated philosophy which included prudence, but the crude variety of hedonism and indulgence, after Aristippus.)

Client-centered therapy is certainly not a matter of relief as an aim. [Relief from anxiety, pain or 'unhappiness' since classical Client-Centered Therapy has no 'aims' other than to follow the client, Ed.] I would say that the primary objective is freedom, informed choice, responsible choice, self-determination — whether or not that includes happiness. Client-centered therapy is a theory of dynamic change, in directions chosen by the client, not prescribed by the therapist. (It should be kept in mind that its optimistic assumptions come from observations about clients in the safe, accepting opportunity of therapy, and these may not realistically apply in ordinary social situations.)

A philosophy of change needs careful understanding. It could be mistaken as adventurist 'change for the sake of change'. It is not a philosophy of romanticism, hardship, or punishment. It is a creative response to *inevitable* conditions of change, due to *inevitable* factors of growth, development, new organisms and combinations.

At this point, it seems only fair to give you my own position. Since I struggled through two previous versions, these are no longer conclusions to be revealed on the last page. Here are some of my opinions.

MACHT THERAPIE GLUCKLICH?

I would say, first, that if happiness is at all a consequence, it is not a *direct* consequence of therapy. Therapy does not *make* happiness. The client may *create* it, as a secondary effect. In spite of its *seeming* to be of ultimate significance, it is not an end-product itself, but a by-product of other positive factors, much as confidence, self-esteem, *accomplishments*, etc.

Second, happiness is not a valid end-in-itself or end-by-itself. If it comes, it is not only a consequence of other factors, but it will be *one consequence among many*. Whatever enables happiness will also enable a wide range of other experiences, such as sadness, loneliness, or whatever life may bring. What therapy makes is the *capacity* for happiness, not the happiness itself.

And if happiness is considered to be a state that excludes these other dimensions of feeling and thought, then, I would say, a psychotherapy that brings such a conclusion is a failure.[1]

Third, however appealing and benevolent happiness may be, I do not consider it to be a worthy ultimate objective of therapy or of life. Instead, I believe that the most important personal objective in modern civilization is: *how to lead an honorable life*.

I have no evidence that any therapy contributes to this objective, or even tries to address it. It is a 'moral' question (in a way that happiness is not). Finding an answer to this question would not guarantee happiness, or serenity, or any other benefit such as social rewards. That is one of the strange features of this moral question. The only motive that makes it work perfectly is a strange idea: *virtue is its own reward.*

This essential motive is completely personal and internal. 'Virtue is its own reward.' I wonder how that strikes you? I found it hard to comprehend, hard to learn, still more difficult to teach, and hard to live by as a principle.

This internal reward gives a special satisfaction. It is a deep and solid feeling, with firm conviction and without doubt or ambivalence. That is rare. The feeling does not diminish in time. That is rare also. From my small experience of it, I recommend this, if you search for ultimate goals.

Let me give you a little illustration. This comes from one side of American life, and I will say something about another side later. Here is a statement from a 65-year-old lawyer, married, two daughters and one grandson. He belongs to a group of volunteers who go to a hospital at different hours of day and night, to nurse (bottle feed) and hold and comfort small infants. Many of these infants are offspring of mothers too ill to care for them, often drug addicts. The hospital staff cannot take good personal care of each baby, so the volunteers do. This man says, 'We just go and give them love, and hold them. I was struck by that act being an important thing to do. If you ever want to do something unselfishly, with no return, without a thank you, this is it.'

There is virtue as its own reward. If this is happiness, I would be proud to think that therapy had some part in producing it. It is interesting that these people, who belong to groups calling themselves Samaritans, The Open Hand,

---

[1.] A psychoanalyst friend says, 'Therapy is the one thing that makes you feel worse but do better.'

etc., are active and numerous. About half of all adult Americans offer some time to a cause. The average volunteer offers about five hours a week. That is one side of contemporary America.

Therapy cannot take credit for the people in this illustration, but then, therapy never claimed to have invented kindness or compassion. We could even ask whether therapy does, in fact, contribute to being a more humane person. I think that it does. More sensitive, aware, empathic? Yes. More appreciative of truth and beauty? Yes. Possessing greater dignity? Confidence? Self-respect and acceptance? More energetic? Yes to all of those. More friendly, though perhaps with fewer friends, now being more selective and sincere.

More hope? Clarity of thought? Creativity? Greater sense of freedom? Better memory? Yes.

More honesty and courage (the two essential features of good therapy)? Yes. Better physical health? Yes.

Why not ask about sleep? It is so important, so vital to health, and even to life. Yes, more restful and recuperative sleep is an outcome. So is the full range of emotions and also their *balance*.

However, you [the members of the Congress, Ed.] raise the question of 'happiness'. Since I was far away and could not ask why, I began to speculate — why ask this question, now. It could be that you have reached a point in your professional practice where your competence and experience enables you to witness a high degree of successful therapy. Or it could be that your personal and professional lives bring you happiness, and you think that clients deserve the same.

Or, it could be a growing optimism in your culture. Finally, after the destruction of war, a long period of recovery, peace and prosperity may suggest that happiness could now be attainable in a culture of affluence as it could never have been in a culture of scarcity and deprivation.

I am asking these somewhat anthropological questions, trying to understand the question, and its meaning in your lives.

While I do not believe that therapy does or should make happiness, you may think otherwise. In that case, I say, 'Beware!' If happiness becomes our goal for therapy, there are many traps.

For one thing, goals may be destructive. They are like weapons of war — you may not intend to use them, but they have their own imperatives, they use you, and shape your methods. Also, your goals may inhibit or exclude the emerging goals that develop in the process of therapy, coming from the clients' freedom and new perceptions. Above all, if you have in mind that the clients' happiness is your goal, you may promise something you *cannot* deliver. And should not. It is not our responsibility.

Our responsibility is to *understand*. If a client complains of not being understood we can work to correct that. But happiness — would you advertise it as the product of the service you provide? I doubt it.

Some other therapists are not so modest or so conscientious. They advertise everywhere. They promise whatever you want: happiness, success, a new husband, a new life. They invite you to Centers full of hot tubs, altered states of consciousness, massage, 'new age' music, electronic muscle stimulation, special goggles to produce a 'stress-resistant brain', etc. On visits to these Centers, you may find warmth and openness, but you may also encounter some of the most closed, rigid, secretive and cold fellow humans. It seems that extreme personalities seek extreme cures. Those who are overly intellectualized, for example, look for body experience, etc.

A spiritual community in Oregon seems to have produced mass happiness. They recently convened for three days of laughter. It also produced extreme violence, hostility, broken bones. I have become suspicious of happiness as well as those who advertise it.

Perhaps this is unfair. Perhaps it is judging a whole by a part. However, it is a very large part — this is the other side of American life. It is a part called 'hyper-reality', in postmodern language, but it is all too real, and suggests where 'happiness' as a goal may lead. We have two large industries devoted to manufacturing and indulging the desire for happiness. One is the entertainment industry. The other is the drug industry. Between them, they threaten the moral and intellectual quality of our nation.

We have generations of young who believe that happiness is a constitutional right to which they are entitled by birth, without effort. Of course, our Declaration of Independence guarantees only the *pursuit* of happiness, but they do not read. (They listen to the popular culture which tells them what they want to hear.)

It goes even further. In the name of happiness, we have a physician's archetype called 'Dr. Feelgood'. They treat the rich and famous, using various chemicals to produce happiness, pleasure, excitement, euphoria, contentment, tranquility. Some of these patients are dying of happiness. Elvis Presley had his own private Dr. Feelgood. For us it is no joke. Once the biochemistry of pleasure centers becomes known, happiness is a commercial product as well as an end-in-itself. The largest cash crop in the rich farm state of California is not oranges. It is marijuana.

California is our fashion center for the hedonistic lifestyle. There, happiness is not enough. Joy is the word. The joy of sex, joy of dance, the joy of living, of learning, politics. In a world where fun has become a commodity, this influence is widespread. Psychotherapy could suffer the worst possible fate. It could become part of the entertainment industry!

I am still wondering, why the question, 'macht therapie glucklich?' I think of Freud's famous statement, which in English translation reads: 'Much is gained if we only succeed in transforming neurotic misery into common unhappiness'.

A very interesting statement. It is one of Freud's most humane and plain-spoken sentences. Unfortunately, psychoanalysis in practice tends to do just the opposite. It transforms ordinary human unhappiness into arcane diagnostic/pathological conditions! But when Freud wrote that, he was thinking about 'Anna O.' and it is probably true that she, and others, with bizarre 'hysterical' feelings and behaviors would indeed be better off to see their distress as part of ordinary human unhappiness, not so different from that of many others. (That is not to say that common unhappiness has ever been readily accepted. It is often punished, and forced into pathological distortions.)

The question is, would we want to leave it at 'common unhappiness'? Is that where therapy should stop, or where it begins? Freud may have been in a social position, in his time and place, where ordinary unhappiness seemed the common fate. It is endemic in psychoanalytic thought that pessimism is close to realism. It could be said that there is a kind of 'cult of suffering' in it.

The cults of sorrow and suffering seem to me as extreme as the 'cult of happiness'. All are unsatisfactory. I am not a proponent of hardship or suffering as necessary to psychological health (though it is impossible to grow from infancy to adulthood without some experience of pain). I believe that psychological health can be achieved by predominantly happy people and also by predominantly suffering people, or the 'once- born' and the 'twice-born', as William James called them. It is, we should note, mainly the 'twice-born' (those who have been more or less wounded and healed) who write the books on clinical theories of personality (and who become therapists).

The struggle to answer or comprehend the question, 'macht therapie glucklich?' reminds me of a similar question with similar complications. 'Does money buy happiness?' Here is a different question. Can money buy *therapy*? Not necessarily — it can pay for *time*, but not guarantee a *process*. Therapy is also possible, quite possible, without payment of money at all. (In fact that is my personal preference.) So it is simply the case that money can assist, within limits, but not guarantee either happiness *or* therapy, and that both may be had without money, if they may be had at all.

The critical word is 'buy'. You cannot really purchase happiness, friendship, or therapy. These things cannot be *taken* from another. Unless they are also given they are not genuine. This is quite true of therapy; it is not a commodity to be bought, but must also be given. There is a third point. Not only must they be given, and taken, but they must be *created*. This is especially true for therapy. Here is a most important point, as to *who* creates: the *client* already makes a giant step just in the decision to undertake therapy. That expression of the motive for change must not be forgotten.

As Erik Erikson points out, many therapists resist seeing this clearly, because it is flattering to think that the therapeutic success is due to their analytic skills rather than to the patient's health and motives. At worst, therapists describe themselves as 'healers', mistaking the healing process in the organism (client) for a special talent of their own.

While therapy does not make happiness, it can facilitate that ability in a client. It can bring the *capacity* to enjoy happiness. It may increase the possibility to *create* happiness. However, as it increases that possibility, it increases *all* possibilities, as light contains the spectrum of colors. Happiness *among* other things, not *without* other things.

Therapy makes for health. More being alive. Greater awareness of the varieties of experience, not of any single constant. Therapy makes for 'affective complexity', a theory related to the reality of relationship. For example, a young man, in the first hours of therapy, talks about his love for his mother. Next, he discovers, 'I thought I loved my mother, but I realize I hate her. I've always hated her.' At this point, the therapist of the 'cynical/realistic' school would say, 'A break-through. There's the real truth.'

No, the client is not finished.

At the end, the client says, 'The fact is, I both love and hate my mother, and for good reason. She is both loveable and hateful. She has done both wonderful and harmful things to me. I suppose that is true of me, too.' That is the reality of most human relations — *affective complexity*.

The one thing therapy does not bring is indifference, or numbness. It brings sensitivity. You can smell the new-cut grass in the summer — also the garbage. As it brings an appreciation of comedy, it will do the same for tragedy. The end result is the integration of clarified ambivalences, and probably a new level of opposing ideas or feelings, again to be integrated. It is not just a cycle, but an evolutionary spiral.

Finally, let me mention an idea related to complexity and health. It is my personal idea of the ultimate outcome in the most successful therapy, but it is achieved at various levels all the time. I call it 'Neurological Innocence'. Not to be mistaken for moral innocence, since the adult who achieves it may have broad knowledge/experience of corruption and evil.

It is not a child's innocence through lack of experience nor is it ignorance, nor stupidity. It is at best a kind of genius.

It is at least a very *sophisticated* innocence. Because it is much like Rogers' concept 'openness to experience' [see Rogers, 1961, pp. 115–17, Ed.]. I will not extend its discussion here, but having already used the example of light and spectrum of colors, I will extend that example briefly.

When we look at a person standing near a red-brick wall, we see the face as 'normal' flesh colored. Color photography will show the face as red-toned flesh color, in the reflection of the redness of the wall. What the camera sees, we screen out. But the eye of the artist sees both; the red-toned face as the camera records it, and the flesh color as we 'normally' perceive it. The artist is not a restoration of the child. The artist can do what the child cannot — switch perceptions at will, represent one or the other or in combination. It means, in neurological terms, clear and open transmission of experience, with balance and control. It is balance to enable either stability or advance.

The balance, ruling out nothing, is essential. One of your great philosophers wrote, 'My memory says I did that; my conscience says I could not have. Memory yields.' What a dreadful loss! Memory is precious. Nothing should yield, not memory and not conscience. In a successful therapy, memory and conscience are both treasured. If they are in conflict, the resolution is not exclusion of one or the other but reconciliation at a new level.

My struggle with your question has been serious and difficult. How could any idea so apparently cheerful cause me such torment? It is because I am afraid to make the mistake of denying to others a bright possibility I do not see for myself? It is bad enough to write false history — it is truly terrible to write false future.

After composing most of this paper, I returned home, and in my library, went to find out whether Carl Rogers had said anything related to your question. In his essay on 'The Good Life', he writes,

> It seems to me that the good life is not any fixed state. It is not, in my estimation, a state of virtue, or contentment, or nirvana, or happiness. It is not a condition in which the individual is adjusted, fulfilled, or actualized. To use psychological terms, it is not a state of drive-reduction, or tension-reduction or homeostasis.
>
> The good life is a *process*, not a state of being . . . It is a direction, not a destination. The direction . . . is that which is selected by the total organism, when there is psychological freedom to move in *any* direction. [Rogers, 1961, pp. 186–7, original emphasis, Ed.]

Perhaps I have done little more than to reinvent the wheel. But it is not a wheel; it is an idea, which needs to be re-examined and reinvented. Just because there is such a thing as humane psychotherapy in the world, this new factor may enable new possibilities. Whether that includes 'happiness' I do not know. Certainly if therapy brings/makes happiness for the therapist, the client is entitled to it as well.

Now we are at the end.

Everything is personal. There is no psychological theory, social policy, collective ideology or 'objective' structure that does not come from, and is not expressed through, individual actions and consciousness. Individual motives, needs, hopes, fears, and satisfactions are the beginning and end. *Everything is personal.*

So, lastly, let me give you my most personal and probably most controversial opinion. *Everyone knows everything.* That is what I believe about consciousness. (It is also an old theory of knowledge.) I believe that you and I know everything about our lives and experience. It is often just too hard to face. Or/and is too complicated for easy thinking and solution, it is cowardly to hide behind the misty gauge of a concept such as 'the unconscious', which is a device for pretending ignorance of what we do not want to know — until, that is, we want to know it.

Earlier I mentioned what I consider the two essential factors in therapy: honesty and courage. With those qualities, and perhaps some help from friends, or caring nonexploitative others (that is what therapists are supposed to be), everything that can be done, can be done. Then we will have psychological freedom, which may itself be another name, a better name, for happiness.

REFERENCES

Rogers, C.R. (1961). *On Becoming a Person: A therapist's view of psychotherapy.* Boston: Houghton Mifflin.

Section 2

A Literalist Approach

EDITOR'S INTRODUCTION

A constant theme in John's work was his dissatisfaction with theories of human behaviour that propose or suggest indirect, hidden, mythical, overly-metaphorical or, in his view, downright *unlikely* processes and explanations. He could see no need for convoluted or over-elaborate theories when a simple everyday explanation, born out of the evidence of ordinary experience will suffice. He called this essentially phenomenological approach to the consideration of human experience a 'literalist' approach. The work in this section is presented in chronological order, to enable readers who wish, to trace any development or progression of ideas (although I cannot find much evidence of substance myself) and it should be noted that the writings cover a span of over twenty-five years.

Chapter 7 was first published in 1970 in *New Directions in Client-Centered Therapy* edited by Hart and Tomlinson. It is a dense volume, packed with seminal papers by a formidable array of writers. The substance of the paper is a vigorous questioning of the 'entrenched esoterica' in psychotherapy ('transference', the 'unconscious' and the florid metaphors used by some therapists). Shlien makes tentative suggestions towards an alternative which are elaborated in his later work.

Both the Hart and Tomlinson collection and Shlien's chapter in it are also amongst the earliest markers of the emerging debate in the approach (still then called 'Client-Centered Therapy') regarding developments of, and divergence from, Rogers' ideas — or, for want of a better word, 'purity' (see for example, Gendlin, 1970a and b; Rogers 1970; Gordon, 1970). In 1977 Rogers first referred to his helping system as 'person-centred' giving further impetus to the debate which led to the (inconclusive) round-table discussion published in *Person-Centered Review* in 1986 and a variety of nomenclature, including John Shlien's own offerings 'Classic Client-Centered' (see p. 220, this volume) and 'inherently nondirective' (Shlien, 2000). John Shlien's passion for purity surfaces in many places in his work, including his principle (see p. 5, this volume) 'Do what you want. *Call it what it is.*' wherein he requires theorists and practitioners who diverge from the prime client-centred principles of non-directivity, the actualizing tendency and the six therapeutic conditions, to call it something different from 'client-centred' or 'person-centred'.

Probably John Shlien's most well-known work, *A Countertheory of Transference* is a further, deliberately provocative, questioning of Freudian orthodoxy and the proposal that a client's experiences be taken more literally — not 'transference' from a previous relationship, but 'originalence' arising in the present one. Therapists are exhorted to seek explanations for their client's experiences of the therapist in their own (the therapist's) behaviour — Shlien writes '"Transference" is a fiction, invented and maintained by therapists to protect themselves from the consequences of their own behavior' (p. 93 this volume). Many of his critics have taken this to mean that John (and by extension, client-centred therapists in general) did not (do not) believe that what psychoanalysts call 'transference phenomena' exist. However, John's critique was of the *explanation* or *theoretical construct of transference* which in his view was mistaken in that it was (i) a general category, and therefore anathemous to client-centred therapy, (ii) archaic and contrary to John's view that the future is more important than the past in determining present behaviour, (iii) unlikely, in that there are many more obvious explanations based in the present relationship and (iv) a convenient get-out for therapists to avoid responsibility for their own behaviour. His main thrust (still waiting to be properly fulfilled) was that we should look at client behaviour and for CCT to develop its own phenomenological, humane and believable theory and vocabulary for clients' experiences, all of the time respecting the uniqueness of the experience of the client in question. In practice this calls for relationships with individuals, rather than grand interpretative theory.

This paper first appeared as Chapter 8 in the 1984 collection co-edited with Ronald Levant (Levant and Shlien, 1984), was amended and resurfaced as the centrepiece of a debate in the journal *Person-Centered Review* in 1987 (see Cain 2002 for the collection including responses). John was particularly pleased that his mentor, colleague and friend, Carl Rogers told him that it was the one paper that he wished he had written himself.

Although the third chapter in this section has been published before, I felt it needed a longer introduction. Readers should note that the original paper was a presentation at the Third International Conference on Client-Centered and Experiential Psychotherapy (ICCCEP), held in Gmunden, Austria, in 1994. It was preceded on the day by John's 'introduction', titled 'Untitled and Uneasy' which is published for the first time as chapter 16 in this collection. Having access to John's lecture notes it is clear that the published version included here was 'tidied up' (minimally) for publication and is nowhere near a word-for-word version of what was said. Having said this, however, it is also clear that we are reading a paper that was written to be *spoken* rather than one that was written to be *read*. This explains both the lumpiness of the prose in places (it helps me to imagine it being spoken) and the absence of references. I have interpolated some of John's additional notes (some were handwritten on his lecture notes) where I think they add to the text.

It brings to life his literalist position as he returns to his attack on esoteric, and in his view, frankly implausible explanations for anxiety. In contrast, he chooses an anxiety that all of us can locate within our personal repertoire, 'embarrassment anxiety' and applies his own literalist explanations. He does not shy away from ordinary explanations on a human scale and nor does he have to, since this is a deadly anxiety. Not only do people claim they might 'die of embarrassment' but others have killed to avoid it. Human emotions cannot be more powerful than this and John elegantly demonstrates that we have no need of exotic theories to explain them.

Also in this chapter is a moving glimpse into John's take on some of the events that shaped the client-centred/person-centred movement. In fact, John rarely let an opportunity go by without making a comment or aside on some aspect of what I would call the integrity of the approach and how it is viewed by adherents and 'opponents'. On pages 125–6 he defends reflection and gives an account of its demise. He was particularly sensitive to attacks on CCT based on incorrect understanding — tellingly he says of Rogers and reflection at the time of Wisconsin:

> . . . after a lifetime of scorn by enemies who ridiculed his method as 'parroting'. Even though he knew that the technique [reflecting] itself can be raised to the level of a refined art (as well as lowered to a 'wooden mockery') he was tired of defending, tired of being typecast and thus seemed to abandon a mainstay of his method. (p. 126 this volume)

I find this one of the most moving passages of John Shlien's writing. Whilst clearly irritated by those who would misrepresent the Person-Centred Approach or appropriate its good name for their own purposes; what shines through is his fierce defence of the healing force of understanding and of person-centred practice but most of all, his fierce defence of his friend, Carl Rogers, and his memory.

REFERENCES

Cain, D.J. (2002). *Classics in the Person-Centered Approach.* Ross-on-Wye: PCCS Books.

Gendlin, E. (1970a). Existentialism and Experiential Psychotherapy, in J.T Hart and T.M. Tomlinson (eds.) *New Directions in Client-Centered Therapy.* Boston: Houghton Mifflin, pp. 70–94.

Gendlin, E.T. (1970b). A Theory of Personality Change, in J.T. Hart and T.M. Tomlinson (eds.) *New Directions in Client-Centered Therapy.* Boston: Houghton Mifflin, pp. 129–73.

Gordon, T. (1970). A Theory of Healthy Relationships and a Program of Parent Effectiveness Training, in J.T. Hart and T.M. Tomlinson (eds.) *New Directions in Client-Centered Therapy.* Boston: Houghton Mifflin, pp. 407–25.

Levant, R.F. & Shlien, J.M. (1984). *Client Centered Therapy and the Person Centered Approach: New directions in theory, research and practice.* New York: Praeger. Reprinted in Cain 2002.

Rogers, C.R. (1970). The Process of the Basic Encounter Group, in J.T. Hart and T.M. Tomlinson (eds.) *New Directions in Client-Centered Therapy.* Boston: Houghton Mifflin, pp. 292–313.

Shlien, J.M. (2000). CCTPCA email discussion group communication.

CHAPTER 7

The Literal-Intuitive Axis
And other thoughts[1]

It is hard to peer into the future of clients who will be living as people in a period of genuine social revolution. Some old problems may disappear, new problems may emerge, with the possibility of different kinds of solutions than those to which we are now accustomed. The environment will become more complex. Like it or not, the great society lies ahead of us, and if it is not great, it will at least be big. As Nicholas Hobbs[2] has pointed out, in this coming society the future of individual psychotherapy is itself somewhat in doubt, perhaps bound to give way to various community mental health efforts based on new models of helping. This poses a problem since, to my mind, client-centered therapy has always had a particularly phenomenological base and will require some theoretical modification or extension to adapt to group contexts. The sources of this theoretical development are not yet clear, but from what we hear of Carl Rogers' current interests in intensive group therapy, he might be one source.

There is another gap. Though client-centered therapy developed out of work with children in the Rochester Clinic it soon became and has largely remained in theory and practice a matter of adult repair. Presently, as surely as one works with groups and larger communities, one is led to thoughts of preventive work in those problems of living which endanger mental health. As soon as one thinks of prevention, one is led to thoughts of working with younger and younger people, eventually children. This is the other gap. We need still more in the way of a theory of child development and of creative education. Again, the sources of

1. First published as Chapter 28 in Hart, J. T. and Tomlinson, T. M. (Eds.) (1970). *New Directions in Client-Centered Therapy.* Boston: Houghton Mifflin. © Joseph Hart, reprinted by kind permission. Originally adapted from a paper given at the Symposium, 'The Future of Client-Centered Therapy', at the American Psychological Association Meeting in Los Angeles, September 1964, with Carl R. Rogers, John M. Butler, and Eugene T. Gendlin.
2. Chapter 7 in Rogers, C. R. (1951). *Client-Centered Therapy.* Boston: Houghton Mifflin.[Ed.]

these future developments are not clearly visible. One wonders why they have been absent and neglected. Economics? Age-graded interests of adult therapists? Apparent need?

Now, as for the idea of change and the directions of change, true prophets are most often those who work toward the fulfillment of their predictions — I would rather try to forecast what might be the 'natural history' of the future, though admittedly this will reflect my personal interests.

I think there will be no single line of development, but that change is assured in several directions. Change as a motif is built into the system by the founder, with his notable distaste for dogma, and by the inventive mavericks attracted to the system. Indeed, during my own early years at the Counseling Center, when Carl Rogers was its leader, I often got the impression that there was a directive: to become neo-Rogerian as quickly as possible. Even so, in the past, client-centered therapists, according to studies by Strupp (1960) and others, have been more homogeneous in their practice than have other schools. This is understandable; intelligent reflections will vary a good deal less than equally intelligent interpretations. But client-centered therapy has had somewhat the quality of a protest movement, with some forced cohesive effects. Now the missionary zeal is tempered, our protests have been drawn into the main stream (on the surface at least), and the organization is big and steady enough to contain what in the past might have been spin-offs. A more heterogeneous set of behaviors is predictable, remaining, I hope, more or less client-centered. With regard to changing of techniques, there is another factor. Techniques become tiresome. Reflection was, and is, a good tool. It takes a surprising amount of skill to apply it deftly and without woodenness, since it is actually quite foreign to our conventional repertoire (such as advice, persuasion, etc.). For those attitudes which Rogers set forth and to which we subscribed, reflection serves to implement as no other technique would. Yet, after 20 years, it is incomplete, a bit restrictive, and tiresome. A technique may be excellent, but if it becomes tedious and confining, the therapist's own need for novelty and originality or for personal expression will force modifications. I do not mean that 'understanding is not enough' or that reflection will be dropped; it will be laced with new variations, and probably be the better for it.

THE FUTURE IN GENERAL

Even though client-centered therapy is entrenched in the universities and more barricaded by research than is any other, it seems to me that we must share to some extent the future of psychotherapy in general. The future in general has been commented on by a number of observers, who have noted a measure of turmoil, confusion, and even 'chaos'. None sees disaster ahead, but to me the situation looks serious. Granted the demand is there; therapy is favorably represented on TV, and studies of the metropolis show a large proportion of the population in need of treatment. (In this connection, let me parenthetically remark that I believe psychotherapy is an urban substitute for a deep and satisfying contact with nature. Indeed, if it were required to prescribe one and only one method of bringing a mental health measure to the public on a massive scale, I would say, give each person a tree of his own to grow and contemplate.) The demand is there, and the profession is growing lustily as a profession. However, that profession may be afflicted by problems attending popularization, and by a 'market mentality' which might be our undoing if we cannot deliver to the mass culture. Already, those long clinic waiting-lists have in them some who have been patients once or twice elsewhere.

Meanwhile, from the inside, Schofield suggests that anxiety and psycho-therapy may have been overrated and oversold; Szasz challenges the 'myth of mental illness'; Leary takes some jabs at the 'psychotherapy game'; and Mowrer tells us that the neurotic endeavor is a shirking of guilty responsibility which most therapy only perpetuates. These are all intelligent men whose messages deserve some attention. From the outside, we have the much publicized critiques such as Eysenck's (1952), still not thoroughly refuted and perhaps not to be.[3] Drill has recently surveyed outcome studies and concluded that currently the results total only ten studies to nine on balance favorable in their effects. Recent research evidence (Rogers, 1967) shows what we have always known — that in the ubiquitous one-third rated 'not improved', some are not only not improved but according to outcome measures, rated lower than their initial status. Something is wrong, though given the general ineffectiveness of all sorts of work in all other fields, we might be foolish to expect otherwise. Indeed, proficiency is bound to be imperfect. It is always a combination of incomplete theory and imperfect practice. The product is like the multiplication of fractions.

A private survey of my own suggests that, in the opinion of therapists in practice, about 20 per cent of their colleagues are judged to be of so little competence that one would not consider referral to them.[4] If this is so, the 70 per cent improvement rate generally reported and generously accepted by critics is remarkable! It means that some therapists are quite efficient. Others are not. We

---

[3.] Chapter 13 of *New Directions in Client-Centered Therapy* by Donald J. Kiesler ('Basic Methodologic Issues Implicit in Psychotherapy Process Research', pp. 237–56) is a reply to Eysenck's critique. [Ed.]

[4.] This was carried out by asking some variant of the question 'to whom would you send a close friend or a member of your family?', It has since come to my attention that Dr. Paul Meehl, using much the same technique, supposes that only one-third or one-fourth of the 'professional helpers' are regarded as competent by their colleagues. [J.M.S.]

are hard put to identify any of these therapists at any point in their career. Further, effectiveness surely fluctuates, and all attempts at evaluation are complicated by problems of inadequate sampling, patient differences, criteria, and so on. Yet this is a problem that we cannot continue to avoid. It points to the question of competence — the personal competence of the therapist. There is probably no such thing as a 'good therapist', whose efforts never fail or whose results are never disappointing, but rather therapists who are more or less good with some people, at some times, and not with others. I think we see one reaction to this problem in the development of new systems. That there were five, then 36, now 100 systems of therapy does not testify simply to the excitement and inventiveness and freedom in the field. It also reflects the failure of *any* system to produce sufficient results *as a system*. A hundred more will not save us while the fault lies not so much in our system as in ourselves.

If this is so, client-centered therapy (once scorned as a homeopathic method of study counsel), with its demonstrably increased range and potency of application, shares this problem. What can we do about it? I predict that in the next ten years the therapist's behavior and personality will be subjected to such scrutiny as has been applied only to patients and clients in the past. Focus on the selection and training of therapists has and will come from many quarters: from group therapy, where he is on public display; from visits by actors and journalists trained to represent patients (two instances have already been reported); from the results of various outcome studies. All this may carry discomfort, potential mismanagement, unjustified sampling, and other abuse. But the therapist, in spite of a good deal of recording and some films, continues to work largely in private with only one true potential collaborator, the client. From this latter source, I believe, will come the next major client-centered effort to find a way to develop and maintain advanced competence in keeping with its general principles. In the past, an apprentice therapist was often judged promising if his behavior matched the teacher model, and supplementarily, if the client responses indicated confirmation of the therapist's understanding. The latter aspect has to be developed and amplified. Our ultimate criterion has to be the client's own perspective. Whatever faults this basis has, it is no more flawed than any other source, and in the end every other criterion *has* to connect with this one. The next step is to take the client in as an active research collaborator. The myth of the naïve subject is fading in the rest of social science. It is absurd now in therapy to assume that the client does not know what is being measured, or what process is being experienced. What I envision is, first, a move toward sophisticated self-study by the therapist and the client, with both trained in introspective and observational methods; second, a new form of collaboration in which the process of interaction is closely examined by these two participants, perhaps with the aid of a third party. When the client and therapist together analyze their own actions and interactions, we will see some new subtleties only dimly perceived or not even suspected before. Of course, this procedure will depart from the ordinary uninvestigated therapy, but so does any other research strategy. For us, the future will either hold a sophisticated rigorous self-study involving candid and intelligent therapists aided and appraised by clients, or therapy will turn more and more to *external* criteria and end as a conditioning operation, since external criteria logically lead to 'behavior modification'.

There will be, then, a serious concentration upon the problem of competence. It will involve intensive study of the therapist, self-study with the collaboration of the client, we hope. With it, much new can be learned. Without it, individual therapy may wither away even as a laboratory, since studies of patient or client outcome cannot support it indefinitely. By no means is this to say that individual therapy is not or cannot be good, when it is often very good indeed, and a source of satisfaction to both clients and practitioners. It may remain as a research laboratory, a training procedure, and a luxury trade item in private practice. However, it cannot continue to meet either its scientific or social obligations without some new developments.

THE LITERAL-INTUITIVE AXIS

Client-centered therapy is much more than a method of therapeutic endeavor. It is also an intellectual-theoretical position — a way of looking at and understanding behavior. The characteristics of this range along an axis which features a highly literal approach at one end, and at the other, a deeply intuitive one.

The intuitive side has attracted many, with its emphasis on feelings, inner experience, the philosophy of phenomenology and its consequent ultimate individualism, man's nature and his relation to nature. When intuitive knowledge is invoked, it is a type of knowing called 'feeling' and it draws on what was always there; the unitary and universal in knowledge, as the slave boy intuitively knew the geometry of the triangle when Socrates led him to it, and as the flower in the crannied wall represents the transcendent whole when understood in depth. There is an organic tone to it. It smacks of soil, sea weed, tree roots; when Rogers dips his toe into the blue Caribbean, he gets an infusion of that oceanic feeling and writes about the personal side of science. It also characterizes something of the mystical or at least mystifying (and this may mean nothing more than that of which we are ignorant or pretend to be) relationship between client and therapist, and is in fact the naturalistic touchstone of client-centered theory.

The other emphasis is the strikingly different literal quality of thought. For me, this is the greater part of the genius of this approach, and would remain as an influence if the conduct of therapy were to cease. This is not merely the instrumentation of theory with technique such as reflection to implement the other's internal frame of reference, or the penchant for verbatim recording of interviews for review. Both are valuable in themselves and as illustrations, but the literal is more than any illustration. It is a quality of description and explanation that aims to simplify operations and translate them into the currency of science. It avoids ceremonial complexities. It shuns the arcane and esoteric, but it is by no means simple-minded. It rejects the deliberate mystique of some therapies and looks for rational alternatives. Ignorance is admitted for what it is. Knowledge is advanced in the form of tentative hypotheses couched in ordinary language rather than a contrived vocabulary. I have always admired Freud's statement, 'Much is won if we succeed in transforming hysterical misery into common unhappiness'. This Freudian wish is in fact the kind of effort which has characterized client-centered therapy, while psychoanalytic thought, by contrast, seems to have moved in the opposite direction toward a metaphorical system.

(a) To illustrate, consider a key concept such as transference. Rogers never accepted it as a necessary condition. He spoke of 'transference attitudes', which need not be cultivated, could be avoided. Butler analyzed transference in terms of learning, anticipatory response, and extinguishing. Shlien called transference 'a fiction, developed and maintained to protect the therapist from the consequences of his own behavior' — which behavior could consist of no more or less than just listening and understanding and sharing the secrets of the client's experience. He accounted for positive and negative transference on the basis of the client's feeling understood or misunderstood — supported by van Kaam's phenomenological study of 'how it feels to be understood'. This major hallmark, transference, has already lost much of its force. The therapist no longer holds the bland and neutral role of a screen upon which all patients' attitudes are simply projections. This now sounds silly. It always was. The predicted future examination of therapist's behavior will reveal much of his contribution to reactions which have heretofore been attributed to 'transference'. It is interesting to note that Franz Alexander's final statement from his research experience ran along these very lines. The most important conclusion that has emerged from this research is the fact that the traditional descriptions of the therapeutic process do not adequately reflect the immensely complex interaction between therapist and patients. The patients' reactions cannot be fully described as transference reactions.

(b) I expect that there will be new literal attacks upon other entrenched esoterica, including the stronghold of the 'unconscious'. This is a concept so fundamental to most psychotherapy, and, as Sartre points out, so attractive as a cover-up for our conventional duplicity and stupidity, that we will have to provide a set of alternative explanations, or come to terms, or go out of theoretical business. The alternative concept of 'levels of awareness' as a continuum rather than a trichotomy was a start. Snygg and Combs (1949) additionally pointed to figure-ground phenomena and also to 'tunnel vision' (narrowed and rigidified perception) under conditions of threat, which is essentially the concept of span of attention as it is affected by emotion. It is thus closely connected to the concept of energy level, a level which fluctuates and thus differs from the Freudian hydraulic system. In conjunction with the interaction of span of attention and energic fluctuation, there are also the variable forces of sensations competing for enough of that attention to become perceptions. To such combinations of concepts as attention, energic fluctuation, and levels of awareness, add variability of self-concept as a filter through which perceptions are screened, and the combined literal explanation of inconsistencies or temporary ignorance takes on considerable power. Finally, consider that the sensory system is composed of multiple input channels (ears, eyes, nose, etc.), all capable of compound reception, while the expressive system is usually limited to a single output (vocal, usually) at one time. This very imbalance of rapidly accumulative multiple input and slower single output makes suppression, at least, unavoidable. All these considerations, along with clues from new 'visual search' studies of scanning and selection, and other strategies from information storage and retrieval theory, should help in the future to provide literal understandings of at least some phenomena previously relegated to the hidden operations of 'the unconscious'. It may be that besides the emotional clearance of free and honest expression in the psychological economy, the literalist inquiry into the multiplicity of thought will require the invention of new apparatus to train and extend expressive modalities — a response piano, as it were, so that the limits of consciousness are released through a keyboard of complex chords instead of a single melodic line.

(c) This more literal stance will probably show itself also in a new understanding of sex and the role of sexual behavior. Client-centered therapy, as many have noted, has been relatively backward in this area. It is as if we invested in self-theory while psychoanalytic libido-theory was sweeping the field. Now there is a 'sexual revolution'. It seems real. Whether it turns out to be harmful or helpful, or leads to a counter-revolution, we cannot yet see, but certainly the restrictive pressures are off. Much of what used to be hidden is now open and perhaps less powerful. Now social-self theory rears its head with more validity. For instance a client who had been almost unselectively promiscuous says, 'I've come to realize that there is a man on the other end of that penis.' This makes life understandable and to be understood in terms of real human interaction and humanity, rather than squeamish interpretations of sexual symbols in dreams. Another sexually active girl, for whom interpretations of sexual repression would be nonsense, says, 'When I really like a man, I let him see me take down my hair.' Lack of sexual experience is not a concern; lack of genuine intimacy is. Another example comes from a brilliant and attractive college student who takes the view that in each new relation she is ready for sex as soon as it feels comfortable, with the idea that if sex is not used as a lure, 'then we can see if we can be friends, if he cares for me as a person, without all that phony and awkward courtship'. Perhaps astonishing, perhaps over-balanced according to our traditional views, and whether this turns out to be a matter of vulnerability and exploitation or a noble experiment in the betterment of human relations we wait to see. But, plainly, self-theory takes on more validity as the force and interest of 'naughty' sexuality wanes. New, more literal understandings may become possible.

Here is a better example. It has to do with an alternative understanding of an 'Oedipal situation'. Oedipal theory has always seemed slightly hysterical to me, and I'm appalled at the force therapists have applied to this pressure point without looking beyond the original theory. A 21-year-old male entered therapy under heavy stress. According to his Rorschach, appraised by an expert and famous clinician, this young man was a suicidal risk, near a psychotic break, ready for hospitalization, and, above all, bore a deep Oedipal attachment to his mother. He certainly was very nervous, very confused. As therapy progressed, he reported and discussed a recurring dream. In his waking life, he was courting an attractive girl with whom he wanted to have intercourse, but of whom he was afraid because of his own inexperience and lack of confidence. In his dreams, he saw himself beginning to make love to the girl, and as he began to lie upon her, her face turned into his mother's face. He was shocked and puzzled. One might think, from the previous diagnosis and the power of Oedipal theory, that there was no more to be said. But, given the opportunity, the young man continued to consider the dream and his feelings about it. Why should he want his mother? 'Really an old bag, after all' — when the girl he was courting was so beautiful. Then he hit upon it — 'Why not! Why shouldn't I want my sex where I get my security? That's it!' There is the crux of the problem for any frightened person — to find both pleasurable adventure and sufficient security together, for severe anxiety is a detriment, sexually and otherwise. With that realization, this young man solved his own problem and, to my mind, made one new contribution toward a theory of sex. What characterized the supposedly Oedipal complex was the essential quality of the experience of security, not the being of mother, who was a metaphorical representation of that security.

(d) As a final comment on this position I submit that psychotherapy can be expressed as the composition of two primary elements — honesty and courage. Such simple terms will never win the Talcott Parsons Award; indeed, these are such simple terms for problems which have such complicated consequences that when they are unresolved, we can only rename the elements just because we lost the battle. Honesty and courage mean the ability to know the facts of experience without flinching, or at least without turning away and denying these facts to oneself, whether or not one chooses to declare them to others. The person who possesses these qualities does not need psychotherapy. He may want friendship, love, help, support, and other environmental benefits, but he does not need psychotherapy. He has a cleanliness of neurological operation, a psychological economy unburdened by deficit financing of layers of defense, and that is the value of the literal elements.

How have the therapies dealt with this basic problem? Psychoanalysis, by the rule of free association (a contradiction in terms if taken literally) meaning no thought held back, and through the royal road of symbolic analysis, sought to penetrate all secrets, distortions, and self-deceits. Forced-choice honesty, that is. Client-centered therapy sought through acceptance, understanding, and safety, to promote 'openness to experience'. Honesty by safe conduct, that is. Whether safety in a privileged environment can produce courage outside it is a question. True, clients grow by facing their pain and surviving. They also develop a psychological integrity which they prize and know they would lose if they allowed fear to drive them back into self-deception. But client-centered therapy accidentally approaches the development of courage in another way. It has been classified as an 'insight' therapy. Originally, insight was a partial objective, but it now receives less and less attention. Client-Centered Therapy has moved closer to becoming an 'action' therapy in this sense: the objective is to develop a *capacity* rather than to attack a particular problem or symptom. We work toward the exercise of a *capacity to see,* not toward particular vision itself. Thus it is not an insight therapy in the sense of tracing causes or understanding particular content. Content has long been considered subordinate to feeling. Experiencing is increasingly emphasized but, again, more as a capacity. This capacity, regardless of content, is what may lead to courage. It is as if we encourage weight-lifting, not to move a particular set of heavy objects into a new arrangement (though that is one of the effects), but to strengthen muscles. That strength can be the basis for courage.

All this leads to an increasing awareness of the component of 'will' therapy. That is not to say that Rank begat Rogers, but that they have much in common. I believe that the simple virtues of honesty, courage, and personal responsibility (though without the punitive cost demanded by some who preach responsibility) may become more and more the context in which growth and successful outcome will be analyzed. Even guilt will lose much of its force as a basis for interpreting neurosis. Most therapeutic theory in the past has been based upon guilt; either this was an error adopted from religious precepts or people have changed. Guilt does not seem very important. People do not seem to suffer much from it. Social concern, yes, and social shame. Perhaps they are not very guilty. They suffer more from being scared and lonely. If it were only guilt, there is plenty of machinery to take care of that: various forms of confession, repentance, expiation, and salvation. But overcoming fear and loneliness — that takes some doing. For the scared and lonely, it is often easier to confess and analyze at length than to face life and make friends.

REFERENCES

Eysenck, H.J. (1952). The effects of psychotherapy: An evaluation. *Journal of Consulting Psychology, 16,* 319–24.

Rogers, C.R. (Ed.) (1967). *The therapeutic relationship and its impact.* Madison, Wisconsin: University of Wisconsin Press.

Snygg, D. & Combs, A.W. (1949). *Individual behavior.* New York: Harper.

Strupp, H.M. (1960). *Psychotherapists in action.* New York: Grune and Stratton.

CHAPTER 8

A Countertheory of Transference

Transference or the 'transference neurosis' is reexamined. This analysis suggests that transference is a defense mechanism used to deny or disguise the reality and natural consequences of the therapist's behavior. Two of these behaviors, understanding and misunderstanding, are featured as archetypical causes of love and hate, unnecessarily called 'positive' and 'negative' transference. The analysis starts with the uneasy origin of the concept illustrated in the case of Anna O. It continues through variations in definition and use of transference, and observations on the self-concept of the therapist. The repetition-logic of psychoanalysis is disputed, and a countertheory is proposed, based on clinical experience and phenomenal evidence of the normal human response to understanding. The act of understanding is described not only as the first cause of 'transference' but also as the essential healing factor, the main contribution and the proper objective of all psychotherapies.

'Transference' is a fiction, invented and maintained by therapists to protect themselves from the consequences of their own behavior.

To many, this assertion will seem an exaggeration, an outrage, an indictment. It is presented here as a serious hypothesis, charging a highly invested profession with the task of reexamining a fundamental concept in practice.

It is not entirely new to consider transference as a defense. Even its proponents cast it among the defense mechanisms when they term it a 'projection'. But they mean that the defense is on the part of the patient. My assertion suggests a different type of defense: denial or distortion, and on the part of the therapist.

Mine is not an official position in client-centered therapy. There is none.

First published in *Client-Centered Therapy and The Person-Centered Approach: New Directions in Theory, Research and Practice*, pp. 153–181. Edited by R. F. Levant and J. M. Shlien. © 1984 Praeger Publishers. Reproduced with permission of Greenwood Publishing Group Inc, Westport, CT.

This chapter in the adapted version, published in *Person-Centered Review,* Volume 2, Number 1, February 1987. Reprinted here with kind permission of the Editor.

Carl Rogers has dealt with the subject succinctly, in about 20 pages (1951, pp. 198–217), a relatively brief treatment of a matter that has taken up volumes of the literature in the field.[1] 'In client-centered therapy, this involved and persistent dependency relationship does not tend to develop' (p. 201), though such transference attitudes are evident in a considerable proportion of cases handled by client-centered therapists. Transference is not fostered or cultivated by this present-time oriented framework where intensive exploration of early childhood is not required, and where the therapist is visible and available for reality testing. While Rogers knows of the position taken here and has, I believe, been influenced by it since its first presentation in 1959, he has never treated the transference topic as an issue of dispute. This is partly so because of his lack of inclination for combat on controversial issues, where he prefers to do his own constructive work and let evidence accumulate with new experience.

Why then should client-centered therapy take a position on an issue of so little moment in its own development? For one reason, the concept of transference is ubiquitous. It has a powerful grip on the minds of professionals and the public. And, while client-centered practice has the popular image of a relatively self-effacing therapist, it holds to a standard of self-discipline and responsibility for the conditions and processes it fosters, and it could not fail to encounter those emotional and relational strains so often classed as transference.

There are many separate questions raised by the assertion at the start of this article. *What* behavior of the therapist? Leading to *which* consequences? *Why* invent[2] such a concept? *How* does it protect? In reexamining the concept of transference how do we, to use Freud's words, 'inquire into its source'?

Throughout we will consider only the male therapist/female patient data. Such was the critical situation when the term was invented. The first five case histories in the 1895 landmark *Studies on Hysteria* (Breuer and Freud, 1957) are Anna O., Emmy von N., Lucy R., Katharina, and Elisabeth. It set up the image of the most sensitive relationship (older man, younger woman) most suspect in the minds of the public (whether skeptic or enthusiast) and the combination most common for many decades.[3] Indeed it is possible that without the sexually charged atmosphere

---

[1] *Transference* does not appear in the index of his earlier *Counseling and Psychotherapy* (1942).

[2] Inventions are human-made. Thus *invent* is used to offset Freud's use of the word *discovered,* which inaccurately implies a fact found or truth revealed.

[3] Social and economic conditions that create anxiety neuroses in women and enable men to become physicians have changed enough to bring about some evening of opportunity. Fortunately, women can now more easily find female therapists. There are also more cross-sex, same-sex, bisex, and other permutations. We know relatively little of these many parallels of the transference model, but may be sure that the concept is now so well established that it will appear as a 'demand characteristic' in its own right. It has become part of the pseudosophisticated belief system of informed clients.

thus engendered, the concept of transference might not have developed as it has, if at all! For it is not insignificant that Breuer, and Freud, were particularly vulnerable. As Jewish physicians, admitted to the fringes of anti-Semitic Viennese society by virtue of their professional status, they could ill afford any jeopardy.

For psychoanalysis, transference seems to be the essential concept: 'sine qua non', 'an inevitable necessity', 'the object of treatment', 'the most important thing we [Freud and Breuer] have to make known to the world', without which 'the physician and his arguments would never be listened to'. In addition, it contains and subsumes all the elaborate support structures: the primary significance of sexual instincts, psychic determinism, the unconscious, psychogenetic theory, and the power of past experience. It is crucial in theory! In practice, it comforts, protects, and explains.

Transference is also supposed to distinguish psychoanalysis from other forms of therapy. Perhaps it is meant to do so, but this becomes moot through contradictions in the literature, which variously asserts that transference is peculiar to psychoanalysis while also common in everyday life. Whether unique or universal, it is in widespread use throughout most psychodynamic systems. One distinction it surely serves: that between professional and paraprofessional, or sophisticate and literalist, and in general between those in and out of power. If transference is no longer the singular hallmark of psychoanalysis, it at least marks those 'in the know', whether novices or not.

It was in Freud's mind 'a new fact which we are thus unwilling compelled to recognize' (Jones, 1953, p. 385). 'Unwilling' does not truly describe Freud's attitude. That word is an artful form of argument to make a welcome conjecture seem an unavoidable fact. Currently, 'unwilling' more aptly describes the attitude of psychotherapists toward reexamination of the idea. But reexamination is necessary if we are to reevaluate the usefulness of the concept.

HISTORICAL CONTEXT

It seems most appropriate to begin this reevaluation with the early history of the concept. The case of Anna O. provides the cornerstone on which the theory of transference is generally thought to be based. More than a dramatic and moving affair, it is of momentous importance to the field, and its effects still influence the majority of theory and practice. Though psychoanalysis and/or other forms of psychotherapy would somehow have developed, all present forms owe much to these few pioneers and their struggles. To honor them properly, it is necessary to study these human points of origin.

The accounts begin in the *Studies on Hysteria* (Breuer and Freud, 1957), first published in 1895, 13 years after treatment ended. Details of treatment were reported cautiously, out of respect for the still-living patient, and for other reasons having to do with questions about the outcome, and growing tensions between Freud and Breuer. Anna O. was, by all accounts, remarkable, and, for that time, so was her treatment. In her twenty-first year, she was described by Breuer and others as a person of great beauty, charm, and powerful intellect, with a quick grasp and surplus energy. Living in a comfortable but monotonous environment at home, she was hungry for intellectual stimulation. She was poetic and imaginative, fluent in German, English, Italian, and French. Much of her waking time was spent in daydreaming, her 'private theatre', She was also sharp and critical, and therefore, Breuer notes, 'completely unsuggestable' (though he routinely used hypnosis), needing to be convinced by argument on every point. She was tenacious and obstinate, but also known for immensely sympathetic kindness, a quality that marked most of her life's work. She had never been in love. In short, she was young, attractive, intelligent, and lonely; it was she who named psychotherapy 'the talking-cure', and she was a near-perfect companion for the also remarkable physician-pioneer in this form of treatment. (He was 38 at the time, admired, loved, respected, and of high professional and social status.) Both deserved all the tributes given, and Breuer perhaps even more. While Freud was the conceptual and literary genius without doubt, and Anna O. the central figure of the famous case, Breuer was probably the therapeutic genius of the time. And that in a new, dangerous exploration where there were few precedents, guidelines, or previous personal experiences.

Through the experience of Anna O. with Breuer, the material used as the basis for the theory of *transference-love* (as it was then called) was gathered, but it was Freud alone who later invented that theory to interpret that material to Breuer and the world. In the meantime, Freud's invention had been fostered by experience of his own with at least one other female patient.

The case of Anna O. is described in 1895 by Breuer (Breuer and Freud, 1957, pp. 21–47), who wrote that he had 'suppressed a large number of quite interesting details' (true), and that she had left Vienna to travel for a while, free of her previous disturbances (not quite so true, for she was taken to a sanatorium where she 'inflamed the heart of the psychiatrist in charge' (Jones, 1953, p. 225), and was temporarily addicted to morphine). By the time Breuer reported the *Studies* a decade later, he could write that 'it was a considerable time before she regained her mental balance entirely' (p. 41). Even so, he had confided sorrowfully to Freud in an earlier discussion that he thought sometimes she were better off dead, to end her suffering. The 'suppressed details' may in part be related to his sudden termination of the treatment and the patient's shocking emergency regarding her 'pregnancy' and his 'responsibility'. James Strachey, editor of the 1957 translation of *Studies on Hysteria*, says Freud told him of the end of Anna O's treatment: 'The patient suddenly made manifest to Breuer the presence of a strong unanalysed positive transference of an unmistakably sexual nature' (Breuer and Freud, 1957, p. 41, fn.). This is a retroactive interpretation, of course, since at the time of its occurrence neither Breuer nor perhaps even Freud yet had any idea of 'transference'. That idea builds, and more complete information is released, as Freud describes the case in both oblique and direct references in lectures and other writings from 1905 to his autobiography in 1925. Still more explicit communications are released in Ernest Jones's (1953) biography of Freud. In 1972, Freeman, a well-known popular writer, published a 'novelized' biography and report of Anna O. and her treatment. (None of these is exact, verbatim, or anything like 'verification data'.)

Even so, the somewhat guarded report by Breuer gives us a privileged view of his work. The editor of *Studies on Hysteria* tells us that Breuer had little need of hypnosis because Anna O. so readily 'produced streams of material from her unconscious, and *all Breuer had to do was to sit by and listen to them without interrupting her*' (Breuer and Freud, 1957, p. xvii; emphasis added). That is *all?* As you will see later, I argue that this is no small thing. It may not seem much to that editor, himself a lay analyst in training, but to the lonely, grieving, and desperate young woman, it must have seemed a treasure. At that period, young ladies were given placebos, referred from one doctor to another, and generally treated with patronizing attention or benign neglect. Breuer and Freud were precious rarities in that they listened, took her seriously. Would that Breuer had done more of that, and had done it steadfastly *through the end*. Listening is behavior of great consequence. The pity is that he felt forced to cut it short at the critical last moments.

Meanwhile, there were many other behaviors and we can only estimate their consequences. He fed her. She was emaciated, and he alone was able to feed her. He could give her water when she otherwise would not drink. No doubt there were other nourishing figures in her life, but he was clearly one himself. He paid her daily visits. She held his hands in order to identify him at times when she could not see. When she was exhausted, he put her to sleep, with narcotics or suggestion. He restored mobility to paralyzed limbs. He hypnotized her, sometimes twice a day, taught her self-hypnosis, and then 'would relieve her of the whole stock of imaginative products she had accumulated since [his] last visit' (1957, p. 36). He took her for rides in his carriage with his daughter (named Berthe, which was also Anna O.'s real name). He read her diary — a notably tricky business either with or without her permission. He forced her to remember unpleasant experiences.

From this alone, would you think that Anna O. had reason (real, not imaginary) for feelings such as gratitude, hope, affection, trust, annoyance, intimacy, resentment, and fear of separation?

Finally, there was the ending. Breuer had been preoccupied with his patient, and his wife had become jealous and morose. There had been improvement, indeed. But also, according to Jones's account, Breuer confided to Freud that he decided to terminate treatment because he divined the meaning of his wife's state of mind. 'It provoked a violent reaction in him, perhaps compounded of love and guilt, and he decided to bring the treatment to an end' (Jones, 1953, p. 225).

Exactly how he announced this decision to Anna O. we do not know. That evening he was called back by the mother and found his patient 'in a greatly excited state, apparently as ill as ever'. She was 'in the throes of an hysterical childbirth' (Jones, 1953, p. 224).

Certainly that is an interpretation of her 'cramps' and utterances that might commonly occur. We have no firsthand information as to what the patient thought or meant. Every report is second- or third-hand, *through* Freud *about* Breuer, and that usually through Jones, who wrote, 'Freud has related to me a fuller account than he described in his writings'. and some of that account is quoted as follows:

> The patient, who according to him [Breuer] had appeared as an asexual being and had never made any allusion to such a forbidden topic throughout the treatment, was now in the throes of an hysterical childbirth (pseudocyesis), the logical termination of a phantom pregnancy that had been invisibly developing in response to Breuer's ministrations. Though profoundly shocked, he managed to calm her down by hypnotizing her, and then fled the house in a cold sweat. The next day he and his wife left for Venice to spend a second honeymoon . . .
>
> Some ten years later, at a time when Breuer and Freud were studying cases together, Breuer called him into consultation over an hysterical patient. Before seeing her, he described her symptoms, whereupon Freud pointed out that they were typical products of a phantom pregnancy. The recurrence of the old situation was too much for Breuer. Without saying a word, he took up his hat and stick and hurriedly left the house. (1953, pp. 224–6)

A somewhat more explicit (but still far from direct or verbatim) report is cited in Freeman (1972, p. 200). Freud writes to Stefan Zweig (a relative of Anna O. by marriage):

> '*What really happened* with Breuer I was able to *guess* later on, long after the break in our relations, when I *suddenly remembered* something Breuer had told me in another context before we had begun to collaborate and which he never repeated. On the evening of the day when all her symptoms had been disposed of, he was summoned to the patient again, found her confused and writhing in abdominal cramps. Asked what was wrong with her, she replied: "Now Dr. B's child is coming!"' (emphasis added).[4]

[4.] One point must be stressed. There is only, but *only* Freud's reconstruction in this momentous history. No other source whatever. How much Freud wanted these data, how much and how often he pressed Breuer for them, we have a few hints. In his autobiography (1948, first published in 1925): 'When I was back in Vienna I turned once more to Breuer's observation and made him tell me more about it'(p. 34). /cont

Freud, speaking of Breuer, added, 'At this moment he held in his hand the key'. but 'seized by conventional horror he took flight and abandoned his patient to a colleague' (Freeman, 1972, p. 200).[5]

Here is one final quotation from Breuer himself in his own report: 'The element of sexuality was astonishingly undeveloped in her. The patient, whose life became known to me *to an extent to which one person's life is seldom known to another,* had never been in love' (Breuer and Freud, 1957, pp. 21–2; emphasis added).

What then 'really happened'? We will never know. Two exceptional (in my opinion, magnificent) people of great intelligence and noble spirit came close to understanding. He knew her well. Probably she knew him better than he thought. The knowing appears to have been precious to both. Understanding failed at a critical point. They dropped the key. It is tragic; so much was lost. Thankfully, we know that both carried on vital and constructive lives for many years.

If you are a woman, reading this will probably bring different reactions than those of the typical man. Perhaps you feel more sympathetic to the patient. If you put yourself in the therapist's place, supposing this could be your case, you know at least that you could think to yourself, and possibly say to Anna O., 'Unlikely that it is my child in the physical sense, since I am woman like yourself, but perhaps you mean that I am somehow parent to your pain, your growth, your condition, whatever.' (If you think that logically a woman therapist would never face such a situation, because of the reality, consider the implications of *that* for transference theory!)

More difficult if you are a man, putting yourself in this imaginary situation. You might say, 'I submitted to voluntary sterilization in order to make my life less anxious, as it were, so it is unlikely, etc.' as above. Not only a condition with which

---

cont/ . . . In 1925 he still speaks of 'a veil of obscurity which Breuer never raised for me' (p. 36). This prodding, however, eventually cost them their friendship. How much Breuer's support meant to Freud we do know. How highly motivated to get this information, which he sometimes says Breuer would never repeat for him, we also know. Yet it is all Freud's reconstruction; and in 1932, when he wrote the cited letter to Stefan Zweig, he still seems wanting of confirmation: 'I was so convinced of this reconstruction of mine that I published it somewhere. Breuer's youngest daughter read my account and asked her father about it shortly before his death. He confirmed my version, and she informed me about it later' (Freeman, 1972, p. 200). To what 'reconstruction' does this refer, that he published 'somewhere' (and *where?*) because he was so convinced yet unconfirmed? Hot pursuit, without a doubt, but the facts are still reported with slight discrepancies, and never by anyone but Freud.

[5.] The key to what? Not necessarily the arcane lock Freud had in mind. Perhaps the door to a more literal and still more courageous exploration, and Breuer might have founded an enlightened form of psychotherapy to advance the field by decades. But he was frightened off by the event, his circumstances, and perhaps his colleague as well.

few readers would identify, but in this case useless, since Anna knows Breuer has recently fathered a child. (There is another possible source of security, transference theory, but it had not yet been invented.)

Meanwhile, return to the fact that it is Dr. Breuer who is directly and immediately involved, and involved with Anna O. What might they be thinking, *meaning*, saying to each other in this perilous moment, at best and at worst? God knows what words she uttered in which four languages (for she was known to speak a 'gibberish' of mixed tongues when ill), nor what she heard, what he said, or what he told Freud was said. Nor what Freud told Jones; nor how accurate Jones's translation (not always, we know). But let us take it that Freud's letter to Zweig is the most authentic; in it, Anna, on one page, says, 'Now Dr. B's child is coming' (Freeman, 1972, p. 200) or, in a slightly different quotation from the same scene, same book, 'Now Dr. Breuer's baby is coming. It is coming!' (p. 56).

Anna might have thought, felt, or said, for example:

Dr. B — a baby. I feel like a baby!

Would you abort my child? Then don't abort my treatment.

You know me so well, but you thought I was sexually underdeveloped, had never been in love, had no romantic feelings — although you knew, for instance, that I loved to dance. Well, I've grown. Thanks to you in good part. Now Dr. Breuer's child has become a woman. I'm ready at last for that sexual release. It is coming! When you were late for our appointment one morning, you apologized and told me [as he had] that it had to be so because your wife was having a new baby and you had to stay up all night. If that is what is more important to you, look, I'm having one too.

Why did you tell me so suddenly that you could not continue to see me? Your reasons sounded false. I know so well your voice, your eyes. What is the real reason? If you must lie to me to leave me, I must lie to you to keep you.

Only hear me out. I mean you no harm as you leave. We have touched. You massaged me, fed me, gave me life, comfort, discipline; made me tell things I would not tell anyone else. I felt loved, and I must tell you in the ultimate way, I love you too. You are handsome, kind, distinguished. If all of this does not justify my excitement and love, what does? Life together is impossible, I know that. Sex is really not that important to me either. But love is. A child would be. I want someone to love. I am in great pain over it.

None of these possibilities begins to describe conversations to which they might have led. But meanwhile, Dr. Breuer, on his part, might have thought, felt, or said something like the following:

What did I do to deserve this?

My God, you are really out of your mind (again).

You cannot think that I . . . (or can you?)

We've never even discussed such a thing (which they hadn't).
It never entered my mind (if indeed it hadn't).
Is this more of your 'private theatre'? Not amusing.
You are punishing me.
Damned embarrassing. I already have problems at home.
This is a trap! How to get out of it.
Here is the ruination of my reputation/family/livelihood/method/hope/
everything.[6]

Or, in a more benign mood:

You don't want me to leave you.
Perhaps I have been both too caring and careless, left you unfairly.
What are you growing, laboring to deliver?
What part did I play?
I am touched and honored that you choose me.
Have I led you to expect more than I can give?

Or, best of all:

You are in pain. Let's try to understand. I will postpone my trip and work with
you.

Freud, as we already know, discussed this case with Breuer more than once. There is some evidence that Breuer felt not only uncertainty about it, but guilt and shame as well. In the late 1880s, years after *Studies on Hysteria* was written, Freud tried to persuade Breuer to write more about it. Breuer had declared the treatment of hysterics an ordeal he could not face again. Freud then described to Breuer one experience so well known now through his autobiography (1948, p. 48) in which he too had faced 'untoward events'. As Jones (1953, p. 250) described it:

> So Freud told him of his own experience with a female patient suddenly flinging her arms around his neck in a transport of affection, and he explained his reasons for regarding such 'untoward occurrences' as part of the transference phenomena characteristic of certain types of hysteria.[7]

[6.] I have personally known psychologists and psychiatrists who far exceeded Breuer's relatively innocent transgressions, that is, their 'sins' by the informal definition, 'included exchange of bodily fluids'. Results included divorce, marriage to the patient, suicide, murderous thoughts and a probable attempt, career changes, and the development of new theories. The late O. H. Mowrer's therapy based on real guilt and compensation (1967) is an example of the latter, as he often announced to professional colleagues.

[7.] This is either the instance that Freud sometimes described in his autobiography and elsewhere, as the patient being just aroused from a hypnotic trance, and with a maidservant unexpectedly knocking or entering, or it is a separate but prototypic scene.

This seems to have had a calming effect on Breuer, who evidently had taken his own experience of the kind more personally and perhaps even reproached himself for indiscretion in the handling of his patient.

Momentarily this comforted, explained to, and protected Breuer, but only momentarily. At first, Breuer agreed to join in the publication and promotion of the idea of transference. As Freud writes many times, 'I believe,' he told me, 'that this is the most important thing we two have to give the world' (Breuer and Freud, 1957, p. xxviii). But then, Breuer withdrew his support for the theory and the complete primacy of sexual etiology of neuroses — support Freud needed and urgently sought. 'He [Breuer] might have crushed me . . . by pointing to his own patient [Anna O.] in whose case sexual factors had ostensibly played no part whatever' (Freud, 1948, p. 6).[8] That Breuer was ambivalent, that he neither crushed nor supported, Freud put down to Breuer's suppressed secret of the case. Breuer may have had serious and sincere doubts on other scores. They agreed to disagree, citing 'the natural and justifiable differences between the opinions of two observers who are agreed upon the facts and their basic reading of them, but who are not invariably at one in their interpretations and conjectures', It was signed 'J. Breuer/ S. Freud, April 1895' (Breuer and Freud, 1957, p. xxx). Breuer, quite possibly intimidated by the nature of his suppressed material and his loyalty to both colleague Freud and patient Anna O., did not press his arguments, whatever they might have been. Freud did, and swept the field. Now we have transference.

DEFINITIONS AND DEFINERS

A few definitions are in order. There are dozens. They change over time and between authors. The main theme is constant enough that the proponent of any form of 'depth psychology' can sagely nod assent, though Orr (1954, p. 625) writes, 'From about 1930 onward, there are too many variations of the concept of transference for systematic summary'.

Circa 1905

What are transferences? They are new editions or facsimiles of the tendencies and phantasies which are aroused and made conscious during the progress of the analysis; but they have this peculiarity, which is characteristic for their species, that they replace some earlier person by

---

8. Breuer knew better. Had he walked into this trap, it is he who would have been crushed.

the person of the physician. To put it another way: a whole series of psychological experiences are revived, not as belonging to the past, but as applying to the person of the physician at the present moment. Some of these transferences have a content which differs from that of their model in no respect whatever except for the substitution. These, then — to keep the same metaphor — are merely new impressions or reprints. Others are more ingeniously constructed; their content has been subjected to a moderating influence — to *sublimation,* as I call it — and they may even become conscious, by cleverly taking advantage of some real peculiarity in the physician's person or circumstances and attaching them to that.[9] These, then, will no longer be new impressions, but revised editions. (Freud, 1959, p. 139)

The new fact which we are thus unwillingly compelled to recognize we call 'transference'. By this we mean a transference of feelings on to the person of the physician, because we do not believe that the situation in the treatment can account for the origin of such feelings. (Freud, 1935, p. 384)

By transference is meant a striking peculiarity of neurotics. They develop toward their physician emotional reactions both of an affectionate and hostile character, which are not based upon the actual situation but are derived from their relations to their parents. (Freud, 1935, p. 391)

There can be no doubt that the hostile feelings against the analyst deserve the name of 'transference' for the situation in the treatment gives no adequate occasion for them. (Freud, 1935, p. 385)

Why should anyone feel hostility toward Freud? 'Actually I have never done a mean thing', wrote Freud to Putnam (Jones, 1957, p. 247). Not many can make this disclaimer, and not all believe it borne out by Freud's record (compare Roustang, 1982).

Still, if he only *thinks* this of himself it is more likely that hostile feelings toward him would be seen as unjustified by his behavior. What matters here is the analyst's proclamation of innocence — a stance that permeates transference theory throughout. While an ad hominem argument is of limited use, there is a principle to which readers in this field must surely subscribe. It is that *every honest theory of personality and psychotherapy must reflect the personality and experience of its author.* How could it be otherwise?

Freud (1935, p. 385) continues this definition:

The necessity for regarding the negative transference in this light is a

---

9. Women are especially good at this, he writes. They 'have a genius for it' (Freud, 1935, p. 384).

confirmation of our previous similar views of the positive or affectionate
variety.

This 'necessity' is part of that strange logic in which the second assertion confirms
the first!

Is transference useful? Yes, it overcomes resistance, enables interpretation; it
is your chief tactical ally. 'The father-transference is only the battlefield where we
conquer and take the libido prisoner' (Freud, 1935, p. 396).

In sum, the patient's feelings '*do not originate in the present situation,* and *they
are not deserved by the personality of the physician,* but they repeat what has happened
to him once before in his life' (Freud, 1927, p. 129; emphasis added). The 'once
before' is experience 'in childhood, and usually in connection with one of his
parents'. As put most simply in *The Problem of Lay Analysis* (Freud, 1927, p.
129): 'The attitude is, to put it bluntly, a kind of falling in love'. We must not
forget, 'This affection is not accounted for by the physician's behavior nor the
relationship nor situation' (1935, p. 383).

So, the analyst is not responsible, the situation is not responsible, even though
there may be some 'real peculiarities' visible in the physician or circumstances.
Transference is a neurotic peculiarity. Whether it is a normal (common) trait also
is unclear, but the transference neurosis is a feature of analysis — that is certain.

There are some updatings. They will not make a basic difference, but it is
worth noting that Fenichel (1941, p. 95) tried to alter the absolute exemption of
the therapist's responsibility when he wrote:

> Not everything is transference that is experienced by a patient in the
> form of affects and impulses during the course of the analytic treatment.
> If the analysis appears to make no progress, the patient has, in my opinion,
> the right to be angry, and his anger need not be a transference from
> childhood — or rather, we will not succeed in demonstrating the
> transference component in it.

Later positions (Macalpine, 1950; Menninger, 1958) suggest that the analytic
situation itself is regressive, and thus somewhat influential if not responsible. Waelder
(1956, p. 367) says, 'Hence transference is a regressive process. Transference develops
in consequence of the conditions of the analytic situation and the analytic technique'
(emphasis added). Waelder's statement directly contradicts some of Freud's basic
definitions, but to what effect?

The qualifications make concessions and corrections, but no one anywhere
questions the basic concept, per se. Oddly, they serve only to strengthen, never to
cast doubt. The situation *is* regressive because it turns all the patient's attention
inward and backward toward earliest experience, and the therapist is made to
seem bland, neutral, indistinct, even invisible. It is like a form of sensory

deprivation. Other forms are elevated into unusual prominence. So it is with the presence and with the pronouncements of the therapist in this regressive situation.

Or, if transference is considered as a matter of 'projection', the question arises, *what is the screen?* The answer was implied, though it seemed not to be recognized, in the first deep crack in transference theory — 'countertransference'. The instant that concept was developed, it should have become clear that the analyst's presence was more than a blank. Presumably countertransference was to be kept at a minimum. Until recently, definitions of and attention to it have been relatively minimal (except for one sector where it seems most nearly innocent, appropriate, and 'natural': that is, work with children).

As Freud began to give attention to countertransference, he viewed it as responsive or reflexive rather than as an originating characteristic of the analyst. 'We have become aware of the "countertransference" which arises in [the physician] as a result of *the patient's influence*[10] on his unconscious feeling' (Freud, 1910, p. 122; emphasis added). This is a far cry from the notion of one of my students, who thinks that transference lies in wait with the therapist and his wishes or expectations, while the countertransference is on the part of the patient! Not so far-fetched as it first seems, for it may be only a reversal of Freud's statement just preceding. Which comes first?

The psychoanalytic positions on countertransference range from treating it as a hindrance to be overcome[11] to welcoming it as a sensory asset ('third ear') (Epstein and Feiner, 1974, p. 1). In any event, one can hardly claim 'no responsibility' on a 'nobody home' basis if it is admitted that somebody, with *some* palpable characteristics, is there. The question now becomes, 'What is the nature of these characteristics?'

The therapist is in truth a person of some distinctiveness, some identity, no matter how discreetly hidden. He has some self-concept — an image of what he is and wants to be. Perhaps the more truly modest and humble, the more he will be surprised by intense idealizations of himself by others. If plain (he thinks), how much more inappropriate for the patient to think him handsome.

[10.] This too is the patient's doing? Does this material not reside in the being of the physician? Or, if an interactive quality, does the transference, in reverse, arise in the patient as a result of the *physician's* influence?

[11.] In a letter dated 1909 about a case now become infamous, Freud wrote to Jung, 'After receiving your wire I wrote Fraulein Sp. a letter in which I affected ignorance' (McGuire, 1974, p. 230) and says of Jung's mishap, 'I myself have never been taken in quite so badly, but I have come very close to it a number of times and had a *"narrow escape"* [in English]. I believe that only grim necessities weighing on my work and the fact that I was ten years older when I came to psychoanalysis saved me from similar experiences. But no lasting harm is done. They helped us to develop the thick skin we need and to dominate "countertransference" which is after all a permanent problem for us' (McGuire, 1974, p. 231).

But perhaps he is not really modest or humble. That may be only a professional attitude. When Freud wrote to his wife Martha, telling her of Anna O.'s strenuous affection for Dr. Breuer and of the consternation on the part of Breuer's wife, Martha replied that she hoped that would not happen to her (a common concern of the therapist's spouse). Freud 'reproved her for her vanity in supposing that other women would fall in love with *her* husband: "for that to happen one has to be a Breuer"' (Jones, 1953, p. 225). Yet it was not really *her* vanity at issue, it would seem, but her concern over *his* exposure. Having first miscast the problem, he then did not quite give the assurance that she wanted,[12] and additionally, it *did* happen to her husband, as the theory predicted that it would. Perhaps it already had. At some point, reported in his autobiography, Freud had discontinued hypnosis after an 'untoward event' of his own. The patient, being aroused from a trance, threw her arms around him 'in a transport of affection'. At any rate, Freud dropped the method of hypnosis (was 'freed of it') shortly after, and took a position behind the couch. Some aspect of self-image certainly was a factor: hypnosis he compared to the work of a 'hod carrier or cosmetician', while analysis was 'science', 'surgery'. Perhaps it was more dignity at stake than modesty.

Though modesty was a thread often pulled. He wrote to Martha, 'To talk with Breuer was like sitting in the sun; he radiates light and warmth. He is such a sunny person, and I don't know what he sees in me to be so kind.'

To Martha herself, 'Can there be anything crazier, I said to myself. You have won the dearest girl in the world quite without any merit of your own'[13] (Jones, 1953, p. 110). Granted that this is the romantic hyperbole of courtship, and that there are fluctuations in mood and tone as situations change, so that we hear this humility from the same powerful genius who called his real nature that of the *conquistador*. Still, the literary license we give to 'without merit' is like that we give to the supposedly indistinguishable therapist who receives what *he* says *he* does not deserve in the service of carrying out the conditions for transference.

'Can there be anything crazier, I said to myself.' Yes, a few things. One is institutionalizing false modesty such as that, by denying the characteristics in the situation and the personality of the analyst — denying so completely that a neurosis is cultivated by and for both parties while it is the very object of treatment. And all in the name of sanity, clarity, and honest scrutiny.

[12.] 'Later he assured her that the anatomy of the brain was the only rival she had or was likely to have' (Jones, 1953, p. 211).

[13.] 'But a week later he asks why he should not for once get more than he deserved. Never has he imagined such happiness' (Jones, 1953, p. 110).

INTERIM THOUGHTS

On the way to proposing a countertherapy, permit me to describe some experiences that, over the years, led me to depart from the common beliefs in psychoanalytic theory that I once held.

1. For 15 years, at the University of Chicago Counseling Center, I worked through the ranks from student-intern to senior faculty and chairman of the Interdepartmental Clinical Program, and occupied the office of my former mentor Carl Rogers after he left for Wisconsin. In such a position, one develops the reputation of a 'therapist's therapist'. It is a privileged learning opportunity. My clientele consisted largely of junior professionals. Three were interns on a psychiatric rotation from the university hospital. They were taught by their medical faculty a good deal about transference. They discussed their experiences as psychiatrists in training. One, a shy, diffident young man, was especially articulate about the onset of transference as he perceived it in a slightly older woman patient. He felt a rising excitement — 'This is it'. He also felt that he was being handed a power about which he was both pleased and embarrassed, and of course embarrassed by his pleasure and embarrassment. Not only was transference theory an 'armor in his ordeal', but a source of *downright satisfaction*. He felt 'as if I were wearing a mask. I smiled behind it. I could have taken it off. I thought of that, but I was too confused about what I'd have to uncover. Behind it, I could be detached, amused, be more thoughtful and responsive.' It was a revealing bit of information on the inner experience of transference in a young adherent of the theory. I wondered how many therapists acknowledge their pleasure so honestly. Weeks later, I took a neighbor and his four-year-old son to the emergency room. My client was on duty. I helped hold and soothe the little boy while Dr. G. sewed stitches in his head wound. We worked in a kind of harmonic unison over this child of French-Iranian extraction, who knew little English and was pained and frightened. We did it well. In our next session, Dr. G. told me that he had felt as if the boy were 'our child'. Did he mean his feminine qualities and my masculine ones (or the reverse)? No. If it must be put in familial terms, we were brothers, he thought. So did I (though neither of us actually had brothers). One might easily see in this an expression of transference and/or countertransference. I found neither. We had an experience that made us feel like brothers.

2. I attended a discussion of religion between Bruno Bettleheim and Paul Tillich. Bettleheim took the general position outlined in Freud's *Future of an Illusion* (1949) to the effect that the urge toward religious belief was a projection of the longing for a father. That seemed most plausible to me. Tillich answered, 'But what is the screen?' Not a weighty reply, to my way of thinking at the time, but increasingly I realized that 'it' cannot be nothing.

3. One evening I overheard a client in the next office. She wept and shouted,

'No one has ever treated me this way before. I love it, I can't believe it, but I'm afraid every time I come.' I thought she was banging on the desk to emphasize her points. At the end of the evening I went to that counselor's office. 'For God's sake, Russ, what were you doing?' He explained, and I heard fragments of a primitive audiodisc recording. The banging was the steam pipes. The client was saying, 'No one has ever understood me this way before. No one. I can't believe it. I love the feeling of "at last, someone knows, someone cares". But when I come back next week, with the rest of my garbage, will you still understand? I couldn't bear it if you didn't.' I do not know the content of what was understood, but was most struck by what understanding meant to her, and thought about it for a long time.

4. I once taught a course with the prominent Adlerian Dr. Rudolph Dreikurs — a hearty, gruff bear of a man. In one class he seemed especially heavy-handed. Students were angry and critical. During the intermission, he said, 'Do you notice the hostility? There is a lot of negative transference here.' I told him my observations, and he was perplexed, crestfallen. He had taught hundreds, even thousands, and no one had complained. They usually loved him.

5. In 1971, during the period of the 'revolution in mental health' (community organization, demystification, 'radical therapy' and politics to fit, and so on), a consulting psychiatrist and practising analyst told me, 'It is amazing. Some of these paraprofessionals I'm supervising can do anything we can do — except the handling of the transference.' I wondered — what would he say if there *is* no 'transference'?

6. Over many years, I have been perceived in many different ways. Humble and proud, kind and cruel, loyal and unreliable, ugly and handsome, cowardly and brave, to name a few wide-ranging contradictions. Someone must be mistaken? No, they are all true. This sense of my self, sometimes selfish, sometimes generous, makes me hesitate before characterizing someone's perception as a distortion. One client dreamed of me as a little boy, one she held on her lap — and I a white-haired father of three grown children, as she knew. But she too was correct (and she had her own reasons for that caretaking dream). There is that childlike side of me. I could cast it off, but keep it for my enjoyment. I have been seen as a lion and a rabbit. True, I can be hard and soft. Is that unusual? Though happy to have been married for 40 years, I could, when young, have fallen in love frequently — with ease, passion, and tenderness. Seriously? Sometimes seriously enough to last another lifetime, probably, but not so seriously that I think I am the only man for this only woman for me.[14] While I do not respect the philanderer because of the damage he is likely to do, reading Jones's (1953, p. 139) judgment that 'Freud was not only monogamous in a very unusual degree but for a time seemed to be

---

[14.] My wife, with good taste and judgment, advises ('after all, this is not your biography') omitting this entire section. I would like to, but a main point of the article is that theory is in part biographical, stemming from thought, observation, and self-concept.

well on the way to becoming uxorious' struck me as curious and doubtful. It is, however, a condition that would more readily incline one toward transference theory — at least as a supporting illusion. But if that is not my condition or my personality, should his theory be my theory?

Then, about my granddaughter. I dearly love this child. From what previous experience do I transfer this affection? Yes, I dearly loved my two daughters and my son when they were three-year-olds, too — but whence came *that?* Sooner or later, experience has to be *de novo,* original. We know from work in comparative psychology that most women and many men show autonomic signs (such as pupillary change) of great attraction to the typical 'configuration of infant' large head and small body. In short, it is an instinct, and it *produces its natural consequences each time for the same instinctive reasons, as if each time were the first.* This child knows, trusts, and loves me, too. Is *her* experience transference? Transfer of what? From where? Is mine transference and hers countertransference? Neither one; the trust is earned, the love is natural. That is the answer.

The real question is, what conditions bring about the original experience, the first of its kind without precedents? Then, what if those conditions again prevail? Put another way, if every perception depends on the past, what if there is no past?

THE NEXT STEP

History of its origins aside, transference is a shorthand term for qualities and characteristics of human interaction. Any shorthand will fail to represent the particulars of a unique relationship. Rather, the shorthand will obscure (in a sometimes comforting way) the realities of the relationship. The concept of 'father figure', for instance, needs to be unraveled; what characteristics is it supposed to represent? What do such concepts as 'parent' or 'infantalizing' mean? In the remaining pages, an alternative view is presented to clarify the realities that the shorthand forms fail to represent.

A COUNTERTHEORY

If transference is a fiction to protect therapists from the consequences of their own behavior, it is time to examine some behaviors — and their normal consequences. This does not start with any implication of villainy. It is simply that since 'transference-love' is the consequence most fraught with concern, and since that was the original instance in development of transference theory (from which all its extensions come), we should examine the behaviors responsible for the development of affectionate and erotic feelings. What is the truth? What are the facts?

First, there is the situation, its true conditions. Dependency is a built-in feature for the petitioner at the beginning, and the treatment itself often promotes further dependency. The patient (or client) is typically anxious, distressed, in need of help, and often lonely. The therapist, presumably, is not. Instead, he holds a professional role (especially if a physician) that ranks at or near the top in sociological surveys of romantic attractiveness to women seeking husbands (ahead of astronauts and other celebrities).[15] The situation is set for intimacy, privacy, trust, frequent contact, and revelation of precious secrets.

Second, it is also the case that there is an ongoing search, on the part of most adolescents and adults, for sexual companionship. It requires only the opportunity for intimacy. One does not need to look into therapy for arcane and mysterious sources of erotic feelings. They are commonplace, everywhere, carried about from place to place. Psychotherapy will encounter sexual attraction as surely as it encounters nature. The simple combination of urge and situation is a formula for instant, if casual, romantic fantasy.

Third, there is a supremely important special factor in a behavior to which most therapists subscribe and try to provide. It is *understanding*. Freud put it bluntly, (of transference) 'It is a kind of falling in love'. Let me put this bluntly too: *understanding is a form of lovemaking*. It may not be so intended, but that is one of its effects. The professional Don Juan knows and uses it to deliberate advantage. That alone may make it an embarrassment to the therapist who does not wish to take advantage and is hard-pressed to deal in an accepting but nonpossessive way with natural feelings that conventionally call for either some response in kind or rejection. Such difficulty does not relieve him of the responsibility. Intentionally he has been understanding, and this alone will, over time, activate in the patient some object-seeking components of trust, gratitude, and quite possibly affection or sexual desire.

In this same context, *misunderstanding is a form of hatemaking*. It works equally well since being misunderstood in a generally understanding relation is a shock, betrayal, and frustration.[16]

[15.] A current viewpoint in social psychology suggests that love, especially sexual love, is the result of status and power factors — 'a love relationship is one in which at least one actor gives (or is prepared to give) extremely high status to the other' (Kemper, 1978, p. 285).

[16.] This should not be overlooked: the therapist wants, and sometimes demands, to be understood by the patient, or client. Whether dealing in reflections, interpretations, or hypnotic suggestion, the therapist wants these understood — he or she feels good about it if they are, and inadequate and 'resisted' if they are not. Indeed, *the therapist may have the same response to understanding as does the patient* — tempered, of course, by wisdom, maturity, self-awareness, and other (not always present) virtues.

Understanding and misunderstanding and their ambivalent interplay are the primary factors in this thesis about 'positive and negative transference', but there are numerous supplementary behaviors. To supplement misunderstanding, for example: waiting, asking for the bathroom key, paying (possibly for missed appointments), cigar smoke, and various other subordinating and infantalizing conditions.

The most convincing evidence for this simple but profoundly effective thesis probably lies in one's own experience. It was, however, called to my attention by a combination of events, such as that overheard client in the next office, and another fortuitous circumstance. A Catholic priest took a year of sabbatical study at the University of Chicago, and I was able to see some of the basic data on which he based his study of how it feels to be 'really understood' (van Kaam, 1959). A seemingly simple question, but of great significance. By chance, the first questionnaire respondent was an adolescent girl, a 17-year-old student in a parochial school. This midwestern bobby-sox type is hardly a match for the sophisticated European Anna O., but they are equally real and, I suspect, would have understood each other. As to how she feels, in substance and spirit, when she experiences understanding, she wrote:

> I felt as if he, my boyfriend, had reached into my heart and had really seen my fears and understood how much my religion meant to me. My whole being wanted to cry out how much I loved him for that understanding. My body felt so alive and I wanted to tell everyone how happy and exuberant I was. I wanted everyone to be happy with me. I wanted to hang on to that understanding and pray it would never be lost to me.
>
> Whenever I am understood by anyone, I feel a fresh onset of love for anyone or anything. I can't sleep right away because I don't want that understanding to fade, and somehow it seems to me that it will probably be lost in the morning.
>
> My body seems to have a terrific pounding sensation and I want to cry out something which I don't know how to express in words. I feel more sure of myself. I want to give. I want to give everything I have to make this person who understands happier. I want to live the full minute of every day. Life seems so much richer when you know someone understands, because to me, one who understands is the one who cares and loves me and I feel love and security and peace. (A. van Kaam, personal communication, 1961)

I submit that this is not an atypical reaction, but simply one heightened by the enthusiastic vigor of an adolescent girl. She tells us how being understood affects a human being psychologically or physiologically. Why should such effects be labeled 'transference'? They do in fact originate in the situation and through the performance of psychotherapy (when that is indeed benevolent). The reaction might better be called 'originalenc..' It is not transferred, not inappropriate. It is the normal and appropriate reaction. It might come about in someone who had never been so understood before. Thus it might come from no past experience, but from a wish that the past had been different, or from the hopes and dreams of the future!

For example, there is the filmed interview between Carl Rogers and Gloria (Rogers, 1965), of which a portion is reproduced below. Near the final section, she feels deeply understood in a way that brings tears and a feeling she calls 'precious'. She wishes her father had been so understanding — but that had not been the case. The typical professional audience witnessing this becomes tense and alert. There is uneasy laughter. They have been taught what to think of this, and the moods range from scornful to sympathetic, for there is a general feeling that transference has reared its head (and the anticipation that Rogers might be caught in a dangerous 'Freudian' situation). It can be read that way. It can equally be read as her response to understanding such as she never had from her father, her wish that she could have a father like that, not like her own. Is that transference?

Rogers, on display and well aware of this issue, makes certain that he does not deny or reject, and while his response may not be the perfect model, it acknowledges her admiring wistfulness, his appreciation in kind of her, and continues in an understanding mode.

> ROGERS: *I sense that, in those utopian moments, you really feel kind of whole. You really feel all in one place.*
>
> GLORIA: *Yes. [Rogers: M-hm.] Yeah. It gives me a choked-up feeling when you say that, because I don't get that feeling as often as I like. [Rogers: M-hm.] I like that whole feeling. It's really precious to me.*
>
> ROGERS: *I suspect none of us gets it as often as we'd like, but I really do understand. [pause] M-hm, that [referring to her tears] really does touch you, doesn't it?*
>
> GLORIA: *Yeah, and you know what else, though, I was just thinking . . . I feel it's a dumb thing that, uhm, all of a sudden when I'm talking, gee, how nice I can talk to you, and I want you to approve of me, and I respect you, but I miss that my father couldn't talk to me like you are. I mean I'd like to say, gee, I'd like you for my father. [Rogers: M-hm.] [pause] [Rogers: You . . .] I don't even know why that came to me.*[17]

[17.] The typical audience thinks it knows why — 'looking for a father'. Popular wisdom says that young women seek 'father figures'. A less popular and somewhat hidden knowledge is that men also may seek 'daughter figures'. Freud might have known this from his dream about 'overaffectionate feelings' for his ten-year-old daughter Mathilde (letter to W. Fliess, May 31, 1897), but such reciprocity, or seeking from both directions, does not so readily fit to transference theory. Whatever motives for either . . . /cont

ROGERS: *You look to me like a pretty nice daughter. [A long, long pause] But you really do miss the fact that you couldn't be open with your own dad.*
GLORIA: *Yeah, I couldn't be open, but . . . I want to blame it on him. I think I'm more open than he'd allow me. I mean he would never listen to me talk like you are. And, ah, not disapprove, and not lower me down.*

'ORIGINALENCE' VERSUS A FORM OF 'REPETITION-COMPULSION' IN PSYCHOLOGICAL THOUGHT

'Originalence' is a not very good word for another way of thinking about the problem. It refers, if you can believe in such a possibility, to new experience. That could mean 'fresh perceptions', or 'first loves' and could also refer to an experience previously known or an act previously performed but new in spite of its appearance of being old. It is an orientation toward present or even future influences on behavior. 'Originalence' is merely a word counterpart to 'transference' and is not designed to 'catch on' as a theory. The purpose here is to balance and then dispense with these particular theories so that the facts can once more be observed with what the phenomenologists call 'sophisticated naivete'.

One of the errors in transference theory is the illogical assumption that any response duplicating a prior similar response is necessarily replicating it. Similar responses are not always repetitions. They appear to us to be repetitions because, in our effort to comprehend quickly, we look for patterns, try to generalize. There is breathing as a general respiratory pattern, but my most recent breath is not taken because of the previous one: rather, for the same reason the previous breath was taken, and the first breath was taken. It is not habit. It is normal function, repeated but not repetition.

In the first instance, the original love of the child for the parent is not transferred from the past. There was no earlier instance. What then? This original love developed for the same sorts of reasons or conditions that will again produce it in later life. Provide those conditions again and they will produce (not reproduce) it again and again, each time on its own merits. The produced experience is mingled with memories and associations, but those are not the conditions. Memories may seem to reproduce. If so, they reproduce the *conditions* (for fear or passion, for example), and it is again the *conditions,* not the memory, that account for the response.

/cont . . . party — whether benign caring, dependency, exploitation, fulfillment or various hopes and desires — the seeking moves in *both* directions. So neither party may be justly accused of entirely uninvited or unrewarded responsibility. This is not necessarily to explain the particular case of Gloria, but to add a statement of general interest in the reanalysis of transference theory.

How did any particular affect come into being in the first place? If love developed through the parents' understanding (of what the child needs in the way of care, in the development of its whole mental life from language to thought), further understanding should elicit love too; but consider, *every second instance might as well have been the first*. Warmth feels good to the body, not only because it felt good when one was an infant, but because it *always* feels good. The need is 'wired in' as an innate physiological requirement. When one tastes a lemon at age 30, does it taste sour because it tasted that way at age three? It *always* tastes sour, the first time at any age, whether or not it ever tasted so before, and all following times for the same but original reason each time.

A QUESTION OF LOGIC

This logic is functional; the logic of transference is historical. The difference is very great. Historical logic in psychoanalysis goes even beyond looking into the past of an individual's life. Anna Freud writes: 'Long ago the analytical study of the neuroses suggested that there is in human nature a disposition to repudiate certain instincts, in particular the sexual instincts, indiscriminately and independently of individual experience. This disposition appears to be a *phylogenetic inheritance, a kind of deposit accumulated from acts of regression practised by many generations and merely continued, not initiated, by individuals*' (1946, p. 171; emphasis added). In contrast, the logic of a present (or future) orientation does not deny the past, but looks at immediate experience, or even imagination.

From experiential evidence, this newer logic explicitly asserts that any therapist has an active and response-arousing set of roles and behaviors. Therapists are loved for what makes them lovable, hated for what makes them hateful, and all shades in between. *This should be the first hypothesis.* Whatever it does not account for may then be described as proof of another phenomenon, such as transference, but understanding and misunderstanding will, I believe, account for the major affects of love and hate.

This does not begin to analyze the complex interactions beyond understanding and misunderstanding. Whatever they are in any given case, there too therapists play their part. The first principle remains; for the therapist to eschew the pretense of innocent invisibility and to reflect upon what, in the situation and his or her behaviors, does in fact account for those 'untoward events' that brought transference theory into being. Adoption of this principle may engender a sense of vulnerability and remove not only the shield but some of the most ornamental of therapeutic trappings as well. This is not the most inviting prospect for the contemporary psychotherapist. It is easier to have an exotic treatment for an intriguing disease. For the patient there may be some allure and pleasure in disguise as well.

Is there no transference, whatever, at any time? Of course there is, if you wish it. The material is there at the outset. It can be cultivated, and it can be forced. Emotional attitudes *will* be expressed, through indirect channels if open expression is discouraged. Like seeds, emotions and perceptions will grow straight and true in nourishing soil or crookedly through cracks in the sidewalk. One can encourage distortions, and then analyze them. It is a matter of choice. As with any fiction, 'transference' can be turned into a scenario to be acted out, creating a desired reality.

At the beginning, there is always incipient prejudice. Upon first meeting, stereotyped judgments and appraisals based on prior experience will be applied to the perception of the new unknown. Some call it 'stimulus generalization'. In a state of ignorance, what else can one do to make meaning? — unless it is the rare instance of those who are able and willing to approach new experience with suspended judgment, and a fresh, open view.

Except in such cases, prejudgment applies. Then if the reality of the new experience is concealed, attention turns inward to make meaning. If, however, the new reality is available to be known as needed, prejudice fades; judgments and appraisals appropriate to that reality will develop. For example, if red suspenders (and it could be blue eyes, swastikas, peace symbols, skin color) are worn by a person you meet, and if you have been mistreated by someone wearing red suspenders, you will be wary of this new person. If you are permitted to know more, and wish to do so, the effect of red suspenders will be canceled or supported or become trivial, depending upon your whole knowledge of the new reality. But if the new reality is concealed, attention searches for focus and meaning and, from a relationship standpoint, projections reign. Transference, or what passes for transference, can then be cultivated. Yet it is neither inevitable nor necessary. It is an obstruction.[18] That some derive benefit from its analysis may come from the concentrated self-examination and the presence of attentive intelligence on the part of the therapist — both of which are possible in at least equally pure form *without* the transference neurosis.

Will there be any change in basic transference theory? Is it possible to bring balance through corrective criticism? Not likely. Such 'balance' is only a temporary concession. The theory itself does not allow for balance. It is too heavily weighted (nearly all or none) because its logic cannot bear disturbance. As for the basic position, it is as entrenched as ever. For the public, it is high fashion and popular culture — diverting and entertaining. For the professional it is a tradition, a convenience, a shield, stock-in-trade, a revealed truth and a habit of thought.

[18.] Without doubt, the transference neurosis is an illness, deliberately contrived to benefit the treatment. Perhaps this is part of what is meant by the statement, 'Psychoanalysis is the disease it is trying to cure'.

How strong a habit of thought is illustrated by an instance described in the study by a sophisticated and sympathetic journalist, Janet Malcolm, under the title 'Trouble in the Archives' (1983). It reports as 'striking example of Eissler's[19] remarkable freedom from self-justification' (p. 132) a case history. 'He treated a wealthy older woman during the years before her death, and was so helpful that, in gratitude, she changed her will and left him a huge amount of money.' He could not accept it for himself and ordered it returned to beneficiaries or donated to charities. However, 'the husband of a relative of the deceased whose legacy had been diminished because of the change in the will, formally objected to the probation of the will. He happened to be an analyst, and his argument was that Eissler had exercised "undue influence" on the patient through "the unconscious utilization of the transference"' (p. 132). Malcolm writes, 'The case history ends with a wonderful twist'. Since the matter had caused painful embarrassment, what had first been seen as a 'loving gesture' was reinterpreted by Eissler as 'an expression of her hatred of him — an expression of the negative transference that had never been allowed to emerge during treatment' (p. 137).

It can be interpreted in other ways as well. The ex-patient may indeed have wished him well, may even have expected that if he could not use the money for himself he could choose to support charitable interests of importance to him. On the other hand, she may have enjoyed the amusement afforded by anticipation of cleverly hurting both her analyst and her relatives with one stroke. Two other observations remain. First, she was treated, even after her death, like a psychiatric patient and therefore a minor or incompetent. She could not exercise her choice about what was, after all, her money, because (a) her judgment was forever suspect, (b) it dispensed something of considerable value to others, and (c) it did not suit those who survived her and who either could call upon or were called upon by transference theory. Second, everything suffers (not entirely without compensation) *except* the concept of transference. One might think that since it was born of embarrassment, it might now die of embarrassment. But no, that is its charm. It merely changes color, never seriously questioned, only reconfirmed.

CONCLUSION

I have offered a brief for a countertheory, not in the sense of a complement or counterpart, as in 'transference and countertransference', but in the sense that

---

19. Kurt Eissler is a towering figure in the psychoanalytic movement, of whom one of his colleagues says, 'Eissler is not lovable, and he knows it' (Malcolm, 1983, p. 152). Yet his patient may have found him so, and rightly, for the very reason of his understanding behavior — when, if, and inasmuch.

counter means opposite, alternative. If transference is a theory, this is the counter. Personality and situation aside for the moment, *the therapist is responsible for two fundamental behaviors — understanding and misunderstanding — which account for love, or for hate,* and their associated affects. These, as well as other behaviors and the situation and personality of the therapist, may account — should first be held accountable — for the whole of what passes for transference.

The power of understanding has been featured to account for the phenomenon called 'transference', That use should not hide the point that it is this very power of understanding (not the transference, transference-love, or love itself) that heals. Understanding makes for healing and growth; misunderstanding makes for injury and destruction.

The proposition that 'understanding heals' does not make understanding the exclusive property of client-centered therapy. Far from it. Client-centered therapy has a constant theme in its focus on understanding: early, in its method of seeking confirmation from the client; later, in its stress on empathy (as a form of understanding and even a 'way of being') and how such understanding is best achieved. That is its emphasis, not its proprietary claim.

The emphasis on understanding is stressed at this final point to indicate that, while love is a blessing, love is not enough. Ultimately, we are trying to account not only for transference-love, or for love in general, but for *healing*. Even romantic love ('falling in', or choosing to be in) gives promise of, and is given in the hopes of receiving, understanding (which may or may not be delivered). Being 'in love' often assumes understanding to exist even where it does not. When love *is* present, it is an environment for or the consequence of *understanding*. Though the two are strongly associated, love does not heal. Understanding heals. It also makes one feel loved, or sustains love already felt, but the healing power is in the understanding.

Knowing that does not make the conduct of therapy easier in the slightest. It may, however, help us to separate therapy from the rest of life. It seems that we can quite well love, and take love from, those to whom we do not devote the considerable or sometimes near-consuming effort to understand fully. *That* is the difference between real life in ordinary relations and equally real life in therapy. If and to such extent as they could be brought together, so much the better; if not, so much the good in either case.

To conclude that it is not love that heals may be a disappointment to many. The role of the healer is appealing. So is that of the benefactor who dispenses love. Therapists and others find these roles all too gratifying. But no, the 'healer' takes credit for a process inherent in the organism, if released, and love is therapeutic or enduringly beneficial only if expressed through understanding. The act of understanding may be the most difficult of any task we set ourselves — a seemingly mundane 'service role' yet requiring kinds of intelligence and sensitivity so demanding that some people are truly seen as gifted. Even that is not the final cause. It still remains for the client to feel understood. Of course, in doing so, clients understand themselves — that is the source of their confirming the understanding.

To realize that it is the *understanding* that promotes the healing will direct us to the remaining problem for psychotherapy and psychology: we do not know the mechanisms by which understanding promotes healing or even the mechanisms of understanding itself. That knowledge cannot come from a theory such as transference, which has been a roadblock and a pointer in the wrong direction for almost a century. That knowledge may not come from *any* present version of psychotherapy, but rather from more neutral realms of cognitive, social, and developmental psychology, or neuroscience, to the ultimate benefit of a new theory and practice.

AUTHOR'S NOTE

This article is a revised version of a chapter in the book *Client-Centered Therapy and the Person-Centered Approach* (Levant and Shlien, Eds., 1984) and I would like to thank the publisher, CBS-Praeger, for permission to reprint it here. It has previously been translated into Italian, French and Hungarian. Working with translators taught me, too late for this chapter, that my writing should have been translated into better English at the beginning. I apologize for difficulties to the reader.

REFERENCES

Breuer, J. & Freud, S. (1957). *Studies on hysteria.* New York: Basic Books.

Epstein, L. & Feiner, A. (1974). *Countertransference.* New York: Aronson.

Fenichel, O. (1941). *Problems of psychoanalytic technique.* Albany, NY: Psychoanalytic Quarterly Inc.

Freeman, L. (1972). *The story of Anna O.* New York: Walker.

Freud, A. (1946). *The Ego and the mechanisms of defense.* New York: International University Press.

Freud, S. (1910). The future prospects of psychoanalytic theory. In J. Strachey (Ed. and Trans.), *The standard edition of the complete psychological works of Sigmund Freud* (Vol. 7, pp. 3–122). London: Hogarth.

Freud, S. (1923). *The ego and the id.* London: Hogarth.

Freud, S. (1927). *The problem of lay analysis.* New York: Brentano.

Freud, S. (1935). *A general introduction to psychoanalysis* (Vol. 1). New York: Liveright.

Freud, S. (1948). *An autobiographical study.* London: Hogarth.

Freud, S. (1949). *The future of an illusion.* New York: Liveright.

Freud, S. (1959). *Collected papers* (Vol. 3). New York: Basic Books.

Jones, E. (1953). *The life and work of Sigmund Freud* (Vol. 1). New York: Basic Books.

Jones, E. (1957). *The life and work of Sigmund Freud* (Vol. 3). New York: Basic Books.

Kemper, T. (1978). *A social interactional theory of emotions.* New York: John Wiley.

Macalpine, I. (1950). The development of the transference. *Psychoanalytic Quarterly, 19,* 501–39.

Malcolm, J. (1983, December 5). Annals of scholarship: Trouble in the Archives I. *New Yorker,* pp. 59–152.

Masson, J. (Ed.) (1985). *The complete letters of S. Freud to W. Fliess 1887–1904.* Cambridge: Belknap-Harvard.

McGuire, W. (Ed.) (1974). *The Freud-Jung letters.* Princeton, NJ: Princeton University Press.

Menninger, K. (1958). *The theory of psychoanalytic technique.* New York: Basic Books.

Mowrer, O. H. (Ed.) (1967). *Morality and mental health.* Chicago: Rand McNally.

Orr, D. (1954). Transference and countertransference: An historical survey. *Journal of the American Psychoanalytic Association,* 621–70.

Rogers, C. R. (1942). *Counseling and psychotherapy.* Boston: Houghton Mifflin.

Rogers, C. R. (1951). *Client-centered therapy.* Boston: Houghton Mifflin.

Rogers, C. R. (1954). The case of Mrs. Oak. In C. R. Rogers & R. F. Dymond (Eds.), *Psychotherapy and personality change.* Chicago: University of Chicago Press.

Rogers, C. R. (1965). *Three approaches to psychotherapy I* [Film]. Santa Ana, CA: Psychological Films.

Roustang, F. (1982). *Dire mastery.* Baltimore: Johns Hopkins University Press.

Shlien, J. M. (1963). Erotic feelings in psychotherapy relationships: Origins, influences, and resolutions. Paper presented at the annual meeting of the American Psychological Association, Philadelphia.

van Kaam, A.L. (1959). Phenomenal analysis: Exemplified by a study of the experience of 'really feeling understood'. *Journal of Individual Psychology, 15,* 66–72.

Waelder, R. (1956). Introduction to the discussion on problems of transference. *International Journal of Psychoanalysis, 37,* 367–84.

CHAPTER 9

Embarrassment Anxiety
A literalist theory

Most theories of therapy contain a theory of anxiety; sometimes two or more. It might be as simple as incongruence between self and ideal. Or it might be as exotic and dramatic as the 'Oedipal complex'. My effort here is to provide a theory of anxiety in keeping with my own 'literalist' position, 'experiential' in keeping with the title of the conference, and as a contribution to our understanding of the fundamental things in life.

I have already subscribed to the view that all theories are autobiographical, and can vouch for the validity of this theory. It may not apply to everyone; some because they are so noble, others because they are so ignoble. We might learn from either of those extremes how to avoid or conquer this anxiety. What recommends the theory besides its validity is that it is literal — not abstract, mythological, literary, or metaphorical. Perhaps that takes much of the fun out of it. But anxiety is not for fun — it is misery, and those who coat it with the amusement of clever symbolic analysis are probably putting a layer of defense between themselves and the real pain of the experience. The experience which I have in mind is embarrassment.

People speak of 'anxiety attacks' and describe them as 'massive and terrible'. I would simply call anxiety, 'that which cripples'. As examples of the characteristic theories, here are some of the more famous ones. 'Separation anxiety' is my literary favorite, developed by Otto Rank. As you know, it relates to the concept of the 'birth trauma', that shock of being rudely ejected from the pleasant homeostasis of the womb. That is a fascinating but inferential theory, abstract and metaphorical. Separation anxiety could have more literal origins: disorientation, loneliness, ambivalence about growth, without reference to birth trauma. These are

First published in the ICCCEP collection *Client-Centered and Experiential Psychotherapy: A Paradigm in Motion*, Hutterer, R., Pawlowsky, G., Schmid, P. F. and Stipsits, R. (Eds.) (1996). Frankfurt: Peter Lang, pp.101–6. Amended and reprinted with kind permission.

experiences that can happen at any time, any age, for any observable cause. And these are real, quite real. There really *is*, for instance, ambivalence about growth. We talk of growth as glorious development, a motive we only admire and enjoy, but, in fact, learning to walk has many bumps and falls, is painful. Luckily, the rewards of independent mobility more than offset the pain. But then, each step in growth has in it the potential consciousness of death, not generally contemplated with pleasure. So separation and growth have ominous overtones without resort to the struggle to be born. And children who are lost have very good reason to feel anxious without *any* previous referent. Of course, parents who have lost their children are also anxious — sometimes more so than the children. *Everyone* lost may feel scared, and everyone has been born, but one is scared because one is *lost* not because one was *born*. It was actually for another reason that separation anxiety was linked to 'birth trauma'. That has more to do with the psycho-genetic outlook of early psychoanalysis. 'Find the origin' was the motif. On that scale, *in utero* is hard to beat. Rank won, to the annoyance of his mentor, Freud.

For Freud had already proposed 'the' basic anxiety — fear of castration. That comes after the child (son) is born and is in competition with father for mother. This might be a metaphor for a power struggle within the family — otherwise, it excludes the female gender. That would be inappropriate, since the majority of early patients were women. But then the formulators of theory were men — some of whom later reasoned that the vagina was a symbolic wound in the service of penis envy. Fascinating as all this may be, attractive and arcane, I consider such concepts to be a form of 'packaging'. Packaging does work. It does attract, may even convince — whether or not it contains the truth.

Here now is another, more literal theory of anxiety, 'that which cripples', with no packaging. It is a major anxiety, traumatic in the instant of its experience, at any age, and with long-remaining consequences of fear that it might be re-experienced. Anxiety, 'massive and terrible', is the result of embarrassment. More accurately, fear of embarrassment. Perhaps eventually, fear of that fear.

At first, embarrassment may sound slight, a small thing, temporary. It is, however, no small thing — not exotic, not glamorous, although you will not see it in any diagnostic manual. Perhaps you will remember more about it when you hear the reported experience of other people.

(a) For instance, there is a 'phobia' called 'fear of flying'. Not a joke to those who suffer from it. They are quite inconvenienced, sometimes disabled by it. Work with such sufferers indicates that it is not so much a fear of sitting in a plane traveling from one point to another. People can grit their teeth, grip the arms of the seat, close the eyes, etc., and complete the trip. What stops them is fear of the embarrassment at being *seen* trembling, sweating, being perceived as cowardly, foolish, perhaps being ridiculed, laughed at.

So, in 'support groups', they take a section of seats in a plane, sit together, have a bearable, even humorous time, and increasingly overcome the disability. They are not impressed nor are they helped by interpretations of the body of the airplane as a womb, or of flying as a sexual metaphor. But if they can look each other in the eye, look at themselves in a mirror, be relieved of the dreadful embarrassment and ridicule they fear, they can, for the moment, and in principle, conquer the fear of flying.

(b) Fear of embarrassment is a major factor in most reports of being 'blackmailed'. Why else would victims pay so dearly for matters often of relatively little consequence?

(c) In a large newspaper poll, people said they would 'rather have a root canal treatment' than purchase a car. Why? Because it was such an embarrassment to haggle over the price, especially with someone who knew all the facts and felt no such uneasiness. (Incidentally, since buying a car has long been a special anxiety for Americans, one psychologist who interviewed Carl Rogers thought it would be a telling and testing question to ask him, 'What if you were buying a car, would you be person-centered, or, how would you be?' (Rogers' answer: 'shrewd'.))

(d) More surprising, it is reported in the Book of Records, and quoted by the New Yorker Magazine, that the fear ranked as the most dreadful by Americans is not death, not fear of mutilation, not fear of divorce. These are three of the four worst fears. The number one rank, by far, is fear of public speaking.

(e) All fears are serious to the sufferer, but here are some which we cannot fail to recognize as very serious indeed. Frequently, women do not report rape or other sexual abuse. For the majority, the reason given is their fear of embarrassment. There is international testimony to this fact.

(f) Similarly, incest, physical abuse, alcohol and drug addiction are all often suppressed by individuals and families for fear of embarrassment.

(g) Expert beggars in the New York subways, when interviewed, said that eye contact was the most effective factor, because only then could they make the fear of embarrassment work for them.

(h) Most shocking to me was the confession of a Vietnam veteran, who said that he was 'too embarrassed not to kill'! He had been with other soldiers who destroyed a village. He was afraid that if he did not join in the murder, they would laugh at him, feel scorn for him. Terrible, is it not, to murder because you fear being embarrassed if you do not follow the crowd? That tendency is common to all sorts of teenage male exploits. It is not just fear of embarrassment, but of ridicule, which is a form of punishment that is well known.

Teachers use a dunce cap on children, and Mao's Red Guards used the same device to torment their teachers.

(i) How bad is this fear? People sometimes say, 'I could have died of embarrassment'. Some actually do! A restaurant owner has reported two cases in which a patron (female) was choking on food. The Heimlich maneuver was used, and after it had only partially succeeded, the woman ran into the restroom (because she had vomited on her dress) and there, behind the locked door, suffocated to death. A second similar case was reported at a garden party.

(j) A man who had claimed to be a good swimmer and sailor took a small sailboat out on the sea in a high wind. He could not control the boat — it capsized, and he was rescued, unconscious, from the water. Why had he not signaled for help from a nearby boat? He told his therapist that he was too embarrassed to admit that he had lied about his sailing ability.

(k) A well-known literary celebrity was depressed, and about to commit suicide. He remembered some pornographic photos in his safe deposit box where he also kept his will. When he thought of the embarrassment their discovery would cause, he postponed his suicide, sailed back to New York from Europe to hide the photos, and by the time he arrived there had changed his mind. In this case, fear of embarrassment saved his life. In others, it has caused death.

These are a fraction of the incidents that could be presented. If they are enough to remind you of the experience, you can reflect upon your own observations.

Some say that this anxiety is a disease of adolescents. Others say that there is a new generation immune to embarrassment. It is true that many topics and behaviors once shunned are now commonplace. TV talk shows in America and Europe present discussions and displays of every kind of oddity and perversion. Some young people, at an age we think typically most sensitive about appearance, wear spiked purple hair, safety pins through the nose, carry a nipple pacifier to school as a pendant around the neck. I think that in place of courage, they use defiance. One young man said to me, 'No one can ridicule us more than we do ourselves — that makes us safe, and scares you.'

Perhaps the fear of embarrassment can be outgrown. I do not know. It would be wonderful to see some serious studies of the phenomenology of embarrassment. Part of the difficulty in such study is that the experience begs or demands *not* to be observed. It wants above all to hide. One of our colleagues, Regina Stamatiadis wrote,

> To be embarrassed is one thing — and being seen to be embarrassed is another. The second is worse, or the worst! I truly believe that a person may prefer to die (but can't), especially when being embarrassed means being ashamed of oneself.

Shame, it seems to me, is closely related, but may be equally powerful in isolation, while embarrassment is more likely to be a public event. Embarrassment is an intensely immediate experience. It is a feeling of being excruciatingly alive and wishing one were not. Of being intensely present, and wanting to be anywhere else. There is no escape. Time stops! One is frozen in place, stiff, paralyzed, exposed with a sense of naked vulnerability, unwanted intimacy and transparency. To the witness(es) the victim says in a silent shriek, 'Don't look'. In response to which the witness, feeling either pain or glee, may feel drawn into the experience. In either case, there is a reverberation of embarrassment. Neither sufferer or witness is actually in a good condition to analyze or report.

[I tried to look up some definitions of embarrassment in my German-English dictionary. 'Short of cash' is one which sounds more like the view of the English lexicographer, but perhaps we are all the same in this respect. 'Confusion' is another definition. That one fits: 'Confusion', says H. S. Sullivan, 'is like a blow on the head with a hammer and "terrifying"', and so it is. Perhaps this discussion is enough to convince you that embarrassment is no small thing and worthy of a place in the theories of anxiety. JMS]

Let me mention now some instances in the history of psychotherapy in which fear of embarrassment has played a role, influencing contemporary ideas and practices. First, you may remember that Freud confidently used hypnosis, until, one day, a maid servant entered the room as a woman patient coming out of a trance threw her arms around his neck. Shortly thereafter, he dropped the technique of hypnosis, saying that it was superficial, and that his was 'not the role of the cosmetician but of the surgeon'. I believe that embarrassment was a factor in his decision.

This was at a time when angry husbands were already voicing jealous suspicions about psychoanalysis and the stolen affections of their wives. And it is worth noting that Freud once said, 'There is an incomparable fascination in a woman of high principles who confesses her passion'. That seems to me an astonishing confession and self-indictment on Freud's part, but true. It was and still is the case that a therapist often meets such ladies, frequently above his own social and moral status, and only in the avenue of his practice. That same fascination, and the embarrassment about it, still exists.

Also, there was the famous case of Breuer and Fr. 'Anna O', a young woman he treated in a most caring way, using hypnosis and cathartic methods, sometimes feeding her, sometimes taking her for rides in his carriage. At a critical point, as he was thinking her treatment should end, he received an urgent call from her mother, and found his patient 'writhing in the throes of an hysterical pseudo-pregnancy'. He quickly fled from the house in a cold sweat (leaving his umbrella, Ernest Jones does not fail to mention), and left the city the next day for a trip to Italy with his wife. It was the beginning of his separation from Freud, who was barely able to persuade Breuer to join in the writing of the 'Studies in Hysteria' that came from their work together. Is it not clear that embarrassment played a part in these events? Remember the fact that both Freud and Breuer were Jewish physicians needing to guard their hard-won reputations in an already somewhat anti-Semitic Vienna. Later, when Freud 'discovered' transference ('invented' would be a better word), he wanted to explain to Breuer this meaning of the embarrassing incident, but for Breuer, the relief came too late. He did not continue in the business of psychoanalysis.

And what about Carl Rogers? One example from his life concerns the matter of technique. At an early point, he developed a method of response called 'reflection' (of feeling, more than of content). It was an enormous aid to the practice of Client-Centered Therapy.[1] He made it teachable and learnable. And do not underestimate the importance of technique in this regard. Beginning therapists are certainly looking for methods of practice, they want to know, 'what do I do, how do I do it?' Methods precede and implement philosophy as means precede ends. In fact, means are ends, at earlier levels, and sometimes the means are the only expression of the ends the clients ever know. Rogers and others of his colleagues refined and promoted this method in much the same way as the psychoanalysts promoted interpretation. Sometime later, he became unwilling to be identified with the method he said had become 'a wooden mockery'. Still later, he asserted, 'I do not reflect!' This was not entirely true. In the first place, shortly after this published assertion, he did a private study of some of his recent interviews, and found that about 75 percent qualified as 'reflections'. In the second place, what he meant by his assertion was that he 'checked his understandings' as an alternative to and/or refinement of 'reflection'. Did embarrassment play a part in his statement, 'I do not reflect'? You have probably read, or heard him say, he 'winced' — it made him 'cringe' to be identified with such a technique. This is an expression of embarrassment, painful embarrassment. What happened to bring this about? Here is my version.

At Wisconsin, Rogers hoped that the project with 'schizophrenics' would be his greatest test and crowning glory. Instead, it became a failure, and a source of personal anguish as well. Why the failure? For one reason (and this was, I believe, a very large factor) the staff team was not prepared to provide Client-Centered Therapy that was adequate to test the hypotheses. Rogers later wrote of 'flaws that were nearly fatal', '. . . I did not take the time to develop a staff that was unified in philosophy and outlook . . .'. That puts it mildly. They were not trained and not committed, it was a staff torn with personal and political as well as philosophical disagreement, and laced with desperate innovations in practice. I must say here, in the most serious way, that it did damage to Client-Centered Therapy, damage from which we have never recovered. Nor do I see the wisdom of allowing that failure to be the basis for prescriptions of our techniques! But to

---

[1] Surprisingly, there is still some loyalty to the method. P. Pentony writes in an article just published [*The Person-Centered Journal, 1*, 3, 1994, Ed.], 'The discovery and development of this response was a major technical innovation in psychotherapy. If he had done nothing else, Carl Rogers would deserve to be remembered for this contribution.'

return this to the topic of embarrassment: there were on that staff two younger men of talent and ambition, on whom Rogers pinned some of his best hopes: Gendlin and Truax.

What did they make of 'reflection'? (You must understand they were both bitterly angry at Rogers and at each other.) After Wisconsin, one, Gendlin, calls reflection, 'the method of saying back'.[2] The other, Truax, employed reflection as part of a 'skill training' program, just the kind of technical emphasis that Rogers hoped to avoid.[3, 4] What a disappointment. Trivializing by one friend, technologizing by the other. This, after a lifetime of scorn by enemies who ridiculed his method as 'parroting'. Even though he knew that the technique itself can be raised to the level of a refined art (as well as lowered to a 'wooden mockery'), he was tired of defending, tired of being type-cast and thus seemed to abandon a mainstay of his method. In so doing, he contributed to the loss of discipline and definition, and to the 'anything goes as long as it is congruent' situation we have now.

In this, I see a sad disillusionment, and a sort of detachment from the public effort of leading a school of thought. In a letter written January 2, 1987 he said, 'I have come to feel that good therapists are few and far between'. That comes from a man who at one time hoped to see widespread applications of this form of counseling and psychotherapy. In the end, he wanted no more to be a model for others, nor to be called upon for approval or endorsement of the ideas of others, but simply to do what he wanted, in his own way. Finally, he came to rely on what he called his 'presence', a healing, 'almost another condition', but not one he could call upon at will, much less model for imitation by others.

There you have it.

I have tried to suggest another theory of anxiety: experiential, not metaphoric; directly observable, not inferential; literal, dynamic, contemporary, not psycho-genetic; so traumatic that people say they would rather face mutilation or death; and with lasting effects.

---

2. I am not sure where this 'quote' comes from and Shlien has probably dramatised it for effect. An almost exact match is found in Gendlin, E. T. (1974). Client-Centered and Experiential Psychotherapy. In D.A. Wexler and L.N. Rice *Innovations in Client-Centered Therapy*. New York: Wiley. The context is important since it is not at all clear to me that Gendlin intended to trivialise empathy here. Gendlin wrote: 'Everyone in the field of psychotherapy knows about the client-centered response, saying back to the person what the person has said.' (p. 214) [Ed.]

3. For details of the skills-based training that begat the 'skills movement', see Truax, C.B. and Carkhuff, R.R. (1967). *Toward Effective Counseling and Psychotherapy: Training and practice*. Chicago: Aldine. [Ed.]

4. For an account of the Wisconsin Project staff team difficulties, see H. Kirschenbaum (1979). *On Becoming Carl Rogers*. New York: Delacorte, pp. 275–318. [Ed.]

It is also the case that some of our leading theoreticians changed their methods and careers because of personal interactions that caused them embarrassment. They, and we, do not live or work in a sanitary laboratory of ideas, but in an atmosphere of personal interactions. Some of these interactions involve this commonplace but powerful experience we call 'embarrassment'. It is not such a small thing. It can cripple, kill, and change the history of ideas.

The study of this subject awaits your attention. The data is near by. It is a kind of 'psychopathology of everyday life' without the cleverness of the sly jokes, slips of the tongue, and the magic paraphernalia of the 'unconscious'.

It does not carry any prescription for treatment, but it should advance our understanding of the human condition, or it will have missed its mark. Even in that case, it would at least be a model for the kind of theory I believe the world needs — literal and true to life.

Embarrassment, the experience and the fear of it, may be a major factor in the lives of your clients. Study of it is difficult, but can be accomplished if we will have the courage, and the 'openness to experience', to *not* do what embarrassment asks us to do. Namely to avert our eyes; pretend that it does not matter; is not happening; as we are so inclined to do partly because of this very embarrassment.

Section 3

Applications
Theory, research and life

EDITOR'S INTRODUCTION

Chapter 10, another unpublished paper, is a further example of how ideas were developed, discussed, evaluated, elaborated, dropped or ignored. As the applications of Client-Centred Therapy expanded rapidly in the late 1950s, with the University of Chicago at the epicentre, it was important to understand whether these wider applications of a method developed for individual therapy had any staying-power. Nicholas Hobbs had opened the debate regarding group psychotherapy in 1951 in Rogers' *Client-Centered Therapy*. John Shlien joined the debate, raising some different issues in this contribution to a 1957 American Psychiatric Association meeting.

He explores, at a fairly basic level, the tensions between an individual therapy method and group psychotherapy — tensions that have never been fully resolved in Client-Centred Therapy (or any other therapy method, in my view), or the wider Person-Centred Approach. This debate embraces the essential nature, psychological elements and aims of the individual versus the nature of groups. The fundamental questions, 'Can we, should we, treat a group as though it were an individual?', 'Is a group a separate entity, greater than the sum of the individuals in it?' and 'What is *group* psychotherapy?' can still be debated with vigour today and we are invited to join in.

The chapter on phenomenology was written for Wepman and Heine's *Concepts of Personality* published in 1963. I have included it here (after a nudge from Goff Barrett-Lennard) because it is a substantial and scholarly effort to address some basic philosophical issues in psychology. Readers should remember that the 1950s and early 1960s saw the seemingly-unstoppable rise of behaviourism in first academic psychology, and then applied psychology, including psychotherapy. John Shlien was not only critical of psychoanalytic theory, but also of behaviourism and this chapter includes a rebuttal of behaviourism, or indeed of any philosophical system which would threaten the 'internal world'. When behaviourists questioned the need for the concept of 'mind', and therefore the discipline of psychology itself, John carefully outlined phenomenology and its relevance to contemporary humanistic psychology. It also serves as a comprehensive introduction for anyone wanting to understand the philosophical bases of the psychological 'turf wars' of the 1950s and 1960s and will enhance the understanding of contemporary person-centred theory for those with no background in philosophy and the social sciences.

'Empathy in Psychotherapy' was written for the excellent compilation *Empathy Reconsidered* (Bohart and Greenberg, 1997) — one of the books responsible for breathing life back into the North American Client-Centred Therapy scene in the late nineties. Chapter 12 is quintessential Shlien: in part a review of the concept of empathy, it presents a theory of empathy and why it heals, offers moving and amusing anecdotes, returns to echo his work on literalism, courts controversy with a couple of mischievous pot-shots and (in my view, almost perversely) leaves it all unfinished, practically ending in mid-sentence. The first time I read this piece I felt breathless and short-changed at the same time. I will not pre-empt the reader's experience of it by further comment.

Robert W. White was a professor in the Harvard Graduate School of Education when John Shlien arrived, having a big hand in the development of the program that John was ultimately responsible for: 'Clinical Psychology and Public Practice'. White was responsible for the theory that competence is intrinsically motivating, i.e. that to experience competence at something is a motivation to continue — a key concept in education. Lack of opportunity to achieve starts the downward spiral of experience of unremitting failure. Actually experiencing that they are good at something can rescue a failing child from this literally hopeless experience of education. John Shlien, along with others at Harvard, helped test this idea in practice. Chapter 13, a paper co-written by his former student and later collaborator Ronald F. Levant, is both a report of work-in-progress and a manifesto for action-research. Here we see one of the richest institutions in the world putting its resources behind a project to help some of the most disadvantaged people on its doorstep. Whether it succeeded or failed is, then, immaterial. It is worth reading to discover that it happened at all.

My intention in including it here is to remind us that there is life and a worthwhile contribution to be made beyond the therapist's consultation room and that the Person-Centred Approach and its practitioners have always sought wider applications, often with a social or community theme. And more than that, this is a statement riven with a wider social responsibility — it is a political statement, commenting on the distribution of wealth alongside exploring respectful relationships and learning environments. As with so many of John Shlien's other writings, it is personally revealing — of the authors; John Shlien and Ronald Levant, of their co-workers at the school, and of the personal roots of the philosophy of their enterprise. Another clutch of resonant, quotable quotes comes from such philosophy grounded in everyday life:

> Philosophically, we find our roots in the educational theories of William James, A. N. Whitehead, John Dewey, Carl Rogers, and of course, Robert W. White. And, on off days, Attila the Hun. Those are roots, but before we develop and prune our own branches, we have had to concentrate on making sure that the kids have breakfast — the beginning of each day's 'curriculum'. (p. 198)

> . . . our philosophy is, 'What we want for our own children, we want for these.' That philosophy both guides us and reveals our shortcomings. (p. 198)

I hope reading this will inspire and boost the confidence of those contemplating organising or participating in any similarly community-oriented, person-centred project, and those wondering how the PCA might connect with the day-to-day lives of ordinary people in settings beyond therapy.

REFERENCES

Bohart, A.C. & Greenberg, L.S. (1997). *Empathy Reconsidered: New directions in psychotherapy.* Washington DC: APA.
Rogers, C.R. (1951). *Client-Centered Therapy.* Boston: Houghton Mifflin.
Wepman, J.M. & Heine, R.W. (Eds.) (1963). *Concepts of Personality.* Chicago: Aldine, pp. 291–330.

CHAPTER 10

Basic Concepts in Group Psychotherapy
A client-centered point of view

THE FUNDAMENTAL NATURE OF CLIENT-CENTERED THERAPY

As an introduction I will describe some basic concepts from the point of view of 'Client-Centered' Therapy. This therapy was described in a witty journal review[1] as 'a type of treatment that consists of saying nothing to a patient, or at most repeating what he says, acting warmly the while'. This is an amusing caricature, but an accurate description would have to grant us more interaction than that. While the therapist eschews much common behavior such as interpretation, evaluating, correcting, persuading, advising, giving information, comforting, prescribing, and thus *seems* relatively passive; he is in fact being very active and, if he is skilled, being downright artful in certain non-directive types of empathic communication — clarification, simple acceptance, and reflection of feeling.[2] This behavior is designed to be therapeutic on the basis of one fundamental concept: that the person who needs help needs only and especially the conditions of genuine understanding and acceptance. These conditions, which are simple, but not easy to obtain, provide emotional safety and intellectual comprehension. With this help, a client (or patient) can understand and express every significant feature of his experience insofar as he needs to do this to achieve psychological comfort and health. Obviously, this assertion makes some assumptions about the capacity of the client for self-direction and growth which are not shared by everyone.

This chapter was written as a rough draft in preparation for a discussion at the meeting of the American Psychiatric Association on May 14, 1957 at Chicago, Illinois.
[1.] I have been unable to trace the review in question [Ed.].
[2.] Footnote 2 overleaf.

PROBLEMS IN CLIENT-CENTERED GROUP PSYCHOTHERAPY

For several reasons, there is relatively little activity in the field of client-centered *group* therapy. Client-Centered Therapy is relatively young, and group therapy is a later stage of development and application in most orientations. Also, group therapy demands more skill, being more complex and public (though it has less prestige) than individual therapy. The number of highly trained client-centered therapists is not yet so great as to meet the demands for individual therapy and leave a surplus for group work. But perhaps the most important reason exists in the psychological concepts of Client-Centered Therapy. These are based on *individual* experience and perception. The 'phenomenological' approach is carried to such a far point that critics have accused client-centered theorists of a solipsistic world view. That is, we are accused of having such a strenuous bias in our being client-centered — seeing things as the client sees them — that we deny any psychological reality except an individual and subjective one. Consider these

---

[2.] 'This conception of the integrative process in psychotherapy has made it possible to re-examine some aspects of the therapist's function, particularly with regard to the widely described concept "reflection of feeling". Part of a reformulation of the therapist's function consists of discarding inadequate concepts. There may have been a time when the concept "reflection of feeling" was a useful working definition of the therapist's verbal activity. To the writer this no longer seems true, and indeed is one of the least satisfactory concepts in the literature of client-centered therapy. In the first place, the term does not describe what is taking place psychologically between counselor and client. In the second place, it suggests a type of communication which hardly seems therapeutic even when it is done. According to a dictionary definition, reflect means to "give back a likeness or image of". This connotes communication in which the counselor remains untouched and uninvolved, and in which the material of communication remains unchanged. Moreover, the social distance implied in such a description does not at all catch the flavor of an effective therapeutic relationship' (Seeman, 1956).

'What is the client-centered therapist doing that is relevant to this integrative process? Briefly, he is helping the client develop and symbolize his immediate organismic experiences. Verbally, the counselor contributes especially to the symbolizing process through his "understanding" responses. Attitudinally, he is freeing the client for fuller communication of a total sort. We might heighten this point by concentrating attention for a moment upon the apex of the process, the instant at which the client arrives at some integrative point, and the instant in which he feels most deeply understood. How has the counselor contributed to this "aha" experience? Very probably the counselor has expressed that symbolization of feeling which is exactly congruent with the client's unformed emotional experience — in short, he has helped complete the integrative act. This formulation thus abandons the relatively meaningless "reflection of feeling" concept and replaces it with a psychologically meaningful description of a function designed to facilitate the activity of experiencing-with-meaning' (Seeman, 1956). This describes the very symbolizing process that creates society itself, according to Burrow (see p. 134), G.H. Mead, J. Piaget and others.

propositions quoted from Chapter 11, 'A theory of personality and behavior' by Carl Rogers in his book, *Client-Centered Therapy*:

(1) **Every individual exists in a continually changing world of experience of which he is the center.** (Rogers, 1951, p. 483)

An important truth in regard to this private world of the individual is that *it* can only be known, in any genuine or complete sense, to the individual himself. (ibid., p. 483)

(2) **The organism reacts to the field as it is experienced and perceived. This perceptual field is, for the individual, 'reality'.** (p. 484, ibid)

One does not 'react to some absolute reality' but to his individual 'perception of this reality' (p. 484, ibid.). In this second proposition — that one reacts to reality as *he* uniquely perceives it — is the key to the perceptual theory and therapeutic practice of this orientation. Since behavior is a consequence of perception, a change in behavior is facilitated by a change in perception. A change in perception is facilitated by adopting the client's point of view — being 'client-centered' — so that he can, with understanding and without defense or distortion, see more deeply, broadly, and truly, about him. Then behavior can change.

Given the individual bias in these two propositions, one wonders how there could be therapy for a group. How can the group have a frame of reference to which to respond, if it is composed of private worlds never completely known to each other? How can the group have a 'mind' beyond that coarse single-mindedness described by Le Bon for the 'mob'? How can the group hear a response, since, as Spencer (1897) put it, 'The group has no sensorium'? How, for that matter, can there be *a group* at all? (And are we certain, in fact, that there is?) At the other extreme the great sociologist, Durkheim, argued that the group came first, and that there could be no individuals until the group, *sui generis,* formed the very idea of personality and the individual. He put it this way, 'Collective life is not born from individual life but it is, on the contrary, the second which is born from the first' (p. 279). And,

With autonomous individuals, as are imagined, nothing can emerge save what is individual, and, consequently, co-operation itself, which is a social fact, submissive to social rules, cannot arise. Thus, the psychologist who starts by restricting himself to the ego cannot emerge to find the non-ego. (ibid., p. 279).

The sociologist poses for the psychologist (he had Freud in mind as he wrote the above, but the question here applies to the theory of Rogers) the question of how to account for the existence of a group, given the assumptions of individual psychology. Surely the group therapist must face this question if he is interested in conceptualising his work — unless he assumes that there is no more involved in it than individual therapy in a group situation.

In the book from which Rogers' propositions are quoted [Rogers, 1951, Ed.], Nicholas Hobbs writes of 'Group-Centered Therapy', this is 'more than the extension of individual therapy to several persons at once; it provides a qualitatively different experience with unique potentialities' (Hobbs, 1951, p. 278). He speaks of the 'therapeutic potential' of the group itself and says, 'Group therapy, and not individual therapy in a group, is the goal' (ibid., p. 305).

We find, therefore, a conceptual conflict — therapy for a group, which can hardly exist in terms of the concept of the individual percept.

Rogers (1951) wisely makes one approach to this problem when he quotes Trigant Burrow (1949):

> Man's consistent relationship to the outer world came about through the agreement of his own sequence of sense-reactions with the sequence of reactions existing outside him . . . Only man's neural conformity to the observable consistency of eternal phenomena has made possible the intelligent consistency of his own behavior in respect to the outer world (p. 101). [Cited in Rogers, 1951, p. 486, Ed.]

Thus the world comes to be composed of a series of tested hypotheses which provide much security. It acquires a certain predictability upon which we depend. Yet mingled with these perceptions, which have been confirmed by a variety of experiences, are perceptions which remain completely unchecked. These untested perceptions are also a part of our personal reality, and may have as much authority as those which have been checked.

A group functions, then, to confirm *individual* sensations and perceptions, and to give them symbols when the experience is common, to the extent that when this takes place a society is formed or exists. Symbols represent mutual experience, whether in war or peace, and thus one point of a common frame of reference. Because symbols can be retained, communicated, thought about, they are the basis of mind.[3] So, though there is no supra-individual group mind, the group is the source of mind insofar as it supplies the (1) confirmation, and (2) symbolisation of mutual experience. Percepts become concepts in this process. *But* there remain unchecked propositions, a part of personal reality, with authority equal to that of the concepts. The individual can never be completely absorbed in the group frame of reference, but can participate in it from time to time. This

---

[3.] Gordon speaks of the 'wisdom of the group' [see Gordon, 1955, Ed.] but he is not assuming a collective mind; rather the multi-faceted and correcting judgment of several minds working on the same problem.

is what makes the group 'organic', and the therapy individual. Were it otherwise, the group would be 'mechanical' and the therapy would be for the group, if such were necessary and possible.[4]

THE GENERAL GOAL OF GROUP THERAPY

An organic group is the aim of the therapist. A main reason lies in what I consider the general goal of group therapy. Specific goals are as diverse as the specific problems of the individuals in the group. There is one goal for the group and its individual members — that is *the experience of freedom*. This is not flag waving, but an assertion of psychological fact. Political and social freedom are important, but do not dictate the goals of therapy. The point here is that freedom is the condition of psychological health.

1. The individual who is most free is the one who is most perceptive of experience, has the widest choice of alternatives, can therefore be most wise, creative, adaptive.
2. The individual who internally *feels* free is the best adjusted.
3. Group freedom is the most meaningful freedom, since freedom in isolation is almost freedom without context.
4. When a *group* experiences freedom, it has a rare and unique experience, for groups usually have leaders, or levels of subordination among members, or are co-operating for common purposes, or hang together out of fear. To describe the nature of a group experience of freedom, or the specific meanings of that experience, is beyond me at this time. It is simply an idea.

SOME PARTICULARS AND PARTICULAR CONCEPTS OF CLIENT-CENTERED GROUP PSYCHOTHERAPY

1. Group therapy must provide acceptance for the individual. If it does not, it will fail. If it does, it may be more potent than individual therapy, since it carries the weight of numbers. However, the ultimate value of acceptance is that which

---

[4.] Durkheim's terms denoting a group of individuals who are different, and who join out of interdependence to make a complex society, versus a group composed of identical beings who are joined because of likeness.

Ian Suttie [1939, p. 97, Ed.] puts a related and basic sociological question to any therapist working with groups, 'Is Society a spontaneous expression of human nature, or an artefact of force?' Are we together because we want to be, or because we are afraid not to be? The client-centered position is simply stated by Rogers when he says, 'Man is basically social'.

comes from self-acceptance, and this too may be deeper following acceptance in a group. Baehr[5] studied three groups of voluntary patients in a hospital who were given individual therapy, group therapy and a combination of the two. All therapy was in a client-centered orientation. All groups benefited, but the group-plus-individual treatment was most effective, individual therapy next most effective, and group therapy third most effective. Perhaps the full acceptance of one person, coupled with mingled types of interaction for stimulation from other, different persons, is best, while the mingled interaction encountered in groups alone is least helpful. Behavior in individual therapy may be of the order of testing, or 'rehearsal' for life, while that rehearsal enacted in a group *is* life.

2. Group therapy is commonly conducted with six to eight clients. This seem to be small enough for intimate interaction, large enough to be public, and taxes the upper limits of the therapist's capacity to attend to a number of different frames of reference.

3. Whether group therapy is economical is an open question. It often requires two therapists, two hours instead of one, and more sessions than individual therapy. The justification should lie in its potency, not economy.

4. It is therapeutic to give help as well as to receive it. A group member receives help from several instead of one, but more than that, he gains self-esteem by helping others. He also learns to listen, and in doing so quiets some of his own turmoil. He also finds that his problems are not entirely unique; this is comforting and to some extent becomes an asset in that he can understand others by virtue of his own troubles.

5. A book by Gorlow, Hoch, and Telschow (1952) details a great number of particular findings from three collaborative researches on non-directive group therapy, covering behavior, dynamics and process. Only one is mentioned here, for lack of time. That is the finding that of all the therapist's techniques, only one, the 'pause', is followed by a significantly greater number of client responses. This leads to a comment on silence in groups. Ricoh said, 'communication is a fetish'. This applies to therapy, especially group therapy. We value talk, as a sign of activity, but when a group reaches the point of being able not just to endure silence, but to use it in comfort, it and its members are well on the way to the experience of freedom and self-acceptance.

As a closing remark, let me venture the opinion that while therapy is unique, it is

---

[5.] I have been unable to trace 'Baehr' or the work referred to here [Ed.].

only so because it contains — in a heightened and refined state — the therapeutic elements found elsewhere in life. These elements are not invented by and for therapy alone — they come from the best of group life in the first place. If group *therapy* can help to put them back into group *life*, so such the better for therapy and for life.

REFERENCES

Burrow, T. (1949). *The Neurosis of Man.* New York: Harcourt Brace.

Durkheim, E. (1893/1947). *The Division of Labour in Society.* (Translated by George Simpson.) New York: The Free Press.

Gordon, T. (1955). *Group-Centered Leadership.* Boston: Houghton Mifflin.

Gorlow, L., Hoch, E.L. & Telschow, E.F. (1952). *The Nature of Nondirective Group Psychotherapy.* Teachers College, Columbia University.

Hobbs, N. (1951). Group-Centered Psychotherapy. In C.R. Rogers, *Client-Centered Therapy.* Boston: Houghton Mifflin, pp. 278–319.

Rogers, C.R. (1951). *Client-Centered Therapy.* Boston: Houghton Mifflin.

Seeman, J. (1956). Client-Centered Therapy. In D. Brower and L. Abt, (Eds.) *Progress in Clinical Psychology.* New York: Grune and Stratton, pp. 98–113.

Spencer, H. (1897). *Principles of Sociology.* New York: Appleton.

Suttie, I.D. (1939). *The Origins of Love and Hate.* London: Kegan Paul.

CHAPTER 11

Phenomenology and Personality

INTRODUCTION

What makes another approach to personality necessary, particularly one which stresses the very subjectivity which others have tried to avoid? Is it just one more reflection of the 'clash of temperaments' in the history of a developing field, or does the answer really depend upon what one considers to be the raw material, and the avenues of access to it, in the study of personality?

At the heart of the need for a phenomenological psychology lies a fact which Kluver (1936) has expressed as follows:

> Whether or not behavior takes this or that direction is, generally speaking, dependent on whether or not this or that *phenomenal* property exists. The fact that something appears phenomenally as 'red', 'larger than', etc., cannot be deduced from the properties of the atom but only from studies of reacting organisms.

To this must be added the generally accepted observation that apparent phenomena differ in their appearances. Since we learn so many of our meanings from our culture — i.e., each other (Blake and Ramsey, 1951), the first fact of inscrutability plays a large part in causing those differing perceptions. It makes communication of meanings weak and uncertain. If the mind could not think silently; if there were outwardly audible and visible signs directly indicating specific mental activities, we would all be rank behaviorists, and the history of psychology, to say the least, would have hinged on a very different set of data. But this is not the case. As things stand, we have both internal and external events *experienced* by the

First published in Wepman, J. M. and Heine, R. W. (Eds.) (1963) *Concepts of Personality*. Chicago: Aldine, pp. 291–330. Reprinted in Hart, J.T. and Tomlinson, T.M. (1970) *New Directions in Client-Centered Therapy*. Boston: Houghton Mifflin. I have been unable to trace the current copyright holders. [Ed.]

total organism; experienced, recorded at some level of awareness, and in some cases, given meaning. The phenomenologist is convinced that much goes on 'inside', and that the behavioristic concept of the 'empty organism' is narrow, and largely spurious. Most of our experience and its meanings exist in 'private worlds,' not expressed on pointer readings. Nor is this to say that phenomenology is only here on borrowed time.

Instruments have been, and will be, developed to probe the silent and private world of inner experience, but men are not likely to become transparent. Much will remain hidden; meanings will differ from person to person; modes of experience and interpretation will change over time for each individual. Physiological indexes of internal states will have immense value for the study of experience, but heart rate, brain waves, pupil size, endocrine output, or whatever comes will only measure increase or decrease without meaning unless the identifying code is first given and then continually validated by the wise and willing knower. As Kohler (1938, p. vii) says,

> Never, I believe, shall we be able to solve any problems of ultimate principle
> until we go back to the source of our concepts — in other words, until we
> use the phenomenological method, the qualitative analysis of experience.

And, the more the knower is wise and willing, the better the accuracy of his information and verification. Thus the approach may be applied to animals and infants, but reaches its more productive stage in the study of language-using humans.[1]

It is not always constructive to haggle over terminology, but neither is it fair to introduce the problem with a term which, if accepted, envelops the reader in a biased frame of reference. We have referred to activity of the human 'mind'. Use of this word, to the behaviorist, is at least a concession and, to the phenomenologist, a minor victory. J.B. Watson abhorred the word, and Pavlov is said to have levied fines upon students using such mentalistic terms in his laboratory. As recently as 1943, Clark Hull warned against the use of 'mind' saying, 'Even when fully aware of the nature of anthropomorphic subjectivism and its dangers, the most careful and experienced thinker is likely to find himself a victim of its seductions', (Hull, 1943). He suggests that this powerful effect be warded off by observing all behavior as if it were produced by a dog, rat, or robot. Gordon Allport, in a vein typical of the 'personalistic' phenomenologist, objects to Hull's precaution as an

---

[1] Zener (1958) advised psychologists to recognize limitations and capabilities which vary both with the phenomena to be observed and the motivation, intelligence, etc., *of the observer.* Not all are equal in this respect. A striking example of possibilities in the upper ranges of observation by a psychologist is to be seen in a brilliant analysis of the 'psychology of secrets' by Bakan (1954). While anyone may make a satisfactory 'naive' subject for certain kinds of experiments, phenomenology can best thrive through investment in sophisticated informants.

affront to human dignity and an avoidance of human realities because it represents 'an addiction to machines, rats, or infants which leads us to overplay those features of human behavior that are peripheral, signal-oriented, and genetic,[2] and to underplay those features that are central, future-oriented, and symbolic' (Allport, 1947).

The quarrel exposed by this conflict over a mere word really revolves around these major issues: (1) Is the human being active or only reactive? (2) Is activity only external or also internal? (3) If it is internal, can 'subjectivity' be reconciled with 'science' (the latter in quotes because it has its fashions too)? We could brush aside the question of terminology by saying simply, 'When you "make up your mind" to read this chapter, we are talking about whatever you made up.' That is true enough, but the phenomenologist characteristically uses mentalistic terms such as 'mind', 'Mind' is clearly returning as acceptable scientific language in the literature (Scher, 1962); and its use or non-use implies a decision about the legitimacy of inner life as proper subject matter. As Kurt Lewin (1951) says,

> Arguments about attributing 'existence' to an item may seem metaphysical in nature and may therefore not be expected to be brought up in empirical sciences. Actually, opinions about existence or nonexistence are quite common in the empirical sciences and have greatly influenced scientific development in a positive and a negative way. Labeling something as 'nonexisting' is equivalent to declaring it 'out of bounds' for the scientist. Attributing 'existence' to an item automatically makes it a duty of the scientist to consider this item as an object of research; it includes the necessity of considering its properties as 'facts' which cannot be neglected in a total system of theories; finally, it implies that the terms with which one refers to the items are acceptable as scientific 'concepts' (rather than as 'mere words').

It matters, then, that we acknowledge the existence of each person's *faculty for knowing*. This is a basic assumption, expressed in an extreme and unabashed statement by a French phenomenologist, Merleau-Ponty (1945), 'I am the absolute source', We do experience — we sense, perceive, think. Though silent and invisible, thought precedes and attends all of our behavior not accomplished through the reflex arc. Precedings are called determinants, attendings are called interpretations, and there is even evidence that thought should not be distinguished from behavior but may actually *constitute* behavior. A dozen years ago, when 'transfer of training' experiments were popular, Beattie used a dart board with a graded target as a performance measure. As usual in such experiments, subjects practiced with one hand, rested, were retested with the other hand in various combinations of practice

---

[2.] Genetic here refers to history, not biology.

periods, hands, and rest periods. Longer rest periods seemed related to improved scores. We have long been given to think of this effect in terms of 'spaced versus massed practice'. But it also suggested 'rehearsal' effects. Finally, some subjects were given imaginary practice, i.e., were instructed to simply sit at throwing distance from the target (after a base-line performance had been established) and to 'think about' throwing for a practice period. These 'merely' rehearsing subjects often improved their performance as much as those who had 'actual' practice trials (Beattie, 1949)! This reminds us that in the behavioristic strategy of focusing upon specifics of input and output, whatever was unseen was considered as undone (a strange and arrogant subjectivity on the part of the experimenter).

Tolman puts our unobserved learning back into proper behavioral perspective with his statement: 'What [the organism] learns is, in short, a *performance* (and each such performance can be carried out by a number of different motor skills)'. (Tolman, 1959, p. 133). The phenomenologist is vitally interested in that internal performance, the process of experiencing. Whether or not the performance is also evident, he believes in the reality of the internal state as a mode of behavior. This mode consists of sensations, perceptions, thoughts, and feelings, all of which constitute experiencing that can only be approached through the standpoint of the experiencer.

The nature of this approach raises some fundamental questions. Is there really a field of study such as psychology, separate from the biological or electrochemical basis of behavior? What is its subject matter, where to find it, and how to deal with it? To illustrate some of these points, here is an accurate report of a true event in a human transaction.

A 28-year-old graduate student in sociology finished his mid-year examinations. He wearily packed a bag and boarded a bus for a vacation journey to visit his family several hundred miles away. Choosing a seat next to the window, he stretched out as well as he could, hoping to sleep through the night since he felt quite exhausted. In his own words, the report continues:

> After an hour or so, the bus stopped in a small town, and a few passengers got on. One of them was a blonde girl, very good-looking in a fresh but sort of sleazy way. I thought that she was probably a farm girl, and I wished she'd sit by me. By God, she did. She was really comely, if you know what I mean, and she smiled a bit so I felt sure she'd be approachable. Oh boy, what luck. I didn't want to be too eager, and I was still exhausted, so we just smiled and talked for a minute. I made sure that she was comfortable, and then sort of dozed off for a little while, hoping to recuperate by the time the driver turned out the lights and meanwhile enjoying my fantasies about the prospects for the rest of the trip. The last thing I remember was smiling at her and noticing that when her skirt slipped up on her knee as she reached up to the back of the seat, she

didn't pull it down. Wow! About four hours later we were pounding along the road in complete darkness when I opened my eyes. Her leg, the outside of it, was against mine, and the way it pressed and moved with the motion of the bus woke me up. This was more than I'd dreamed of. I was terribly excited, and when I stirred a little the steady pressure of her leg didn't move away. By this time, I had a terrific erection, and the more I thought about this cute little babe pressing against me, the worse it got. I was just about to reach out and touch her when we pulled into a gas station for a stop, and when the light came through the window, *she* wasn't there at all! She must have left while I was asleep. A fat man with a growth of beard and a dead cigar dropping ash on his vest was sprawled next to me, sound asleep. It was *his* leg pressing against me, and he was so fat and slovenly that even when I drew myself away, his sloppy flesh stayed against me. I was so dumbfounded — disappointed too, and the funny thing — I lost that erection almost immediately, got up and moved to another seat. What a let down.

From this event in someone's private life, we can draw several conclusions which bear an introduction to phenomenological thought.

First, there is such a thing as psychology. It operates in such a way as to influence behavior, and it cannot be accounted for simply in terms of physics or biology. Again quoting the extremist Merleau-Ponty, 'The body is not a fact, it is a situation'. An erection is a signal of a notable reaction to something in the environment — what? Not, in this case, the pressure of so many p.s.i., nor that in combination with body temperature of a certain degree, nor both those in combination with motion and friction of a specifiable sort. Those elements remained. The erection-behavior did not. Something interior changed when a certain group of stable physical sensations were given a different meaning as the perception of the experiencer was alerted. What had been exciting became revolting.

Second, it tells us that if we are to study that which is peculiarly psychological, the primary subject matter must be *experience*. Experience is subjective, i.e., it takes place within the opaque organism of the experiencer, and *may* not be public or even repeatable.

Third, from this it seems clear that the approach to this subject matter is to learn the secrets of individual perception, and sometimes of hidden consequent behavior. Whether the secrets are intended to be so, or are merely screened from view by the normal separatedness of people, they are private.

Thus, fourth, is implied a methodology which must be largely dependent upon our ability to obtain the hidden and private data, via some part of the family of introspective methods, or to deduce via such comparative experimental methods as 'stimulus equivalence' those discriminant perceptions which lend themselves to this technique. Most of the investigations will have to rely on some form of self-report; this would seem a special weakness to some, but as William James (1950, p. 191) points out, 'Introspection is what we have to rely on first and foremost and always' and as for its weakness, *'introspection is difficult and fallible; and the difficulty is simply that of all observation of whatever kind'.*

Fifth, there is implied in this illustration a definition of pathology according to the phenomenologist's approach. Pathology would consist of a lack of awareness of one's own experience; of not knowing or understanding it; of being in a state of self-deception. Putting it more simply in perceptual terms, to see clearly is the greatest good — the blind spots are evil.

Sixth, we see in this example the 'real life' nature of the context in which this approach can operate and from which it typically draws its data. The world and any part of it is a laboratory for the naturalistic observation. Its characteristic problems are the major attitudinal states which move men mightily — for example, pride, shame, grief, love, passion, loneliness, hatred, freedom, boredom, anxiety, despair, being and well-being, death, pain.[3]

BACKGROUND AND CHARACTERISTICS

TOWARD A DEFINITION — FIELD AND STREAMS

What is phenomenology, exactly? Exactly, no one can say. It is an old term, now stewing in its own liberal metaphysical juice, which has to allow such scope for change and individuality that during the first phases there could be almost as many phenomenologies as there are phenomenologists.[4] This is simply because the essential concern is *meaning*, and meanings can vary extensively. At the moment

---

[3.] Pain is a particularly interesting and ephemeral quality, in spite of its pervasiveness. As such, it is a striking illustration of the need for a phenomenology. Everyone 'knows' what pain is, but no one can feel another's pain (though the closer the involvement between people, the more a loved one's pain causes behavior in the observer; this comes close to being the behaviorist nightmare, 'the interaction of two 'minds'). For all its ubiquity, and its frequent use in experiments, no one can 'objectively' measure pain, or even accurately localize it or its source in many instances! The same stimulus, such as an electric shock of given intensity, by no means causes the same response in two subjects. Finally, outward behavior, ranging from stoicism to malingering, may or may not express inner experience of pain.

[4.] In practice — in the practice of classifying, anyway — this lack of organized principles does not seem to hold. It is possible to group types of phenomenologies, usually in three or four categories, ranging though 'classical', 'existential', 'pure philosophical', 'eidetic', 'transcendental', 'psychological', etc. (Spiegelberg, 1960, p. 642; Landsman, 1958).

the term is a large envelope containing a confusing mixture of philosophies, psychology, science, myth, and fad. There is, as Boring (1950, p. 408) says, 'room in phenomenology for acts as well as content; it is a tolerant discipline'.

This tolerance is to its credit, and is also its peril. Always there is precaution against premature formulation of hypotheses, allowing for the 'unprejudiced' naturalistic observation of events. MacLeod (1951) speaks of 'a disciplined naivete'; Gibson (1959, p. 461) of 'cultivated naivete'. European phrasing is more extreme: French psychologist Merleau-Ponty says, 'The whole effort is to recover naive contact with the world', while the German philosopher Eugene Fink speaks of the 'shock of amazement at the fact of the world . . . a stunned amazement to which he assigned the function of converting the trivial into what is worth questioning' (Spiegelberg, 1960, p. 600). But which trivia are worth the conversion? *The Place of Value in a World of Facts* (Kohler, 1938) demonstrates the unavoidable subjectivity which makes phenomenology liable to the same criticism it has leveled at behaviorism. The only advantage lies in awareness of the prejudice and the possibility of deliberately suspending or reversing it, or 'bracketing' it, to use Husserl's term. The bigger problem is to find the correct balance of discipline and naivete, of course. The fresh eyes of innocence and the free curiosity of the fascinated naturalist need to be combined with the sophistication of the practiced researcher — combined with, but not subdued by. That is part of the thrust of reviving phenomenology.

The word to which so many lay claim derives from the Greek *phainesthai*, 'to appear', or 'to appear so', or 'as it appears', It is instructive to note that in the original usage, the phenomenal was 'that which is known through the senses and immediate experience' rather than deduction. This is still the case. One binding theme running through all variants of phenomenology is the preoccupation and fascination with the facts (or the data) of immediate experience. This characteristic of both the original and present usage is often taken to pit 'common sense' against 'deduction', thus supposedly making phenomenology a hopeless anachronism in the realm of science. Kimble (1953) points out, for example, how 'common sense' tells us that the world is flat; science that it is round. The method of direct intuition, or that which is known through the senses, then, would be basically a source of error. But even on the level of description, it is not common sense which fails; it is our constricted scope of vision which feeds in limited information. If one can look at the ocean from a mountain top, or take a picture of its surface with a wide angle lens, the application of a straight edge will tell us via 'common sense'[5] that the world has a curved surface. If common sense could not confirm the shape of the earth's surface in just this way, there would indeed be a conflict,

---

[5.] Anyone who has read Piaget's studies of intelligence will realize that it is a mistake to identify 'common sense' at only the lowest level of development.

and 'phenomenology' would have to disavow and separate itself from 'science.'

The important point is that what we see tells us *our* truth — the 'world-for-us' rather than *the* truth — the 'world-as-is,' but that the distinctions are not necessarily opposed or impossible of reconciliation. The original Greek philosophies separated the *Phenomenal World* from the *Ontal World* of permanent being and the *Ideal World of* permanent truth, with the Phenomenal World containing changeable and developing aspects, dealt with as perceptible aspects or appearances rather than their 'true', ideal, fixed or substantial natures. We have inherited the idea that these worlds are all orthogonal to each other as a matter of fact, rather than as a matter of logical convenience or preference.

Phenomenology has a prejudice. It clearly holds that, psychologically speaking, man is the measure of all things, each man the measure of all his things, and that the reality to which he responds is his own. The frequent accusation of solipsism does not apply. Neither does Hume's philosophy that no matter exists independent of mind, the mind being nothing but representations. Kant is more to the liking of the phenomenologist with the notion that there are phenomena, and they are all we know, but there is more beyond.

The current general philosophy in American personality study would probably run to this effect: there is external reality, which we more or less distort, though it exists absolutely while its appearances are relative. But, to the purely phenomenological psychologist, does 'real reality' matter? Is there anything in psychology to study except the perceptions of individuals? Psychologically, 'real' things have only a relative existence. *Phenomena* are absolute (not permanent, but for the moment absolute); *they* control behavior since it is predicated upon *them;* when *they* change, behavior changes. (Behavior, not things, concerns the psychologist. If this makes 'behaviorists' of all of us, so be it, only with the reservation that behavior is covert as well as overt.)

There is a limit to the profit one can take from philosophical speculations in this field. Neither the historical or functional connections between European philosophies and American psychologies are clear or prominent. MacLeod suggests that one might read Kuenzli's (1959) collection *The Phenomenological Problem* and conclude that phenomenology is an indigenous American product. But the German philosopher, Edmund Husserl, is generally credited as the main instigator of the movement. Whether he had a direct effect on modern personality theory as it developed in the group identified with Rogerian practices is a moot question. It may well be that we have here the spectacle of independent invention rather than cultural diffusion, and that the current preoccupation with Husserl is a retrospective tracing of geneology by a successful native development.

Rogers already displayed a phenomenological, almost ethological attitude when he published his first book on *Counseling and Psychotherapy* in 1942. Although the idea of the 'internal frame of reference' was not yet featured, the remarkably phenomenological technique of 'reflection', as a 'natural' non-controlling environment was, and the book shows unmistakable signs of intention to comprehend the inner world of the client without disturbing the natural course of events — a 'disciplined naivete', that is. At this time, Rogers had not heard of Husserl, nor had he yet read him when the second book *Client-Centered Therapy*, with its phenomenology showing loud and clear, was published in 1951.[6] Snygg and Combs, whose 1949 book, *Individual Behavior*, is an outstanding demonstration of a personality theory based on the concept of the phenomenal field, had certainly influenced Rogers, but there is no reference to Husserl in their work. (The updated edition of 1959, however, contains four references to Husserl.) Their work has been called, 'A remarkably independent new type of phenomenological psychology' (Spiegelberg, 1960, p. 638). He adds, 'Rogers' own approach also shows its phenomenological ingredients without any commitment to its philosophical ancestry'. (What ancestry? It is very hard for a historian to accept the notion of independent invention.) These American developments lean heavily on Snygg's earlier article (1941), the import of which is expressed in its title, 'The Need for a Phenomenological System of Psychology'. Snygg, originally a behaviorist, is reported by Spiegelberg as having been influenced toward phenomenology by his contact with Kurt Lewin and Wolfgang Kohler. Certainly both of these men knew Husserl's work, but Lewin is said by Spiegelberg to have been influenced 'much more prominently' by the phenomenology of Carl Stumpf than by Husserl. As for Kohler, he discusses Husserl extensively, critically, and is one of those who interprets Husserl's first principle of 'logical requiredness' as having 'little to do with psychology' (Kohler, 1938, p. 48). Husserl was often considered anti-psychological, and his major translator and interpreter, Farber (1943, p. 567), tries to heal this 'misunderstanding'[7] which had been nourished by 'Husserl's own repeated efforts' to distinguish phenomenology from psychology. Husserl does have a demonstrable connection with the existential

---

[6.] Personal communication.

[7.] It is well worth-while to quote his summary of Husserl's position:

'(c) There are a number of things which phenomenology conspicuously does not do or mean. (1) It does not "tear the meaning loose from the act". (2) It does not deny or reject the external world. (3) It does not try to answer all questions, and is not intended to be all-inclusive as a method for all purposes. (4) It is also not intended to be a substitute for other methods, and above all, for those involving factual and hypothetical elements. (5) It does not deny inductive truth, nor does it fail to distinguish between different types of 'truth'. (6) It is not a trap for metaphysical purposes . . .

(d) In contrast to these misunderstandings there are a number of things that phenomenology does do or mean. (1) It is the first method of knowledge because it begins with "the things themselves" which are the final court of appeal for all knowledge . . . (2) It views everything factual as an exemplification of essential structures and is not concerned with matters of fact as such. (3) It deals with not only "real essences" but also . . . /cont.

form of phenomenology[8] through his student Heidegger, and thus to Sartre, Camus, Rollo May, Tillich, and others prominent in this stream of the movement.

As a final note, it is worth comment that van Kaam (1959) finds William James a source of the stream. He quotes J. Linscohten ('one of Europe's leading existential phenomenologists'), who in turn quotes the diary of Husserl for proof that 'the father of European phenomenology admits the influence of the thought of the great American, James, on his own thinking' (May, 1961, p. 14). James, we may be sure, had a direct and deep influence on all of the American 'self-psychologies'. (His writings on the subject have not been surpassed. They are the best single source available yet.)

The intent of this review is not to chauvinistically plant a flag on new territory. For, one thing, it is very old territory which has been crossed by many travelers. The point is rather to free us of philosophical domination where those philosophies have little or no real connection with the psychologies bearing the same name, especially since 'the very vaguest speculation has sometimes found shelter under the roof of phenomenology'. (Kohler, 1938, p. 68). Husserl's philosophy bears to clinical phenomenological psychology about the same order of relation as does Wundt's (or Titchner's) classical introspection to the modern forms of self-report. To understand phenomenology, it is more illuminating, and more in keeping with the very style of this approach, to look at its characteristics rather than to trace its history.

FURTHER TOWARD A DEFINITION — SOME COMMON CHARACTERISTICS

Since phenomenology is not yet gathered together in a sufficiently homogeneous body to be identified, it is composed of like-minded people,[9] with similar attitudes, objectives, and methods, working rather independently in a gathering 'third force', as Maslow sometimes calls it (May, 1961, p. 52). To help delineate this gathering,

---

cont /. . . with "possible essences," (4) Direct insight, evidence in the sense of the self-giveness of the objectivity is the ultimate test for it. (5) Despite the "reduction" the phenomenologist still has a brain (an "evolutionary" brain) in the same sense that he breathes. That statement is as true as it is irrelevant to the method.'

[8.] An embarrassment to some 'respectable' phenomenologists as it is embarrassed itself by the Beatnik or Left Bank Existentialists, who also cherish immediacy of experience, self-consciously examine their own despair, etc.

[9.] One wonders who to name by way of illustration: Lewin, Rogers, G. Allport and perhaps F. Allport, Maslow, R. May, Bruner, Cantril, Patterson, Snygg, Jessor, as well as many others mentioned elsewhere in this chapter. And Freud, before 'hardening of the categories' set in. Since these independent types seldom declare themselves, especially when the movement is still so ill-defined, others will appear more clearly in the future, as association does not imply guilt.

we turn to some characteristic interests or attitudes on which there has occasionally been some issue.

The scientific posture

In relation to science, there is a position which demands redefinition of what 'sciencing' means. Phenomenology calls for intensive descriptive analysis — a description that often leads to an impatient demand for its supposed opposite, explanation via the 'definitive' experiment. Science cannot be confined to the experimental alone, but must include exploration and discovery. This 'naturalistic observation' is being reintroduced with a new power as 'the foundation of all science' (Butler, 1962, p. 178). Zener reminds us that science consists of far more than confirming already observed relationships. A science not reviewing its problem area is dying, and he suggests 'that twentieth-century psychophysics has exploited the capital of phenomenological distinctions made in the nineteenth century — and [I] am apprehensive that no new comparable wealth of phenomenal distinctions relevant to more complex perceptions is presently being accumulated' (Zener, 1958, p. 364).

Science is subject to such change in fashion over time and even in locality that its objectives can always be questioned. Buytendijk quotes Cantril in this regard:

> The aim of science is often defined as the attempt to increase the accuracy of our predictions. While the accuracy of predictions is clearly a most important criterion of progress in scientific formulation, emphasis on prediction alone can easily obscure the more fundamental aim of science covered by the word *understanding*. (David and von Bracken, 1957, p. 198)

Prediction and control are often found linked together in the literature. The phenomenologist gives second place to prediction, as just indicated, and may reject control altogether. First, control is not science — it is just politics, or management. Second, if exercised in experimentation it is limiting and unfair, since it makes the task of scientist all too easy, and too meaningless. The isolated reaction of the eye blink to the air puff is controlled, specific, but insignificant. The limited behavior of the man in a six-by-four cell is more predictable but less valuable to human beings because he is less human as he is more controlled.[10] Wellek says, 'It is the task of psychology to teach men to understand themselves and each other better. Understanding presupposes phenomenology. It is itself a phenomenological act, an experience' (David and von Bracken, 1957, p. 293). It

---

10. The 'control group' as a comparison technique, or the 'control' of variables holding some steady while others vary, is not the control referred to here.

is this understanding *(Verstehen)* of fully human beings which constitutes the aim of this branch of science.

Understanding comes about through description, or is a concurrent process. Must description be opposed to explanation? What better explanation could there be than a complete description? If one really understands, if the description is fine enough, this reveals the mechanism, and explains *how* — but not why. 'How' is the scientific question. 'Why' belongs to the child or the theologian. A fine-grained description of the digestive process tells us everything about the process from input *(subjectively* called 'food') to output *(subjectively* called 'waste'). Any explanation of 'why' beyond that means 'purpose of this process'. That could be 'because the person needs fuel', or 'the food wants to be transformed into another state', or 'God orders this process between person and food for the sake of either, both or neither but a third purpose to which they are incidental'. Thus it is quite reasonable for MacLeod to put the question of science simply as 'what is there' without regard to 'why', 'whence', or 'wherefore' (Kuenzli, 1959, p. 156).

Reductionism

There is a strong anti-reductionistic bias characteristic of this movement. One finds objections to 'reductionism' to biological drives (hunger, etc.), to simpler mechanisms, to lower forms, of things to each other. Jessor (1961) believes that the banishment of experience took place as psychologists sought safety in a 'methodological objectivity' which forced a three-pronged reductionism: '(a) behavioral — the employment of arbitrary (physical) micro units of stimulus and response, unlikely to enable meaningful constitution by the human organism; (b) physiological — employment of units logically remote from experiential significance for the human organism; (c) phylogenetic — the use of lower organisms for whom language is, of course, unavailable'.

The general view is that man must be understood *as a totality.* To understand parts separately does not describe the totality they would form. Man has a special nature (his 'being', currently called) which defies atomistic understanding in the way we have understood inanimate things and some lower forms of life. Half a piece of chalk is still a piece of chalk, only smaller; half a planarian worm is half of one worm, but still a worm in itself; half a man is not a man at all.

R. May (1961, p. 18) argues that man cannot be reduced to 'drives' since 'the more you formulate the forces or drives, the more you are talking about abstractions and not the existing, living human being'. Opposition to simple stimulus-response reductionism has been steady since Dewey first wrote his objections to the reflex arc concept as the basis of all behavior. The phenomenologist is sure that between the physical properties of S and the R stands a whole system of potential choices in the prepared and evaluating, not passive organism, not at all likely to be moved on a simply stimulus receptor basis.[11] Responses may have multiple determinants, or single stimuli may have differential responses, or the organism may be downright selective about what stimulus it perceives, or even seeks out (Fiske and Maddi, 1961).

Also opposed is the genetic reductionism which tries to reduce not only complex forms to simple ones, but later states to earlier ones (Kuenzli, 1959, p. 153). The phenomenologist tries to take the fact as it is given, and to let it be as big as it is, rather than to cut it down to his size, or to the size of his measuring instruments.

The existence of this anti-reductionist bias as it applies to the genesis of behavior points to another closely related characteristic. So far as time orientation and determinism, the phenomenologist tends to be ahistorical. Their position is simply stated as, 'the past is relevant only as it lives in the present'. This refers only to the *psychological* past, of course. 'The behavior's field at any given instant contains also the views of the individual about his past and future . . . The psychological past and the psychological future are simultaneous parts of the psychological field existing at a given time' (Lewin, 1951, pp. 292–310). While it is not true that 'the past is a bucket of ashes', neither is man a prisoner of the past — indeed, besides heavy emphasis on present and immediate functioning without historical reconstruction, there is some inclination to see behavior as future-oriented more than past-restrained. Ideals, goals, striving, 'self-realization' figure prominently in the literature of this group.

Anti-statistical?

Is there an anti-statistical character to phenomenology? There has been, and may still be. Quantitative methods are not worshipped in the qualitative temple. The phenomenologist works on problems of *individual* behavior. He focuses on the unique, the atypical, but not the average, since groups do not perceive through a mass sensorium. By and large, group correlational methods will not tell the phenomenologist exactly what he wants to know either, since he wants to know *exactly*. There are statistical methods now developed for individual cases, and they are used with keen appreciation (Stephenson, 1953; Rogers and Dymond, 1954). Still, what the phenomenologist seeks is absolute certainty about individual

---

[11.] For the reader who is not acquainted with an actual statement of the contrasting view, the statement by Kimble (1953, p. 158) is quoted here.

'For all practical purposes, it is possible to construct a science of psychology in which the organism is considered as empty. For my own part, I can conceive of a psychology based on stimulus and response events entirely, one in which the existence of the organism is a completely unimportant fact. The scientific account will, after all, deal with behavior in the abstract.'

To the 'experientialist' this statement must sound incredible, but, in fairness, the whole of his article should be read.

circumstances, not probabilities about groups of nonidentical units. In a symposium on 'Clinical vs. Statistical Methods in Prediction', Meehl, representing statistical theory, described two six-shot revolvers, one containing five bullets and one empty chamber, the other one bullet and five empty chambers. Which would you choose to hold to your temple? Snygg, representing the clinical view, is not interested in the safety of numbers or the advantage of chance, therefore offered to choose the more heavily loaded gun with only one empty chamber, if he could know this particular gun to his clinical satisfaction and on that basis judge that the empty chamber was next to be fired. Wellek (1957, p. 291) puts his relation of qualitative to quantitative analysis this way:

> The assertion that description cannot yield any generally valid results is itself something subjective, an untenable dogma. If somebody can count correctly or incorrectly, he can also describe something rightly or wrongly. If a correct calculation is universally recognized, then a true description should be similarly accepted.

Mind-body?

In relation to the biological, phenomenology holds a somewhat tenuous position. If 'the body is not a fact but a situation', it cannot be considered separate from its environment. As a biological substrate, it is the object of much thought in phenomenological work, especially among the perceptual specialties where neuro-anatomical structures are sought. But even there, the structures are pointed out by the functions — apparent phenomena. At the same time, it is well recognized that different structures 'create' for the animal different environments — and thus different phenomenal worlds — as with simple or compound eyes, to mention an elementary example. Many phenomenologists are of the opinion that man does not live merely in order to survive, but rather to achieve some human value — 'self-realization' or some form of spiritual development. Part of the reservation in regard to biological 'bedrock' stems from an emphasis on the social and cultural forces in shaping of behavior (for example, in the behavior of the person who starves to death in a 'hunger strike'), but another comes from the anti-reductionistic bias applied to the reasoning about humans from lower and simpler forms of life. This will undoubtedly continue, but, meanwhile, keen biological research is demonstrating that the simple forms are not so simple as often thought. Best (1963) mentions the example of the half-blinded (one-eyed) bee, flying in a circle, therefore thought to be an 'autonomous' governed by asymmetric stimulation to its one remaining 'photoelectric cell'. Yet the bee has been shown to have a language 'for communicating precise navigational information'. The primitive worms which he trained in a Y maze showed signs of wanting freedom more than food at certain points, leading to the postulation of bio-phenomenological concepts such as 'protoboredom', 'protointerest', 'protorebellion'.[12] However, until self-consciousness is demonstrated in lower forms, the clinical and social psychologist will probably maintain the concept of unique capacity for experience in the human being and may continue to consider it super-organic.

Freedom and human values

In the continuing debate between freedom and control, the phenomenologist is always found to be favoring some aspect of choice, will, decision, responsibility, as opposed to unadulterated determinism (Rogers and Skinner, 1956). This is not a stand based on punitive moralizing about blame, but an emphasis on the qualities of emergence, or 'becoming' as well as 'being'. Freedom of action is considered to have more than political tones — it is a psychologically healthy condition for growth, i.e., the man most free has the widest scope of choice, therefore he (and his free culture) is in the best position to make adaptive responses to changing conditions. That conditions will change is also a conviction of the typical phenomenologist. Novelty is considered to be a feature of the environment, and evidence is rapidly accumulating to indicate that the organism will actively search for new experience (Fiske and Maddi, 1961). Man as a free and active agent is vividly described by Merleau-Ponty (1956), again expressing the extreme view:

> I am not a 'living being' or even a 'man' or even a 'consciousness' with all
> the characteristics which zoology, social anatomy or inductive psychology
> attributes to these products of nature or history. I am the absolute source.

[12.] In connection with new findings in 'protopsychology' and old thoughts on freedom, it is especially interesting to add Hebb's comments on the increasing autonomy of the 'higher' evolutionary levels:

'I hope I do not shock biological scientists by saying that one feature of the phylogenetic development is an increasing evidence of what is known in some circles as free will; in my student days also referred to as the Harvard Law, which asserts that any well-trained experimental animal, on controlled stimulation, will do as he damn well pleases. A more scholarly formulation is that the higher animal is less stimulus-bound.

Brain action is less fully controlled by afferent input, behavior therefore less fully predictable from the situation in which the animal is put. A greater role of ideational activity is recognizable in the animal's ability to "hold" a variety of stimulations for some time before acting on them and in the phenomenon of purposive behavior. There is more autonomous activity in the higher brain, and more selectivity as to *which* afferent activity will be integrated with the "stream of thought", the dominant, ongoing activity in control of behavior. Traditionally, we say that the subject is "interested" in this part of the environment, not interested in that; in these terms, the higher animal has a wider variety of interests and the interest of the moment plays a greater part in behavior, which means a greater unpredictability as to what stimulus will be responded to and as to the form of the response' (Hebb, quoted in Scher, 1962, p. 726).

My existence does not come from my antecedents or my physical or social entourage, but rather goes toward them and sustains them.

Lest that seem too strident or distant a view to be taken seriously, here is a statement of equally assertive force from Rogers' (1963) most recent comments:

. . . man does not simply have the characteristics of a machine, he is not simply in the grip of unconscious motives, he is a person in the process of creating himself, a person who creates meaning in life, a person who embodies a dimension of subjective freedom.

Humanists tend to gather in this movement. They are interested in human beings as persons, albeit sometimes sensitive to accusations of 'softness' (as if it referred to heads as well as hearts). Words such as 'prizing' and 'respect' commonly appear in the literature dealing with their conduct of human observations. The attitude is similar to that displayed by naturalists toward birds, deer, or other species which fascinate them. Out of this desire to let the object of study be free, methods develop as set by the problem rather than to suit available instrumentation — a slow and difficult process.

Behaviorism

The position with regard to behaviorism is somewhat in flux at the moment, with the bare possibility of areas of reconciliation or synthesis, but there has been basic tension and mutual antagonism for decades. This fundamental opposition has already been mentioned. It is common opinion that the 'behavioral tide is ebbing'. Jessor points to a shift in the literature on motivation as one sign (White, 1959) and to reconstruction in the philosophy of science (Feigl, 1959) as another. Not only has behavioristic learning theory and research proved to be largely sterile but 'behaviorism and its canons of scientific procedure have failed in what must be considered the primary task of psychology — the scientific reconstruction of the person as we know him in ordinary life' (Jessor, 1961). One of the main logical criticisms of behaviorism's 'false objectivity' is that it always assumed the stimulus to have a peculiarly independent status — physical, invariant, and stable in its meaning, almost as if it had chosen itself to engage in the experiment (and *then* frozen). This notion is not the straw-man invention of the phenomenologist. It has been suggested, for instance, by Davis (1953, p. 10), for physiological psychology:

For a 'stimulus' (external event) to qualify under the proposed canon, it would have to be something which an experimenter could ascertain without there being any organism for it to work on.

But such a system would require that the experimenter himself were not an organism. For, as Koch (1959, pp. 768–9) points out:

> If stimuli and responses are acknowledged to depend for their
> identification on the perceptual sensitivities of human observers, then
> the demand for something tantamount to a language of pointer readings
> . . . must be given up . . . If, further, the requirement is asserted that S be
> specified in a way which includes its inferred meaning for the organism,
> then *any* basis for a difference in epistemological status between an S-R
> language and what has been called 'subjectivistic' language is eliminated.

Those who wishfully think that 'behaviorism is dead' are mistaken.
Phenomenology may have a chance to come alive in a climate no longer dominated
by pseudophysics in psychology, but behaviorism is now moving into significant
areas of human behavior (Krasner, 1962), and even reformulating a 'subjective
behaviorism' (Pribram, 1962). (Of those earlier behaviorists who are being
discarded, Hebb (1954, p. 101) says, 'These men were narrow — they were
wrong, and without them, without the simplification they achieved, modern
psychology would not exist'.) What is very likely to remain is the strong opposition
of internal and external views of the subject. Even when the same event is under
discussion, these two views remain in conflict, For example, when the 'externalist'
describes the *reinforcement* of the operant conditioning process (conducted by the
outside observer), the 'internalist' claims that the significant part of the process is
the intervention of the operant[13] (which emerges from within through the effort of
the actor). (See Shlien and Krasner, in Strupp and Luborsky, 1962, p. 109.)

The 'essential structure'

One final characteristic formulated by most writers on phenomenological theory
is that it should be the study of essences, or essential structures. This has to do
with the notion that when one describes acts of meaning, there should be a
definitive reference to the meant things. These meant things or their representations
in awareness (ideal concepts) are thought to have cores, or centers of stratified
structures, which centers are *irreducible categories*. These are the 'things in
themselves', not translatable into any other perception (Tymieniecka, 1962,
Chapter II). For the most part, the stratified structure model is applied by European
phenomenologists. Wellek applies this notion to studies of hypnosis. A subject is
asked, during deep trance, to do something in conflict with his values. Refusal to
execute the command in a post-hypnotic state is taken as evidence of a core

---

[13.] In this regard it is of interest to note that in studies of 'imprinting', ducklings *must* be
permitted to waddle after the decoy, from which Hess concluded that: 'the strength of
the imprinting appeared to be dependent not on the duration of the imprinting period
but *on the effort exerted by the duckling*' (Hess, 1958). (My italics.)

region which cannot be overcome (David and von Bracken, 1957, p. 290). Piaget is interpreted as illustrative of this model in his studies of intelligence, finding higher mental adaptations (stages) not reducible to lower ones. Anthropologist Levi-Strauss is likewise interpreted as having made use of the stratification model in kinship studies (Tymieniecka, 1962, pp. 38–44). With few exceptions (Gendlin, 1962), American phenomenologists have not understood or used Husserl, and this aspect of stratification or essential structures has not been followed in any deliberate way. It may be making an appearance in the factor analytic studies by Butler and others (Butler, Rice and Wagstaff, 1962 and 1963) or in descriptive statements about the core of the phenomenal self (Snygg and Combs, 1949, p. 126), but is mentioned here chiefly because 'essences' have figured in most theoretical descriptions of phenomenology, and may yet turn out to be a genuine part of the empirical system.

CHARACTERISTICS IN METHOD

Any system depends for its progress on methods. Phenomenology, like the rest of psychology, has been somewhat ill-equipped in this regard, although some truly ingenious thinking has gone into Gestalt studies of phenomena, into studies of perceptual constancies, stimulus equivalence, the family of introspective and projective methods, empathic techniques, and some statistical methods applicable to individual percepts.

The overall problem is that of subjectivity. All methods in this approach depend more or less on the response of the experiencer, and often on his own report (admission or assertion) of it. Quantitative analysis does not take the curse off, nor does the controlled experiment. Subjectivity has hung like an albatross around the neck of the phenomenologist, since it has been almost synonymous with 'unscientific'.[14]

Much has been said about the subjective-objective axis. It is based on a dualistic philosophy of separation between the knower and the known. 'Subjective' is thought to mean the representing experience; 'objective' refers to what is represented. But one person's experience can be the object of another's representation (or we can experience our own experience) so that experience itself is not subjective beyond rescue, nor the known object so separate from experience that it has a life of its own. It is not necessary to continue the 'history of philosophy [in which] the subject and its object have been treated as absolutely discontinuous entities' (James, 1947, p. 52). It seems much more reasonable (to the phenomenologist) to assume that subjective/objective is a matter of degree,

---

[14.] Excellent references are Jessor, 1956; Bakan, 1954; Zener, 1958. What has passed for 'scientific' has been concensus, stated in numbers and fortified by apparatus.

not of kind. (This holds with the understanding that he is not trying to study the physical world, or a class of things, but the psychological individual.)

A curious line of thinking led to what now appears to be a false division, deeply imbedded in our ideology. Cantril and others who have developed a 'transactional' point of view have shown that most of the behavior we analyze takes place in an *intersubjective* situation. So-called objective stimulus and so-called subjective response hardly deserve to be seen on two different levels since the latter defines the former. Further, the observer of the 'subject' is himself a responding reactor: he is subjective about his 'object' toward whom he was to be 'objective' by simple virtue of the other *being* an object. What we really have, then, is a situation composed of two subjective viewers, either of whom might be called more objective *when viewing the other*. ('There is the objective — mind as it may be seen by others — and the subjective — mind as he [the cyberneticist] experiences it in himself', Ashby, 1962, p. 305.) Some scientific virtue was supposed to reside in distance from the observed according to a formula which seems to run: (a) distance makes the observer impersonal; (b) impersonal attitudes make the other an object; (c) thus, distance and impersonality contribute to 'objectivity'. Is this true?

It seems quite possible that distance could make for less objectivity, if by that we mean reliable and accurate representation of the phenomenon being observed. Too much distance could only lead to 'projectivity', since the original object would be out of sight. Should the observer then better be the one in the very center of the experience? Is there some optimum distance? This leads to a rephrasing of the question, which should really be 'who can be the most distant?' or 'who can make the other more an object?' but simply 'who is the best knower?' That person is closest to the truth. The problems then become: (1) Does he know? (2) Will he tell? (3) Has he the capacity to describe? If we are to have a science of experience, it will come mainly through the efforts of the skillful, intelligent, nondefensive and/or courageous persons who can know experience well and communicate knowledge, for verification and general comparisons, if possible. The current methods are approximations of that possibility.

Introspection

Introspection is supposed to have ended, with a whimper, when behaviorism outlawed it. That was one special, classical form. Bakan, as already noted, has revived the deliberate use of the method, by name, in a promising approximation which demonstrates the possibilities mentioned above. But also, Boring has pointed out that 'introspection is still with us, doing business under various aliases, of which the *verbal report* is one'. This verbal report is so ever-present and of such unavoidable significance that everyone must find some sort of accommodation to it. Spence (1944, p. 57) is willing to say that, 'the phenomenological approach has its advantages, particularly in the complex field of social behavior of the human adult. It is obviously easier to gain some notion as to the relevant variables by asking the individual to verbalize them than it is to employ the procedure of trying to hypothesize them from knowledge of past history.' At any rate, this shows some trust in the possibilities of communication, at least for convenience. Hilgard (1957, p. 4) goes farther:

> Some extremists believe that private experiences have no place in science; they believe that such experiences belong to the province of the artist or poet. But most psychologists hold that these private experiences are just as much a part of the real world as more observable activities; and they accept the *verbal report* of these experiences as data for science.

Skinner (1953, p. 282), who stands guard more sternly, is only willing to allow for some linguistic clues, as he writes by the light of the burning straw-man:

> The verbal report is a response to a private event, and may be used as a source of information about it. A critical analysis of the validity of this practice is of first importance. But we may avoid the dubious conclusion that, so far as science is concerned, the verbal report or some other discriminative response is the sensation.

True, the verbal report is not the sensation.[15] Neither is the pointer reading. But then, neither is Skinner's observation of behavior the behavior itself! Nor is his report of it his observation! The verbal report is not alone in its failure to *be* the experience it attempts to signify, and the *questions about its validity apply to all types of observations*. No sign is its referent — even the knowing is not the known, nor is the process of experiencing the experience, but it is as close as one can get, and quite close enough, I assert, for psychological study. Under certain conditions, I trust my thoughts, feelings, and even expressions of them, quite as much or more than I trust my (or your) observations of the direction of a pigeon's head, or a tennis ball's behavior in flight. (Remember, these things do not speak for themselves.)

All agree, some reluctantly, that there are private events. Most agree that there is private awareness of them. Can these events be considered as behavior? Not by the behaviorist, unless external signals are considered sufficiently representative to be accepted in the local and current framework of science, or 'ways of knowing'. Why such lack of trust in the verbal report? There are good

---

[15.] We dislike being limited to 'sensation', the least of our concerns — and to the term 'verbal report' — a slighting and pseudoscientific reference to the full potency of language in communication, but, for the moment, it is sufficient to accept the behaviorist's terminology.

reasons. One is that we have multiple thoughts for one voice, so that not all internal behaviors can be simultaneously expressed. Another is that we know, from our own experience, that the verbal report can be false. We have accidentally or deliberately made it so, and observed this. However, cannot the verbal report be true? It can, and can be more true than our outward behavior, and this we know from our experience also. It is more difficult (except in simple sensations and expression such as 'ouch') to report the truth, if only because mistakes are easier to make than to avoid, but the verbal report cannot be said to have *by its nature* a low or negative correlation with the private event it represents. (It is odd that the determinists who rule out 'free will' also distrust the verbal report, as if the behaver does have the capacity to falsify at will, if he is not merely stupid.)

Whatever stance one takes toward it, the verbal report is fundamental, and the latest technical advances are simply elegant extensions of it. This includes such excellent tools as the semantic differential (Osgood et al., 1957) and the Q-sort (Stephenson, 1953; Butler and Haigh, 1954; Shlien, 1962a). Introspection means, according to James, 'looking into our minds, and reporting what we there discover', and these techniques are manipulatable data language for 'reporting what we there discover'.

Another problem in the verbal report, somewhat neutralized by tools such as those above which provide the semantic frame of reference, is the difficulty in overcoming the lack of precision in even the extensive vocabulary. It is partly for this reason (that we are only semi-articulate) that the poet in Hilgard's statement seems to have special access to private experience. What we lack is not so much the experience, or access, but the poet's refined and heightened imagery and his very hard work to formulate it. Our failure to have *le mot juste* ready at hand seems to put experience beyond accurate description. We only see the nature of our ordinary failure when we look at its exaggeration, in aphasia. It is next to impossible for one to describe the exact shade of feeling, meaning, color tone and intensity, etc., to another, especially in complex experience. There are, for simplification, yes/no answers, but then the phrasing of the question becomes complex. There is also the possibility of matching techniques, such as color matching, or with words, to match judge's perceptions of the speaker's meaning.

Kluver (1936) offered an experimental technique based on matching of response values (stimulus equivalence and nonequivalence), for the study of personality. It has been little used, though it would seem to hold some promise still. Interestingly enough, many of his early observations were drawn from the field of ethology, which has a clear but little recognized connection with phenomenological principles.

F. J. J. Buytendijk, whose early work with toads is cited by Kluver, has moved from animal observation into some of the most elusive human qualities, in his 'Femininity and Existential Psychology', for example (David and von Bracken,

1957, pp. 197–211). Von Uexkull, one of the founders of ethological method, is often quoted in the literature of phenomenology, since his concept of 'private worlds' or environments for each species and even each animal is very much to the phenomenological point (Tymieniecka, 1962, pp. 121–3). McKellar (1962, p. 636) in his chapter on introspection remarks, 'To some extent, the ethologists like Tinbergen and Lorenz have reintroduced the methods of the naturalist into psychology'. Principles of ethology as described by Hess (1962, p. 160) are highly compatible with those of phenomenology:

> Study of [animal] behavior must begin by obtaining as complete a knowledge as possible of the behavior of the species during the entire life cycle . . . because *all facts on behavior must be acquired before any hypotheses are formulated* . . . [Ethologists] have come to this conclusion because behavior is so multiform that a wealth of evidence can always be compiled in support of any theory, no matter how capriciously constructed. (My italics.)

Though the 'entire life cycle' is beyond the reach of the study, immediate experience, the other ideas, including the intent to study the animals in states which most closely resemble the natural habitat, without fear of the observer, fit phenomenology well.

Empathy

It was noted earlier that the Rogerian technique of 'reflection' is almost ethological in its effort to preserve just such conditions as are described above. This technique was a remarkable invention, though it has been maligned by caricature and wooden application. It not only aims toward allowing free emergence of the dynamics of interaction without interference, but expresses perhaps better than any other form of interaction that much used and discussed quality, 'empathy'. Empathic understanding is described as one of the primary modes of knowing another and as a method in promoting personality change and development. According to Rogers,

> A second necessary condition of psychotherapy, as I see it, is the experiencing by the therapist of an accurate and empathic understanding of the client. This means that he senses and comprehends the client's immediate awareness of his own private world. It involves sensing the cognitive, perceptual, and affective components of the client's experiential field, as they exist in the client. Where the therapist is adequately sensitive, it means not only recognizing those aspects of experience which the client has already been able to verbalize, but also those unsymbolized aspects of his experience which have somehow been comprehended through subtle non-verbal clues by the delicate psychological radar of the therapist. The skillful therapist senses the client's world — no matter how hallucinated

or bizzare or deluded or chaotic — as if it were his own, but without ever
losing the 'as if' quality. (Shlien, 1961, p. 304)

van Kaam (1959, p. 70) calls this 'co-experiencing':

> The understanding person shares at an emotional level the experience of
> the subject understood. The prefix 'co-' represents the awareness of the
> subject that the person understanding still remains another.

Rogers defines the act precisely in Koch (1959):

> *Empathy.* The state of empathy, or being empathic, is to perceive the
> internal frame of reference of another with accuracy, and with the
> emotional components and meanings which pertain, thereto, as if one
> were the other person, but without ever losing the 'as if' condition. Thus
> it means to sense the hurt or the pleasure of another as he senses it, and
> to perceive the causes thereof as he perceives them, but without ever
> losing the recognition that it is *as if* I were hurt or pleased, etc. If this 'as
> if' quality is lost, then the state is one of identification.

Empathy, or co-experiencing, has not been thoroughly described or researched,
but it is well known *as an experience.* It may be put in terms such as those already
quoted, or in what we are given to call 'mystical' (though this seems to refer more
to our ignorance or sheepishness than to its quality) ways such as those described
by Buber (1947):

> A man belabours another, who remains quite still. Then let us assume
> that the striker suddenly receives in his soul the blow which he strikes;
> the same blow; that he receives it as the other who remains still. For the
> space of a moment he experiences the situation from the other side. Reality
> imposes itself on him. What will he do? Either he will overwhelm the
> voice of the soul, or his impulse will be reversed.
>
> A man caresses a woman, who lets herself be caressed. Then let us
> assume that he feels the contact from two sides — with the palm of his
> hand still, and also with the woman's skin. The two-fold nature of the
> gesture, as one that takes place between two persons, thrills through the
> depth of enjoyment in his heart and stirs it. If he does not deafen his
> heart he will have — not to renounce the enjoyment but — to love.
>
> I do not in the least mean that the man who has had such an experience
> would from then on have this two-sided sensation in every such meeting
> — that would perhaps destroy his instinct. But the one extreme experience
> makes the other person present to him for all time. A transfusion has
> taken place after which a mere elaboration of subjectivity is never again
> possible or tolerable to him.

Not everyone will recognize or remember this quality of experience, and still fewer admit it, but some would vouch for it as an actuality (Shlien, 1961, p. 316). At least we realize that we hesitate to cause pain (or else enjoy causing pain) because we believe that the pain of others resembles our own. At least, that.

If this type of description gives uneasiness, one can find more solid comfort in recent physiological studies (Greenblatt, 1959; DiMascio et al., 1955, 1957; Dittes, 1957) which suggest physiological evidence of 'co-experiencing:'

> Studies of different doctor-patient dyads have shown us that the doctor is quite as reactive as the patient. [Findings] . . . suggest physiological rapport at least for *some* of the emotions experienced by the patient. It is further worth noting that the *rapport phenomenon was most striking when the doctor was 'actively listening' and less striking when he was distracted or 'not listening'* . . . (our italics). (Bebout and Clayton, 1962.)

Lacey (1959), in his review, comments that 'these are surprising data, and . . . may imply, as the authors [Coleman, Greenblatt and Solomon] seem to feel, a "physiological relationship" between the therapist and patient revealing a process of "empathy"'.

To Rogers, empathy is not just *a* way of knowing but perhaps *the* primary method in comprehension of all phenomena. He speaks of empathy as a way of knowing both the other, and also oneself, via empathy turned inward. While objects (stones and trees) have no experience to share, even 'objective' knowledge is related to empathy. Empathic understanding in that case is directed toward the reference group which objectifies, by consensus, one's experimentally derived information. Empathy, then, is the fundamental way of knowing, and its direction may turn inward or outward (Rogers, 1957, 1963). It is of singular importance in this methodology. There are two elements of knowing: (1) feeling, or the pathic way (from *pathetos,* able to suffer or subject to suffering) which is the process of *understanding,* and (2) seeing (from *spectore,* to look at), which is the process of spection, intro or extro, or *perceiving.* Together, these two are ways of knowing for phenomenology, if not for all of science.

PERCEPTION AND PERSONALITY

PERCEPTION

This is often called a perceptual approach to personality.[16] Rogers (1951, p. 307),

---

[16.] Basic references for the interested student are Combs and Snygg (1959); Rogers (1951, 1957, 1959); Patterson (1959); and Gendlin (1962).

for instance, writes of the actual 'reorganization of visual perception' during therapy in contrast to the loose descriptive analogy implied by such phrases as 'seeing things differently'. Combs and Snygg (1959, p. 20) base an absolute law of behavior on perceptual experience: *All behavior, without exception, is completely determined by, and pertinent to, the perceptual field of the behaving organism*. Does this sound like S-R theory writ large, with 'perceptual field' standing for 'stimulus'? For clarification, they add, *'By the perceptual field, we mean the entire universe, including himself, as if it is experienced by the individual at the instance of action'*. So, to the extent that the entire universe can be reduced to an identifiable stimulus in a given moment of experience, we are in bed with the enemy. Should we simply acquiesce to the inevitable and say 'good night', or try to avoid the scandal?

No scientist, looking for lawful descriptions of behavior, wants to turn away from cause and effect. But by now, many phenomenological reservations have appeared; indeed these are precisely what and all that distinguish phenomenology and S-R theory. We come to the perceiving situation with differing needs. These are well known to affect the perception of the stimulus. We also come with a different history of experience. We may even bring different perceptual structures, either in physiological capacity or psychological expectancy. What we react to is not someone else's stimulus, but *our* total perception of *our* phenomenal world. In elegantly contrived visual demonstrations, Ames has shown that 'what is perceived is not what exists but what one believes exists' (Combs and Snygg, 1959, p. 84). 'Seeing is believing,' if one can see, but 'believing is seeing', too. We construct our phenomenal world to fit expectations. Reik (1962), working with college 'drop-out' students finds it the rule that they 'describe mothers as being in delicate health, liable to become ill at any moment. What is important here is not what the parents are like in actuality, but that the student's conception of them produces a very real upset in his inner world.')

It might seem that all of these individual differences in perception are the result of the variations in need, structure, past experience, and aim or expectation, thus all 'distortions'. Many are, but we do not derive all differences from parataxic errors, like the blind men describing the elephant. It is worthwhile to note Bronowski's description of the 'clock paradox' based on relativity theory, which proves that two clocks, moving with respect to one another, run at different speeds. It is demonstrated that two observers of a moving light, one moving with it and the other standing still, will have time pass *at different speeds for them*. If time did not, then the speed of light would have to vary (Bronowski, 1963). In the field of perception, then, it is not just cultural relativity or egocentrism which causes differences (though these factors must account for most of the variance) but also unavoidable physical relativity.

Because of these relativities, the perceptual system organizes on the basis of what are called 'perceptual constancies'. These constancies are assumptions to the effect that actions will take place as we have become accustomed to them in the past. Thus we tend to judge depth or distance by apparent size of a familiar object, or we catch a baseball that we did not see after it arrived at a point two feet from our glove. 'Constancies' make us subject to optical illusions, but for the most part they make it possible to carry out relatively stable operations in a constantly active and changing environment (Ittleson and Cantril, 1954).

Before turning to a definition of personality, something should be said in the way of a definition of perception. Definitions are only opinions, of course. One opinion would be that all impingement of stimuli (such as light or sound, upon receptive nerve cells) is perception. A distinction made by J. J. Gibson (1963, p. 1) is important. '*Perception involves meaning; sensation does not*' (our italics). To clarify this a bit more, we would say: radar reflects; a phototropic cell senses; and a mind perceives. Ours is a perceptual theory of personality in that it deals with *meanings,* and requires cognitive apparatus.

PERSONALITY

Now a definition of personality is in order. While these definitions are not sheer snares and delusions, neither are they scientific revelations. They are only a part of the system. In this system, personality must have some relation to the subjective, and to the perceptual. It reflects the very shift which has taken place in psychology as described by Bruner, Goodnow and Austin (1956, p. 106) who note that,

> The past few years have witnessed a notable increase in interest in and investigation of the cognitive processes . . . Partly, it has resulted from a recognition of the complex processes that mediate between the classical 'stimuli' and 'responses' out of which stimulus-response learning theories hoped to fashion a psychology that would bypass anything smacking of the 'mental'. The impeccable peripheralism of such theories could not last long. As 'S-R' theories came to be modified to take into account the subtle events that may occur between the input of a physical stimulus and the emission of an observable response, the old image of the 'stimulus-response bond' began to dissolve, its place being taken by a mediation model. As Edward Tolman so felicitously put it some years ago, in place of a telephone switchboard connecting stimuli and responses it might be more profitable to think of a map room where stimuli were sorted out and arranged before every response occurred, and one might do well to have a closer look at these intervening 'cognitive maps'.

This well describes what has been developing throughout the chapter. Phenomenology could never have adopted a 'switchboard' model. It could and did adopt the image of a map. That is how the 'self-concept' or 'self-structure' is often described — as a map to which the person refers when he is about to make a move. This map is, in fact, one of those 'perceptual constancies' which helps to stabilize behavior, and it is also one of the reasons for the emphasis on self-consistency (Lecky, 1945). Personality is one's view of himself, the self-concept, by which he tends to order and interpret his internal and external experiences.

Rogers (1951, Chapter 11) developed theory of personality and behavior based on the phenomenal self, stated in a set of 19 propositions which are abstracted in a summary by Shlien (1962a). Some of these fundamentals have already been mentioned in the earlier discussion.

1. Each person is unique. No one else can ever completely know his experience. Since each person's neurological capacities and life history combine in unique ways, the closest approach to another's experience is to see it through his own eyes, insofar as possible. Some of his experience is consciously symbolized. Some is at lower levels of awareness, where it has a lesser influence, perhaps a less controllable influence, on behavior.

2. Behavior is a consequence of perception. The organism reacts to reality as it is perceived and defined *by that organism*. The 'objective evidence' of the thermometer notwithstanding, he who thinks the room hot opens the window; who thinks it cold closes the same window. Who sees a light red, stops; sees the same light green, goes; sees an object as delicious, eats it; sees the same object as refuse, avoids it or sickens from it. Whatever 'it' may be — by consensus, physical measurement, or philosophical proof, the way in which 'it' is perceived will determine behavior toward it.

3. From this, it follows that if one wants to promote a stable change in behavior, one must change the *perception* of the one who is behaving. (Unstable changes can be forced from outside, but enduring alterations motivated by internal shifts depend on new perceptions.)

4. The perception of threat is always followed by defense. Defense may take many forms — aggression, withdrawal, submission, etc. — but it is the general and categorical response to danger.

5. Perception is narrowed and rigidified by threat. (Experimentally, the phenomenon of 'tunnel vision' can be evoked by threat.) Narrowed and rigidified perception blocks change in behavior. Threat, therefore, does not permanently change behavior. It only arouses defenses. Attacking the defense system is likely to complicate it, causing more of the psychological economy to be devoted to defense, still further restricting perception and inhibiting change.

6. Of the whole perceptual field, a portion becomes differentiated as the self. *This is the self-concept.* The self-concept has dimensions, and the dimensions have values. Thus the self-concept may be one of weakness

or strength, for instance. Lovable — hateful, lucky — unlucky, worthy or contemptible, are other examples of dimensions which influence behavior. They influence behavior because the interpretation of the self leads to a reactive interpretation of the external object. For instance, if one feels strong, a boulder is a weapon to push into the treads of an armored tank; if weak, the same boulder is a refuge to hide behind. If one feels sick and helpless, the nurse is a creature of mercy, appealed to for comfort. The same nurse may be seen as a temptress, to be sexually pursued, if the patient sees himself as well and sturdy. All experience is evaluated as friendly or dangerous, interesting or boring, possible or impossible, etc., depending *not* upon the nature of the experience so much as upon the *self-concept of the experiencer.*

7. As experiences occur, they are related to the self-structure, and depending on it, each experience will be (a) symbolized accurately, perceived consciously, and organized into the self-structure, (b) ignored, though sensed (as a sensation) because it has no significance to the self, or (c) denied or distorted when symbolized because it is threatening to the self.

'CONSCIOUS AND UNCONSCIOUS' ASPECTS

Throughout this chapter, we have been thinking primarily about ways of knowing. The statement in 7c (above) leads us to consider also remembering and forgetting, and selective attention and inattention.

The issue of the 'unconscious' tends to distinguish two clinical divisions — the psychoanalytic and the phenomenal — though not all Freudian concepts are completely foreign to phenomenology, and not all phenomenologists reject the unconscious. Those few who do not are mainly proponents of projective techniques, who rest their *interpretations* heavily upon psychoanalytic dynamics, though they rest their operational *assumptions* upon phenomenology. Thus L. K. Frank, writing (in the company of phenomenologists) about the 'private world of personal meanings' (Kuenzli, 1959, p. 96), would readily agree that 'we see things not as they are, but as we are'. However, he expresses doubts, held by most adherents of projective techniques, that the individual either has a clear understanding of himself, or would reveal such understanding in the face of social pressure. Or, as H. A. Murray puts it, 'the most important things about an individual are what he cannot or will not say'. This succinctly states the problem — is it a matter of cannot, or is it will not? There is no doubt that Murray values the interior experience. But the phenomenologist will more readily depend on the face value of the testimony or self-report of the individual. Is this his strength or his weakness? It depends in part as to whether he can create conditions that do not force concealment but favor revelation. It also depends on whether or not he postulates an inaccessible unconscious. Patterson, for instance, 'sees no need to postulate an unconscious' and finds support in studies and opinions which conclude 'that a man's expressed opinions and values are more indicative when it comes to prediction than are projective techniques' (Patterson, 1959, p. 255). A similar finding is reported in a study of the 'role of self-understanding in prediction of behavior' (Rogers, Kell, and McNeil, 1948).

It may be that the dimension of rational-irrational is the great divide between those, like Murray and Frank, who are generally phenomenologists, and those otherwise like-minded theorists who do not adopt the unconscious. Allport, for instance, considers humans to be 'characteristically rational. Irrational aspects appear in the undeveloped personality of the child, or the mentally ill' (cited in Fiske and Maddi, 1961). Rogers believes that man, as a healthy, fully functioning person, is 'exquisitely rational' — even his defenses have a certain wisdom about them.

In the main, then, the phenomenological position is in some opposition to the concept of 'the unconscious'. There are knotty problems involved, which may be analyzed in terms of learning, differentiation, remembering, or forgetting, with self-consistency, and Sullivan's concept of 'selective inattention', brought into play — but which are beyond the scope of this chapter.

From the standpoint of the existential phenomenologist such as Sartre (1953), the unconscious is a rejected concept, representing 'bad faith'. As such, it is simply an avoidance of responsibility, via suppression rather than repression, 'playing the game' of mental illness. The ideas of Rogers, Snygg and Combs, and others of their school can probably be expressed in this way: two elements, 'span of attention' and 'level of awareness' operate within an energy system in which energy levels are raised and lowered, and attention directed and focused, by emotions. A favorite example in the perceptual analogies commonly used is that of angle of vision as affected by threat. Normally, under relaxed conditions, the angle of vision is wide enough to permit peripheral perceptions at 80+ degrees to either side when the viewer looks straight ahead. Under conditions of intense emotion (of which threat is one) the phenomenon of 'tunnel vision' can be induced. The view becomes narrow, as if the viewer were looking through a tube. In that event, the peripheral scene, which is no longer perceived, is not 'inaccessible'. It is simply out of sight until normal vision is restored.

Span of attention and level of awareness are thought to enlarge and constrict, or rise and fall, according to the energy available at a given time. If sensation is distinguished from perception according to Gibson's previously noted idea, then sensation registers at a very low level of awareness. There are many sensations which, depending on energy available, we do not immediately or perhaps ever (the process can be delayed) turn into perceptions. To the extent that sensations enter awareness at all, they vaguely influence behavior. A soldier on watch in a jungle slaps only those mosquitos actually noticed. The remainder contribute to some general impression of feeling to one of uneasiness,[17] much less significant than his fear for his life. As he is pinned down by enemy fire, the mosquitos may become ferocious, but fade as perceptions long after, at rest in his lawn chair, he may viciously swat and spray, vowing to kill all mosquitos, hating them for sensations caused years ago, now raised to perceptions in a different situation.

The idea of an energy level model is perhaps especially appropriate to a neurological system, but that is not its justification. Its value is in the distinct and important difference between it and the so-called 'hydraulic' model as Freud's concept of the unconscious is often described (MacIntyre, 1958, p. 22). If, as Freud thought, the 'sum of excitations' in the nervous system is constant (like the volume of blood in the circulatory system, for instance), then an experience, when forgotten, must go some place — some place 'out of consciousness'. The hydraulic model makes a 'reservoir' an absolute necessity. In an energy model, where the sum of excitations is *not* constant but varies according to variation of intake and metabolic rate, forgetting and remembering are functions of a variable process. Once perceived, an experience moves in and out of consciousness *in time,* not in space. The forgotten does not move to an inaccessible location. It stays where it is, and the amount of light cast upon it grows dim, as it were.

Theoretically, given complete absence of threat, and a resultant complete freedom of energy from defensive activities, memory would be as complete as the needs of the moment dictated, limited only by the levels of awareness permitted by energy available at that moment. Such conditions are seldom if ever achieved, and then only temporarily, since the press of new experience and changing social environment alters the situation, re-creating 'normal' levels of stress. Perhaps just to the extent that these ideal conditions are approximated, the phenomenologist is justified in taking at face value the self-reports toward which his methodology points and which others so distrust.

---

17. William James (1950, p. 607) observed that 'if you make a real red cross (say) on a sheet of white paper invisible to an hypnotic subject, and yet cause him to look fixedly at a dot on the paper on or near the cross, he will, on transferring his eye to a blank sheet, see a bluish-green after-image of a cross. This proves that it has impressed his sensibility. He has *felt* it, but not *perceived* it.' Some sensations, such as the weight of this book on your finger tips, may become perceptions if attention is so directed, or if the amount of available energy varies in such a way as to increase sensitivity. Obviously, in social situations which are often complex and fast moving, many high level sensations or low level perceptions are experienced and forgotten in the rush of events on the fluctuations of energy levels.

MOTIVATION

Unconscious or not, motivation is one remaining problem. Presumably the definition of motivation does not differ much throughout these chapters — it has to do with what the person is trying to accomplish through his behaviors. There is only one basic motive to which all behaviors are ascribed in this system. It is called 'growth', or 'self-enhancement', 'self-realization' (Butler and Rice, 1962). Combs and Snygg (1959, p. 46) put it as *'that great driving, striving force in each of us by which we are continually seeking to make ourselves ever more adequate to cope with life'*. Rogers (1963) adds, 'Whether the stimulus arises from within or without, whether the environment is favorable or unfavorable, the behaviors of an organism can be counted on to be in the direction of maintaining, enhancing, and reproducing life. That is the very nature of the process we call life.'

CONCLUSION

There is, by way of summary, a story about a psychologist which is somewhat legendary in the Chicago area. It is a commentary upon many elements which have been discussed: language, personal meanings, frames of reference, motives, private worlds, methods of observation, etc. And it points out that it is not always true that the human mind thinks silently. It can, but it sometimes thinks out loud, from which we can learn if we listen.

The upper-class parents of a small boy were worried. Their son was quiet, sensitive, lonely, nervous, afraid of and highly excited by other children. He stammered in the presence of strangers, and was becoming more shy and withdrawn. The parents were embarrassed and did not want to expose their fears, but wanted some professional advice before the child entered school. The father solved their dilemma by calling a college friend whom he had not seen for years, and who had become in those years a well-known clinical psychologist. For 'old times' sake' an invitation for a weekend in their suburban home was extended, and, with some curiosity, accepted. After dinner, the mother 'casually' mentioned their concern about the child; the father amplified this and suggested that after lunch the next day, the boy might be observed at play for a psychological appraisal. The visitor understood now the purpose of his visit, asked appropriate questions about history and behavior, and prepared to take up his assignment. He watched, unseen, from a balcony above the garden where the boy played by himself. The boy sat pensively in the sun, listening to neighboring children shout. He frowned, rolled over on his stomach, kicked the toes of his white shoes against the grass, sat up and looked at the stains. Then he saw an earthworm. He stretched it out on the flagstone, found a sharp-edged chip, and began to saw the worm in half. At this point, impressions were forming in the psychologist's mind, and he made some tentative notes to the effect: 'Seems isolated and angry, perhaps over-aggressive, or sadistic, should be watched carefully when playing with other children, not have knives or pets'. Then he noticed that the boy was talking to himself. He leaned forward and strained to catch the words. The boy finished the separation of the worm. His frown disappeared, and he said, 'There. Now you have a friend.'

REFERENCES

Allport, G. W. (1936). The personalistic psychology of William Stern. *Charact. and Pers.*, *5*, 231–46.

Allport, G. W. (1947). Scientific models and human morals. *Psychol. Rev.*, *54*,182–92.

Asch, S. E. (1953). *Social psychology.* New York: Prentice-Hall.

Ashby, C. (1962). What is mind? Objective and subjective aspects in cybernetics. In J. Scher (Ed.), *Theories of the mind.* Glencoe, Ill.: Free Press.

Bakan, D. A. (1954). A reconsideration of the problem of introspection. *Psychol. Bull.*, *51* (2), 105–18.

Beattie, D. M. (1949). The effect of imaginary practice on the acquisition of a motor skill. Unpublished M. A. dissertation, University of Toronto.

Bebout, J. F. & Clayton, M. (1962). Toward a concept of shared experiencing in psychotherapy. *Counseling Center Discussion Papers*, Vol. 8, No. 10.

Beck, S. J. & Molish, B. (Eds.) (1959). *Reflexes to intelligence: a reader in clinical psychology.* Glencoe, Ill: Free Press.

Berenda, C. W. (1957). Is clinical psychology a science? *American Psychologist*, *12*, 725–9.

Best, J. (1963). Protopsychology. *Scientific American*, *208* (2), 54–75.

Boring, F. G. (1950). A *history of experimental psychology.* New York: Appleton-Century-Crofts.

Boring, F. G. (1953). A history of introspection. *Psychol. Bull. 50*, 169–89.

Blake, R. & Ramsey, G. (Eds.) (1951). *Perception: an approach to personality.* New York: Ronald Press.

Bronowski, J. (1963). The clock paradox. *Scientific American*, *208* (2), 134–48.

Bruner, J. S., Goodnow, J. & Austin, G. A. (1956). *A study of thinking.* New York: Wiley.

Buber, M. (1947). *Between Man and Man.* London: Kegan Paul.

Butler, J. M. & Haigh, G. V. (1954). Changes in the relation between self-concepts and ideal-concepts. In C. R. Rogers & R. P. Dymond (Eds.), *Psychotherapy and personality change.* Chicago: University of Chicago Press.

Butler, J. M., Rice, L. N. & Wagstaff, A. (1962). On the naturalistic definition of variables: an analogue of clinical analysis. In H. Strupp & Luborsky (Eds.), *Research in psychotherapy*, Vol. II. Washington, D.C.: APA.

Butler, J. M., Rice, L.N. & Wagstaff, A.K. (1963). *Quantitative naturalistic research.* New York: Prentice-Hall.

Coleman, R., Greenblatt, M. & Solomon, H. C. (1956). Physiological evidence of rapport during psychotherapeutic interviews. *Dis. Nerv. System, 17*, 2–8.

Combs, A. W. & Snygg, D. (1959). *Individual behavior: a perceptual approach to behavior.* New York: Macmillan.

David, H. & von Bracken, K. (1957). *Perspectives in personality theory.* New York: Basic Books.

Davis, R. (1953). Physiological psychology. *Psychol. Rev.*, *60*, 7–14.

DiMascio, A., Boyd, R. W. & Greenblatt, M. (1957). Physiological correlates of tension and antagonism during psychotherapy. A study of 'interpersonal physiology.' *Pyschosom. Med.*, *19*, 99–104.

DiMascio, A., Boyd, R. W., Greenblatt, M. & Soloman, H. C. (1955). The psychiatric interview: a sociophysiological study. *Dis. Nerv. System*, *16*, 2–7.

Dittes, J. E. (1957). Galvanic skin response as a measure of patient's reaction to therapist's permissiveness. *J. Abnorm. Soc. Psychol.*, *55*, 295–305.

Farber, M. (1943). *The foundation of phenomenology.* Cambridge, MA.: Harvard Univ. Press.

Feigl, H. (1959). Philosophical embarrassments of psychology. *Amer. Psychologist, 14*, 115–28.

Fiske, D. & Maddi, S. (1961). *Functions of varied experience.* Homewood, Ill.: Dorsey Press.

Frank, L. K. (1959). Projective methods in the study of personality. In Kuenzli, A. (Ed.), *The phenomenological problem.* New York: Harper.

Gendlin, E. (1962). *Experiencing and the creation of meaning.* Glencoe, Ill.: Free Press.

Gibson, J. J. (1959). Perception as a function of stimulation. In S. Koch (Ed.), *Psychology: a study of a science,* Vol. I. New York: McGraw-Hill.

Gibson, J.J. (1963). The useful dimensions of sensitivity. *American Psychologist. 18*, 1–15.

Greenblatt, M. (1959). Discussion of papers by Saslow and Matarazzo, and Lacey. In F. A. Rubinstein & M. B. Parloff (Eds.), *Research in psychotherapy.* Washington, DC.: APA.

Hebb, D. O. (1954). The problem of consciousness and introspection. In B. Adrian (Ed.), *Brain mechanics and consciousness,* Oxford: Blackwell Scientific Publications.

Hess, E. H. (1958). Imprinting in animals. *Scientific American, 198*:81.

Hess, E. H. (1962). Ethology: an approach to the complete analysis of behavior. In *New directions in psychology.* New York: Holt, Rinehart and Winston.

Hilgard, F. R. (1957). *Introduction to psychology* (2nd ed.). New York: Harcourt, Brace.

Hull, C. (1943). *Principles of behavior.* New York: Appleton-Century.

Ittleson, W. & Cantril, H. (1954). *Perception: a transactional approach.* Garden City: Doubleday.

James, W. (1947). *Essays in radical empiricism: a pluralistic universe.* New York: Longmans.

James, W. (1950 edition). *Principles of psychology.* New York: Dover Press.

Jessor, R. (1956). Phenomenological personality theories and the data language of psychology. *Psychol. Rev.*, 63 (3), 173–80.

Jessor, R. (1961). Issues in the phenomenological approach to personality. *J. Individ. Psychol.*, *17*, 27–38.

Kimble, G. (1953). Psychology as a science. *Scientific Monthly, LXXVII (3).*

Kluver, H. (1933). *Behavior mechanisms in monkeys.* Chicago: University of Chicago Press.

Kluver, H. (1936). The study of personality and the method of equivalent and nonequivalent stimuli. *Charact. and Pers.*, *5*, 91–112.

Koch, S. (Ed.) (1959). *Psychology: a study of a science,* Vol. III. New York: McGraw-Hill.

Kohler, W. (1938). *The place of value in a world of facts.* New York: Liveright.

Krasner, L. (1962). The therapist as a social reinforcement machine. In H. Strupp & Luborsky (Eds.), *Research in psychotherapy,* Vol. II. Washington, D.C.: APA.

Kuenzli, A. B. (Ed.) (1959). *The phenomenological problem.* New York: Harper.

Lacey, J. I. (1959). Psychophysiological approaches to the evaluation of psychotherapeutic process and outcome. In E. A. Rubinstein & M. B. Parloff (Eds.), *Research in psychotherapy.* Washington, D.C.: APA.

Landsman, T. (1958). Four phenomenologies. *J. Individ. Psychol.*, *14*, 29–37.

Lecky, P. (1945). *Self-consistency: a theory of personality.* New York: Island Press.

Lewin, K. (1951). *Field theory in social science: selected theoretical papers.* D. Cartwright (Ed.). New York: Harper.

MacIntyre, A. C. (1958). *The unconscious.* London: Routledge and Kegan Paul.

MacLeod, R. B. (1951). The place of phenomenological analysis in social psychological theory. In J. H. Rohrer & M. Sherif (Eds.), *Social psychology at the crossroads.* New York: Harper.

May, R. (1961). *Existential psychology.* New York: Random House.

McKellar, P. (1962). *The method of introspection.* In J. Scher (Ed.), *Theories of the mind.* Glencoe, Ill.: Free Press.

Merleau-Ponty, M. (1945). *La phenomenologie de la perception.* Paris: Gallimard.

Merleau-Ponty, M. (1956). What is phenomenology? *Cross Currents, 6,* 59–70.

Osgood, C., Suci, C. & Tannenbaum, P. (1957). *The measurement of meaning.* Urbana: University of Illinois Press.

Patterson, C. H. (1959). *Counseling and psychotherapy: theory and practice.* New York: Harper.

Polanyi, M. (1958). *Personal knowledge.* Chicago: University of Chicago Press.

Pribram, K. H. (1962). Interrelations of psychology and the neurological disciplines. In S. Koch (Ed.) *Psychology: a study of a science,* Vol. 4. New York: McGraw-Hill.

Reik, L. (1962). The drop-out problem. *The Nation, 194* (20).

Rogers, C. R. (1942). *Counseling and psychotherapy.* Boston: Houghton Mifflin.

Rogers, C. R. (1951). *Client-centered therapy: its current practice, implications and theory.* Boston: Houghton Mifflin.

Rogers, C. R. (1957). The necessary and sufficient conditions of therapeutic personality change. *J. consult. Psychol., 21,* 95–103.

Rogers, C. R. (1959). A Theory of Therapy, Personality, and Interpersonal Relationships, As Developed in the Client-Centered Framework. In Koch, S. (ed.) (1959) *Psychology: A Study of a Science, Vol. 3. Formulations of the Person and the Social Context.* New York: McGraw-Hill, pp. 184–256.

Rogers, C. R. (1961a). *On becoming a person.* Boston: Houghton Mifflin.

Rogers, C. R. (1961b). Two divergent trends. In R. May (Ed.), *Existential psychology.* New York: London House.

Rogers, C. R. (1963). The actualizing tendency in relation to 'motives' and to consciousness. Nebraska Symposium on Motivation.

Rogers, C. R. & Dymond, R. (1954). *Psychotherapy and personality change.* Chicago: University of Chicago Press.

Rogers, C. R., Kell, B. L. & McNeill, H. (1948). The role of self-understanding in prediction of behavior. *J. Consult. Psychol., 12,* 174–86.

Rogers, C. R. & Skinner, B. F. (1956). Some issues concerning the control of human behavior. *Science, 3231,* 1057–66.

Sartre, J.P. (1953). *Existential psychoanalysis.* New York: Philosophical Library, Inc.

Scher, J. (Ed.) (1962). *Theories of the mind.* Glencoe, Ill.: Free Press.

Shlien, J. M. (1961). A client centered approach to schizophrenia. In A. Burton (Ed.), *Psychotherapy of the psychoses.* New York: Basic Books.

Shlien, J. M. (1962a). The self-concept in relation to behavior: theoretical and empirical research. In Stuart W. Cook (Ed.), *Research Supplement to Religious Education,* July-August.

Shlien, J. M. (1962b). Toward what level of abstraction of criteria? In H. Strupp & Luborsky (Eds.), *Research in psychotherapy,* Vol. II. Washington, D.C.: APA.

Skinner, B. F. (1953). *Science and human behavior.* New York: Macmillan.

Spence, K. (1944). The nature of theory construction in contemporary psychology. *Psychol.*

Rev., 51, 49–68.

Spiegelberg, H. (1960). *The phenomenological movement: an historical introduction.* Hague: Martinus Nyhoff.

Snygg, D. (1941). The need for a phenomenological system of psychology. *Psychol. Review, 48,* 404–24.

Snygg, D. & Combs, A. W. (1949). *Individual behavior.* New York: Harper.

Stephenson, W. (1953). *The study of behavior.* Chicago: University of Chicago Press.

Tolman, B. (1959). Principles of purposive behavior. In S. Koch (Ed.), *Psychology: a study of a science,* Vol. II. New York: McGraw-Hill.

Tymieniecka, A. (1962). *Phenomenology and science in contemporary European thought.* New York: Farrar, Straus and Cudahy.

Van Kaam, A. L. (1959). Phenomenal analysis: exemplified by a study of the experience of 'really feeling understood'. *J. Individ. Psychol., 15,* 66–72.

Wellek, A. (1957). The phenomenological and experimental approach to psychology and characterology. In H. P. David & H. von Bracken (Eds.), *Perspectives in personality theory.* New York: Basic Books.

White, R. W. (1959). Motivation reconsidered: the concept of competence. *Psychol. Review, 66,* 297–333.

Zener, K. (1958). The significance of experience of the individual for the science of psychology. In *Minnesota Studies in the Philosophy of Science,* Vol. II. Minneapolis: University of Minnesota Press.

CHAPTER 12

Empathy in Psychotherapy

Vital mechanism? Yes. Therapist's conceit? All too often. By itself enough? No.

In the English language, the word *empathy* is an abstract noun, of a peculiarly Germanic origin and influence. Being abstract, many definitions of empathy are afloat. As a personal quality, it is widely distributed, perhaps on the order of the distribution of eyesight. Everyone who experiences empathy is entitled to propose a definition. Mine is simple. Empathy is one of several essential forms of intelligence, an experiential form of such importance to adaptation that social and physical survival depends on it. It is a normal, natural, commonplace capacity, almost constant and almost unavoidable. Its nature does not determine its use. It is not in itself a 'condition' of therapy, but probably a precondition.

Empathy is an enabler. It may be necessary, but it is certainly not sufficient. Because it is not a rarity, it cannot be a private preserve of professional practice, but may be part of our professional vanity. Those who think, like Kohut, that it is a 'definer of the field' must then consider the majority of human beings as operatives in this field — a welcome thought to those of us who believe that principles of psychotherapy are simply refinements of the best in ordinary human relations. Those who think that empathy assures gentleness, benevolence, or reciprocity should consider that empathy can be an instrument of cruelty. The sadist, and especially the sado-masochist, makes intense use of empathy, albeit without sympathy. The sadist knows your pain, and takes pleasure in it. The hunter who 'leads' his flying target soars with the bird to kill it. Empathy does not always go hand in hand with sympathy.[1]

© 1997 by the American Psychological Association. First published in *Empathy Reconsidered: New directions in psychotherapy* edited by A. Bohart and L.S.Greenberg. Reprinted with permission.

[1.] Surely on the highway you have met that other driver who knows exactly what you want to do — change lanes, pass or turn — and deftly, persistently prevents you from doing it. That is empathy without sympathy.

It can, in fact, be a weapon of war, an advantage in every form of competition as well as in cooperation. The quarterback who throws the football goes with the ball, runs along with his receiver, who in turn may stand with the one throwing the ball to him. Unlike the hunter and bird, this empathy is interactive and relatively benign. The champion tennis player knows where a well-hit ball will land before it gets there and feels the tension of the strings, the sound and compression of the ball, and the hopelessly out-of-place position of his or her opponent. In short, empathy may be used to help or to harm, and it does not automatically communicate its activity or intention. It may not have any 'intention' of its own, other than to function, like any vital organ.

The manner in which this noun was invented is one source of confusion. It begins in a linguistic system that permits the combination of more than one word into a single new entity. For example, there is feeling, and there is the feeling of, or with, and so on. In the case of empathy, there is 'feeling in', or feeling into. In German they are combined into one word, a style for which the language is made famous in jokes, but which may have a real effect on the manner of thought, as well. When 'in-feeling' became a single combination, it was immediately capitalized *(Einfühlung)*, as are all German nouns, and thus became a new word, instantly, as if it were a new idea. Package is to concept as medium is to message. But *empathy,* the English translation of the active or verblike noun *Einfühlung,* is inert at its beginning. It will have to work its way up (or down) to the active form 'empathize'.

We posit a universal human capacity for empathy. Surely the French do not lack for it, as a nation or as a culture. But, as in many cultures, there is no such word in their language, just as there was none in German prior to the combined-word *Einfühlung* or in English prior to the introduced translation 'empathy'. Following World Wars I and II, and given the cultural antipathy to anything less than French (especially German), French translators have struggled with the word. 'A sympathetic penetration' is one phrase (in Swiss French). 'Affection' is another. The current solution is simply to spell the word *empathie,* meaning whatever English speakers mean by that. The Italians have long used the word *simpatico* in a general way, much as we now use empathy, and it may be that the more expressive climates and cultures did not need to invent a word to represent their sensitivities, as did the Teutonic German and British Anglo-Saxon tribes with their more brusque or formal manners.

Language influences thought, and thought influences action — sometimes the influence runs in reverse directions — but when a word is translated from its original setting, where it may have some specificity, it loses that specific meaning and becomes even more abstract. How and when did we get our version? This happened circa 1910 when E. B. Titchener, living in the United States, translated *Einfühlung* as empathy. Although Titchener was English, he studied in Leipzig with Wundt (the name of Wundt comes up constantly as a central influence in the culture that gave us *Einfühlung*). It was Wundt who defined the subject matter of psychology as 'immediate experience', and Titchener who spent most of his life investigating 'introspection', which are both viewpoints of great import in the floundering advancement of clinical psychology. Titchener's was sometimes called 'existential psychology'.

Empathy was a somewhat playful word at the beginning. Titchener considered that it exercised 'the muscles of his mind'. (He mixed his metaphors, as well.) *Einfühlung* was not related to pain so much as to appreciation, or even enjoyment. The 'pathy' in empathy introduced a significantly different association: with 'patheos': illness, suffering, or 'to suffer with'. Thus, although nicely clinical, it also appeared to have some distance from the word and idea of 'sym-pathy', and so offered psychologists an operation somewhat distinct from ordinary sympathetics by ordinary people. Then as empathy spread into the popular culture, it moved from being a noun to becoming a modifier, 'empathic' (as in empathic understanding), and from this, to becoming a verb, 'to empathize'. The Cartesian credo, 'I think, therefore I am', which had undergone so many transformations in psychology and comedy (I talk, therefore I feel; I dream, laugh, therefore . . .) turned into the vulgar psychological misconception of 'I empathize, therefore I am therapeutic'. What an unfortunate mistake. A noun has changed into a verb, and an attitude into a technique. How? It is done by the extraction and mechanization of procedures.

It may help to go back to another example, again from sports — good clean fun with no hidden psychological undercurrents. It is active, therefore visible in ways that intellectual empathy is not. An archer travels with her arrow; and this travel starts before the arrow flies, as she estimates distance, trajectory, strength, and so on. From the moment of release, the archer is in the space between arrow and target. Empathy is involved throughout the process of shooting an arrow.

However, there are machines that will compute the factors of speed, power, distance, and wind, as well as fire the shot. This is not empathy; this is sheer and mere performance. It is based on experience and knowledge derived from empathy, much as a thermometer is based on subjective human response to gradients of hot and cold, but it is merely derivative, cannot adjust, or invent, or even tell right from wrong performance.

When attitude becomes technique, empathy becomes a product in the marketing of psychology, a part of the entertainment vocabulary, and a sort of performance art for therapists. They have 'extracted the procedures'. Those who believe they are well-equipped with empathic sensitivity boast about it, and those who feel ill-equipped consider it a 'deficiency syndrome' to be repaired by sensitivity training. In our time, psychotherapy is featured in theatrical venues — professional films, TV talk shows, and dramatic cinema — that lead to the unfounded belief that what is most dramatic is most effective. Empathy is now a popular, if vulgarized, form of support and unreliable sincerity. The adolescent putative father in a sitcom tells his pregnant girlfriend who fears an abortion, 'I really empathize with that.' The president tells his TV audience of unemployed, 'I feel your pain.' A Columbia professor of law advises the prosecution in a televised murder trial to 'try to empathize more with the victims'. What does he have in mind? Empathy with the dead? Why not? It's something to think about. Or is he just confused, thinking that it is the same as sympathy?

Therapists and others now talk less about how well they understand someone. Instead, they perform 'feats of empathy'. Take, for example, Paul Goodman, a brilliant writer, theoretician, and sponsor of The Living Theater, one of the authors of the book *Gestalt Therapy* (Perls, Hefferline and Goodman, 1951). He writes that when, as a therapist, he is dealing with jealousy, 'I empathize completely. I can predict the next sentence' (Stoehr, 1994, p. 200). This is one of the more benign examples of 'empathy as performance art'. And it must be said that Goodman is worth serious attention as one of the more intelligent and articulate people in the field, even though he is an unconventional representative of it. He is really no more unconventional, no more theatrical, than his colleague Fritz Perls, whose ideas *became* conventions, except for his lesser-known original theory of 'Dental Aggression' (Stoehr, p. 82). In that connection, and not incidentally, Perls studied theater direction under Berthold Brecht in Berlin, where Brecht wrote, in *The Three Penny Opera*, 'What keeps a man alive? He feeds on others' (Brecht and Weill, 1934). Nor is this to suggest that the theatrical inclination is only in Gestalt therapy circles.[2] Sometime in the late 1950s, when Carl Rogers had become famous enough to be interviewed by *Time* magazine, the writer-editor asked what category this material would best fit. Rogers considered the available choices: art, literature, business, medicine, and so on, and said, only half-jokingly, 'How about theater?'

True, there is often high drama in psychotherapy. Too often that is exploited as entertainment. It does not excuse those therapists who boast about how empathic, or congruent they are. They have too easy a time of it with their self-proclaimed performance. And because it is their internal state, we have to take their word for it. Furthermore, even though it may indeed be true that a high degree of empathy is present, empathy is not enough. Empathy is not a theory of therapy, not even one of the 'conditions' proposed by Rogerians. It does not

---

[2.] Neither is it mere conjecture. Taylor Stoehr's book (1994) provides explicit testimony from Lore Perls that Fritz Perls' 'first love was the theater' and in my opinion it is evident that he never left it but imported that interest into his practice of psychotherapy. The same book presents a number of comments on the exercises in 'Dental Aggression': 'You had to see him in action, eating his patients alive, to understand what dental aggression was all about' (p. 134).

require 'contact between two people, one of whom is anxious'. It does not require two people; empathy is exercised in flying a kite. So, although empathy is an important and perhaps essential factor in the service of understanding, it is not in itself the hoped-for consequence of understanding.

Nor is empathy difficult to achieve. It happens. The problem is how to use it wisely and well. In my opinion, empathy has been overrated, underexamined, and carelessly though enthusiastically conceived — in short, treated like the Holy Grail, as 'received knowledge'. It may instead be a sort of dodge, a 'therapeutic costume', an act heavily tinged with pride and vanity. Empathy has been taken as both a means and end; it has become an easy substitute for the real motive, and the real work, in therapy — sympathy and understanding.

Sympathy — 'feeling for' — is a type of commitment. Empathy is not. Is it perhaps time to call sympathy 'an unappreciated way of being'? In my view, it works at a higher stage of moral development than empathy. In fact, empathy may have no more moral status than does the circulatory system. Understanding is a volitional effort and a service that empathy is not; if there is 'empathic' understanding, then it is the understanding that promotes the healing from within (within being the only possible source). The difficult task is to understand. Empathy alone, without sympathy, and even more, without understanding, may be harmful.

It is important to give recognition to empathy for all that it is, but it is also important to make sure that it does not, by thoughtless substitution, undermine and even obliterate the positive values of sympathy and understanding. This effect goes beyond the realm of psychological practice. A whole society is currently affected, slowly losing the vocabulary and consciousness of compassion. Insofar as concepts and practices in psychotherapy create this loss, they are helping to cause the illnesses they mean to cure.

INNOCENCE ABROAD: HISTORY RIDES IN A DUMBWAITER

Partly by accident, a coincidence of timing and interest, I was privileged to be a participant observer, a sort of bystander and witness, to the development of the theory of empathy as it took place at the University of Chicago after World War II. The university was a neighborhood composed of unique circumstances. George Herbert Mead, who had studied in Germany with Wilhelm Dilthey, had left his 'social interaction' tradition there, with Blumer and others who had compiled his posthumous collection of lectures into the book *Mind, Self, and Society* (Mead, 1934). The Division of Social Sciences was full of intellectual and interdisciplinary ferment. Bruno Bettleheim, who lived a few doors away, made a local name for himself as a master of antipathy, which actually helped define empathy by way of demonstrating its contrast. Heinz Kohut was just arriving from Austria (and lived in the next block), although it would be several years before he published his thoughts on empathy. He had not studied with Freud directly but did see him once at the train station in Vienna, when Freud was leaving under great duress to take his daughter Anna to safety in London, along with parts of his library, which contained some writings of Theodore Lipps. In addition, Martin Buber lectured in Rockefeller Chapel a few years later. With all of this, the university was a setting for the conjunction of several stars, who by and large avoided one another, sending their lines of influence through students. I was one of those.

Carl Rogers, already a major figure there, was beginning one of his most productive periods. He had a keen intelligence, a great talent for recognizing and assembling ideas and research findings, and a rather new theory and practice of psychotherapy that gave him such prominence that his advocacy would assure wide attention to a new idea. As the artist historian Ewa Kuryluk said, 'Sometimes history hibernates; at times it runs like a gazelle.' This was the time of the gazelle.

My special interest was cultural anthropology, particularly the 'sociology of knowledge'. Rogers and his school of thought, about which I was skeptical, were tempting opportunities. It was the period in which he was formulating and compiling his book *Client-Centered Therapy* (Rogers, 1951), which contained a major theoretical statement and a powerful philosophical position. I attended some of his courses and seminars and, through this, had the privilege of many casual meetings with him. His honesty, forthrightness, and decency won my respect to such a degree that I felt it would be a sort of betrayal to analyze this material from a sociological framework, which would have missed the most important substance of his work.

So, my interests turned back to prior questions: What do we know, how do we know it, and how does anyone understand another person? At our next meeting, I handed Rogers the book *The Philosophy of the 'AS-IF'* (Vaihinger, 1924). It is a theory of knowledge and of the treatment of ideas as fictions that we must imagine as being real, in order to discover their meanings. It was my hunch that there was value in this theory and that Rogers would have a better grasp than mine. At the same meeting, I also told him about another reading that had struck me as hilarious, written by or about the ideas of a psychologist named Theodor Lipps. To illustrate the idea, the writer, whose name I cannot recall, used the example of Viennese gentlemen who carried walking sticks and rolled umbrellas while they strolled the avenues. Why the canes? To replace the tails men had lost as they evolved from monkeys — extensions of themselves that they needed to feel their surroundings. We thought it funny, and we laughed at the writer's need to relate social science to that most-respected scientific establishment, Darwinism. But two things in the discussion were serious. One was the idea of extending oneself, found in both Vaihinger and Lipps. The other was the word used by Lipps, *empathy*. It caught our attention like a magnet, much as it currently has for the field of psychology. It seemed a word we dimly knew or recognised, or were waiting to hear.

It was in the air, but new to me, and I believe to Rogers, too. We talked about it, and we talked about the 'couvade', and the yawn, and so on. We had both seen the photographs in *Social Psychology* (Allport, 1923/1937) showing spectators who lifted one leg and strained with the pole vaulter as he tried to clear the bar above their heads. So we knew of empathy as 'ideo-motor', or sympathetic imitation, or something of that sort. We also knew of Titchener's work on introspection, but we certainly had not heard of his invention of this term or of any of his descriptions of empathy. It would have surprised us.

In my self-absorbed way, I took the idea of 'extensions' to heart and recalled such experiences as my juvenile-delinquent driving days. With friends, we drove cars through narrow passages, trying to barely 'click' the fenders against walls, trees, and other fenders. How can that be done? Your body, your self, extends into the body of your car. You are spread out into its dimensions, its wheels, fenders, and even the engine. You are in the machine. A scrape against the car is a scrape against yourself. In fact, you have such a sensitive feel for the speed of the engine and of the transmission that you sense the moment of synchronization of those two and can shift gears silently, without even using the clutch. I explained this to Rogers. He was interested but dubious — a more careful and methodical driver one seldom sees — and he was more interested in concepts and in people.

The next time we met, it was Rogers who was excited. Though wearing hat and coat and ready to leave, he beckoned me into his office, handed me the Vaihinger book without comment, and said, 'You know what we were talking about the other day? You ought to read Martin Buber, *I and Thou*. Have you heard of that?' I had not, but he pushed me out the door, saving me a confession of ignorance. The book was checked out of the Divinity Library, and by Russell Becker, a close friend and colleague of Rogers, the husband of Rogers' loyal secretary. Actually, it was the wrong book. The relevant work was Buber's *Between Man and Man* (Buber, 1933). Three paragraphs from that work were circulated to the staff a few weeks later (and will shortly be reproduced here to illustrate a significant difference between Rogers and Buber). What was not reproduced was Buber's statement on the page following these paragraphs, which contained his rather scornful dismissal of empathy. Speaking of his idea of 'inclusiveness', which is the relation between humans, and also between man and God (see Karen Armstrong's recent book, *The History of God*, 1993), Buber wrote, 'It would be wrong to identify what is meant here with the familiar but not very significant word 'empathy'. Empathy means, if anything, to glide with one's own feeling into the dynamic structure of an object, a pillar, or a crystal or the branch of a tree, or even an animal or man, and as it were, to trace it from within' (Buber, 1933, p. 97). But I did not read this page until some years later, nor did Rogers.

Buber was far ahead of us, closer to the original usage of the word *empathy*, and unlike psychologists, not in need of a 'clinical' view of this term.

Now we began to meet with a more regular focus on empathy. Rogers was engrossed in finishing his book and in some difficult clinical work as well. My work was to collect more ideas, more material for discussions. Late in 1948 a 1,000-page book on personality was sent by its author, Gardner Murphy, to Rogers, and this stupendous tome was handed to me. It had considerable information on empathy and sympathy, stating that the two were 'difficult to separate' (Murphy, 1947), a point that did not sit well with Rogers. He had deep misgivings about the idea of sympathy, basically because he thought it smacked of 'feeling sorry for, or looking down upon', both of which were reprehensible, or at least disrespectful attitudes, in his view. He also feared that being overly sympathetic might lead to an 'indulgent' attitude on the part of the therapist. Above all, he wanted to avoid any tendency to pity, which he considered to be not a kindness, but something approaching contempt. He spoke of the lasting effect of his visit to China as a young man with a missionary group, where he saw humans treated as animals, beasts of burden, and humans as prisoners who groveled. It made him sick with rage and made him 'wish he had a gun'.

I was taking a course with Professor Blumer to study the ideas of G. H. Mead. To my mind, it was a great and influential theory, which espoused 'taking the role of the other', but Rogers particularly disliked the notion of a 'role'. Although Mead used the term *sympathy* throughout, never empathy, I thought then and still do think that he was describing, early on and in wonderfully astute observations, an empathic process in every phase; he was describing the learning of the language and rules of the game, of social customs, in short, the whole of being human.

I brought in material from still another seminar, this one with the great biopsychologist Heinrich Kluver. Like Mead, he had studied in Germany, but of course he was born there, and knew Wundt, Titchener, Wertheimer, Kofka, and many others, including even Lipps. He was a man of enormous sophistication and modesty. In fact, he was quite shy. Like Kohut. Like Rogers. Intimate and expressive relationships were an effort, but also a delight to them. The class took place in his animal laboratory, where he studied the phenomenology of perception, working mainly with monkeys, to locate the neurological sites and mechanisms of perception. Sometimes he used himself as an experimental subject and related some of his experiences (Kluver, 1966). One afternoon in New Orleans, he had taken the drug mescaline and had gone for a walk. He had looked up at a wrought-iron balcony, and felt himself 'becoming that wrought iron. I took its shape. I WAS that wrought iron.'

We five students stared. This was 1949, and we had never heard of 'psychedelics'. But was this empathy too? I reported to this class, and then to Rogers, an incident from my childhood, around the age of nine or ten, when I had become a leaf. Resting on the grass, reading the *Wizard of Oz*, I had looked up to see a curled leaf, in a boatlike shape, slowly floating down from a high branch. As it rocked and turned in the air, I had become that leaf. I had understood why, given my shape and weight, I had to fall with a rocking motion. It was a physical and conceptual experience, that is, I had learned physics and logic from it. When the leaf landed, I became separate from it, happy and content. This had not seemed extraordinary. Didn't everyone do this? (I think so.)

Rogers did not like this story. He admired Kluver but may not have approved of drug use. I am certain that he did not at that time like the idea of self-induced hallucination. (Thirty years later, perhaps, yes.) He was working with two clients who were experiencing hallucinations. One of them, the 'easy' one, I later 'inherited'. The other, unbeknownst to me, was causing him a terrifying degree of stress. (That would have some bearing on his reservations — the 'as-if' — about empathy, and the distinction between Rogers and Buber.)

Meanwhile, in another section of the university, empathy was a concept commonly read about and discussed by graduate students (my wife among them) in art history. One assigned reading was *Abstracksion and Empathy* (Worringer, 1908/1948), first published a year before Titchener introduced the term in the United States. Its concept and language is quite explicit and well-thought-out within its field, even dealing with 'negative' as well as positive empathy. However, because it deals with art, which is considered by most to be 'inanimate', the idea of empathy did not make its way across the Quadrangles — about 600 yards — from one department to the other. If only we had known. The Foreword in Worringer's book describes his chance meeting with Georg Simmel at a museum in Berlin, where they talked about the idea of empathy. Georg Simmel! My hero! Revered as the Leonardo of sociology, he was first translated by Albion Small, a founder of the Department of Sociology at the University of Chicago. Our work in psychology might have been enlightened years earlier if Art and Science had been exchanging ideas, for Wispé's superb chapter (Wispé, 1994) on the history of empathy dates the idea back to 1873, with the work of Vischerin, again in the field of aesthetics.

None of this meant much, it seemed, to Rogers. For one thing, he did not care much about history, or origins, or social science in general, for that matter. He cared about individual psychology and contemporary meanings, some of which he was trying to create. At the same time, he was under intense personal pressure. I was not yet an 'insider' and did not know much of this until a few years later. Nor did I comprehend the greater effect until still later, when it was published in the biography *On Becoming Carl Rogers* (Kirschenbaum, 1979). (I did, however, know enough to avoid being interviewed by Kirschenbaum, not wanting to discuss or withhold material that Rogers himself, to my surprise, had chosen to reveal in the book.) In that, the reader can learn of a period, somewhere 'during the years 1949 through 1951', when Rogers was afraid that he might be going insane, and might be 'locked up and start to hallucinate' (which may have some bearing on his negative reaction to Kluver) and, in desperation, 'ran away' on a trip with his wife that lasted over two months (Kirschenbaum, 1979, pp. 191–2). He speaks of his work with a client with whom he 'felt trapped' (how true) and felt that

> many of her insights were sounder than mine, and this destroyed my confidence in myself, and I got to the point where I could not separate my 'self' from hers. I literally lost the boundaries of myself. The situation is best summarized by one of her dreams in which a cat was clawing my guts out, but did not wish to do so. (Kirschenbaum, 1979, p. 192)

Reading these pages some time after 1980 was a shock to me. I already knew about the case, having been told about it by some older staff members. And I had actually met this woman; what is more, in my own mind I had always referred to her as 'the cat woman'. She had stepped out of Rogers' office, and we passed in the hall. She'd said she 'had to come back to see Carl again in a couple of hours' and invited me to lunch. She seemed both beseeching and commanding. I did not like her face. She once had perhaps been beautiful, but now, in early middle age, she appeared seductive and menacing, with her flat, symmetrical face, and dark-blue, slanted eyes. I made some excuse about lunch. She had followed me to the first-floor research room and there talked about some research she had recently completed. She was very astute. It was a great study of learning, under conditions of actual practice compared with imaginary practice. I thought she must be Carl's research colleague from another university (Canadian, perhaps) and made a note about the research for future quotation. Although she timidly was seeking friendship, she was oddly possessive about the Counseling Center, the arrangement of the desks, the dirty curtains, and so on. This so annoyed me that I later told Carl about the research, meaning to get her academic address, but also complained about her possessiveness, and said, 'Who the hell does she think she is?' He looked stricken. I will never forget his eyes. He shook his head, wiped the cup of his famous thermos bottle, screwed it on, and quietly said to come back for a talk next week. A few days later, he was gone. What a blunder, mine.

To get some idea of 'who she thought she was', one can read that section of the biography (Kirschenbaum, 1979). Writing this 45 years later, I have a much more sympathetic understanding of this intelligent woman, trying to make her place in the world and to find recognition, trying to find relationships in a strange place, this being perhaps at the period of her final visits, while she probably had a sense of losing her struggle. She may well have been feeling as much desperation and anxiety as was her therapist.

How does this relate to Rogers' ideas about empathy? In the book *Client-*

Centered Therapy, Rogers makes his first published statement about empathy. There he describes the act of assuming 'the client's frame of reference' and calls it 'empathic understanding' (Rogers, 1951, p. 29). This is not empathy per se, but a particular type of understanding, distinct from the types of understanding that come from external frames, such as diagnostic, or judgmental, or suspicious interrogation. Furthermore, the counselor must '*communicate something of this empathic understanding to the client*' (italics added). Rogers then quotes a passage from a previously unpublished, but now deservedly famous, statement by Raskin, which is about a kind of understanding that represents 'the non-directive attitude'. Although it does not use the term *empathy,* the description forecasts the present-day concept.

Raskin concludes with the words, 'because he [the counselor] is another, and not the client, the understanding is not spontaneous but must be acquired, and this through the most intense, continuous and active attention to the feelings of the other, to the exclusion of any other type of attention' (Rogers, 1951, p. 29). Important to note, such understanding is an act of attention, an effort, and not at all the kind of instant, immediate, spontaneous understanding that many associate with the word *empathy.* Rogers (1951) then adds to Raskin's statement a most interesting qualification, saying that this

> experiencing with the client . . . is not in terms of emotional identification . . . but rather an empathic identification, where the counselor is perceiving the hates and hopes and fears of the client through immersion in an empathic process, but without himself, as counselor, experiencing those hates and hopes and fears. (p. 29)

Plainly, empathic is still a modifier, adjective, or adverb, not the supposedly active noun *empathy.* But the difference between 'emotional' and 'empathic' is not clear, then or now. What is clear is that Rogers is putting distance between the feelings and experiences of the client and his own. Later, he would entirely abandon the idea of identification of any kind, when, around 1956, he drafted the 'as-if' clause (Koch, 1959). I do not know the exact timing of his thoughts as he made these distancing revisions in published writing, but they do follow his experience with the client about whom he was so disturbed, and when his own identity was so threatened.

Turning back to Buber, here are the three paragraphs that so impressed Rogers around 1949 to 1950.

> A man belabors another, who remains quite still. Then let us assume that the striker suddenly receives in his soul the blow which he strikes; the same blow; that he received it as the other who still remains still. For the space of a moment he experiences the situation from the other side. Reality imposes itself upon him. What will he do? Either he will overwhelm the

voice of the soul, or his impulse will be reversed.

A man caresses a woman, who lets herself be caressed. Then let us assume that he feels the contact from two sides — with the palm of his hand still, and also with the woman's skin. The two-fold nature of the gesture, as one that takes place between two persons, thrills through the depth of enjoyment in his heart and stirs it. If he does not deafen his heart he will have — not to renounce enjoyment — but to love.

I do not in the least mean that the man who has had such an experience would from then on have this two-sided sensation in every such meeting — that would perhaps destroy his instinct. But the one extreme experience makes the other person present to him for all time. A transfusion has taken place after which a mere elaboration of subjectivity is never again possible or tolerable to him.[3] (Buber, 1933, p. 196)

Reference has already been made to the theme of 'inclusiveness' in Buber's approach to an 'empathic' relationship. In 1957, he and Rogers met, and that meeting is published (Anderson and Cissna, 1997). In it, Rogers asks Buber, ' "How have you lived so deeply . . . and gained such an understanding . . . without being a psychotherapist?" [Buber laughs; audience laughs]' (p. 17). It is indeed a funny 'throwaway' question from Rogers, the former Divinity School student, who knows and welcomes the fact that many 'untrained' humans have keen sensitivities, to the theologian who also knows and welcomes that. Buber explains (p. 20) that he did in fact study three terms in psychiatry — 'first in Leipzig, where I was a student of Wundt' (again, Wundt) and afterwards in Berlin with Mendel, and Zurich with Bleuler. He did not intend to become a therapist:

It was just a certain inclination to meet people. And, as far as possible to, just to change if possible something in the other *but also* let me be changed by him. At any event, I had no resistance — I put no resistance to it. I already then as a young man — I felt I had not the right to change another if I am not open to be changed by him, as far as it is legitimate. . . I cannot be, so to say, above him, and say 'No! I'm out of the play. You are mad.' (p. 21)

He then describes more experiences in which he was suffering for a friend who

---

[3.] It is my hope that the reader will study Buber's words more than in one reading, to imagine, reflect on, visualize, and perhaps remember. These words express profound levels of thought. Rogers wanted to move closer to this position, but something prevented that, at least in early writing. Also, note that Buber's second paragraph is, in part, about sexuality. It is strange that psychologists, so preoccupied with both sex and empathy, have little to say about their connection. One exception is in *The Talk Book*, by Gerald Goodman (1988), who expands on the above paragraph by Buber in a more prosaic paraphrase.

had been killed in the war, 'imagining the real', feeling it not just in an optical way of imagining but 'just with my body' (1933, pp. 42–5). Most telling, most relevant to this comparison, is the description of 'a tragic incident' in which a young man came to seek his advice. Buber was preoccupied and talked with him but did not really 'meet' him. The young man went away and committed suicide.

For Buber, there is no 'as-if'. He does not want that. It would preclude the possibility of the 'I-Thou'. Buber is willing to be changed by the other. That is the choice of 'inclusiveness'. His tragedies — grief, guilt — and his fears, hates, and hopes are not the same as those of Rogers. Thus, for one person, Rogers, it was essential to preserve boundaries; for the other, Buber, it was to dissolve them. Therefore, these two, among the greatest humanists of our time, espouse different theories of empathic understanding. If there is nothing else to be drawn from this, we can at least conclude that all personality theory is autobiographical. Variations on a theme stem from differences in personal experience. Everything is personal.

In addition, if they do not know each other's particular experience of tragedies, hopes, and fears, they will not readily understand the basis or meaning of each other's theories of self-in-relationship, although they might have had (in fact, they did have) more theoretical similarities than are apparent in their writings and in these dialogues.

Finally, it is worth noting that when Rogers became involved with large 'person-centered' groups around 1970, and no longer felt such personal responsibility for the individual client, or need for such detachment, he was sometimes so moved that, as he put it, he 'wept buckets of tears'. Not 'as-if' but quite real tears, I am sure. And with both Rogers and Buber, we have seen that reaction to failure or disappointment with self sometimes determined theory that later influenced the professions and the world at large. Fortunately, this only applies to the subsidiary issue of the 'as-if' not the general theory of empathy. Unfortunately, there is no such general theory.

A CASE OF 'REVERBERATIVE' EMPATHY

Although empathy works as a more or less constantly active system, found everywhere in daily life, clinicians look for special displays in 'clinical' cases as if they were exceptional. Here is a bit of such material. Why this particular case? Because it has been published — cited as an 'exquisite' example of empathy, most of it recorded, dramatic to the point of obscuring its defects — and because it contains a special theory of psychological disintegration in the psychotic state (Shlien, 1961). When Rogers read it for the second time, some years after his experience in the Wisconsin 'Schizophrenia Project', he called the theory 'a work of genius'. So it is, this theory being taken directly from the writings of a certified genius, Jean-Paul Sartre, in his study of the lie, self-deception, and the consequent loss of self (Sartre, 1956).

During months of strenuous therapy, I learned many things that enter into the experience of empathy — the smell of fear, for instance. That smell is stark, intense, and common to the patients who are subjected to electroconvulsive shock. Many expect to die, strapped down and helpless, to lose consciousness, and never regain it. This patient felt that way. He thought I had ordered that treatment (although I had distinctly forbidden it, a ward physician ordered it to subdue violent outbursts), and Mike, the patient-client, wanted to kill me in return. I didn't blame him.

Lacking space, not much can be reported here. Mike was a former Navy frogman, very strong, a carpenter by trade, and usually good-natured. Easily goaded into foolish escapades, he had been in two other hospitals before his parents committed him (after promising him it was 'just a visit') to the rather gruesome state institution where I consulted. He heard his thoughts coming out of the television set. His mind was transparent; he was the object of an experiment by the FBI; he raged, wept, begged, denied, was sly, and was life-threatening. Often during interviews, guards were stationed outside my office door by the hospital director (who was also my client). Mike and I went through hell together — he in his own hell, I in mine with my own fears, and both hells intermingled. Eventually there came a time when he understood that much more about his life and had so much more control that he was given a grounds pass, and we could meet on the lawn, alone and safe.

At some point during the last of these meetings, he began to cry softly, saying, 'They talk about love and affection. I know what that means. The only good thing I ever had [his engagement to a girl] was taken away from me, broken up.' He blew his nose, dropped his handkerchief, and as he picked it up, glanced at me. He saw tears in my eyes. He offered me the handkerchief, then drew it back because he knew he had just wiped his nose on it and could feel the wetness on his hand. We both knew this, and each knew the other knew it; we both understood the feel and the meaning of the handkerchief, the stickiness and texture, the sympathy of the offering and the embarrassment of the withdrawal, and we acknowledged each other and the interplay of each one's significance to the other. It is not the tears, but the exquisite awareness of dual experience that restores consciousness of self (and not a word was spoken during this episode) (Shlien, 1961, p. 316).

In our final meeting on the lawn, Mike said, 'I went to church yesterday, Doc, and I said a prayer that this would never happen again. I said a little prayer for you, too, that you could help me and always be well yourself.' Of course I was touched, as he was, but did not simply express our mutual appreciation. I said, 'It sounds like you are trying to say goodbye, Mike, and to leave us feeling OK about each other.' Without this, there would have been only empathy, not empathic understanding. Yes, he explained, he absolutely had to get out of here and could not come to see me at the university. Where he lives, 'a person has to be goofy to go to a psychiatrist'. He was discharged before I could see him again.

The significant empathy in this was relational, interactive empathy. The rest — the kite, the straining rope, the rendering of meaning to art — is only basic. What you see in this episode on the hospital lawn is a series of mutual, reciprocal, complex 'reverberations'. Although it need not be wordless, it is, and takes place at a speed beyond our ability in speech. I know his sincerity, his fear, his desperate hope, and his recognition of my caring for his welfare and know that he cares for mine. There is something full of grace in his gesture with the snotty handkerchief and something ungainly, not 'graceful', about it at all. It has the ambivalence that characterizes most of life. He knows that I saw his offer, wanted and did not want to accept it, and why, and that I understood, he understood — we understood, in a series of 'bouncing between us' consequences, for each and for both.

What does this mean to us? It means public confirmation, and internally, self-affirmation. These 'reverberations', in infinite regress (or progress), tell Mike that he can know, he does know, he can be known, understood, and can reciprocate in kind. For Mike, knowing means sanity, no less. To me, it suggests that, although 'growth motive' is a wonderful and spirited idea, it is more elementary — that the animal lives to grow, but the relationally construed person lives to know. Knowing confirms being, existence, and humanity, and for the insane, confirms the restoration of sanity. But knowing takes some degree of communicated confirmation.

In silent empathy, those bouncing 'reverberations' not only take up a large portion of consciousness but also cost us subterranean uneasiness and a good deal of energy for the storage of these unsettled and unconfirmed understandings. It is almost like living with half-truths; hard to make use of these largely voiceless, invisible, unconfirmed signals. What is more, the organ of empathy is not so familiar, not so palpable, or distinct. It takes the whole of the mind-body composite, and it is often wordless. This most certainly does not mean thoughtless. Quite the opposite! True, empathy is more sensational than perceptual, but that only means it requires still more in extra effort of 'cognitive processing' for humans who want to examine and understand their experience, rather than simply to have it.

Empathy operates on data such as smell, sight, and sound: the smell of fear; the sight of tears, of blushing, and of yawning; and the sound of cadences, tone, sighs, and howls. It operates at what we might think of as primitive levels, cellular, glandular, olfactory, chemical, electromagnetic, autonomic, postural, gestural, and musical — rhythmical, more than lexical. If such modalities seem far-fetched, consider the pupil of the eye. For a long time, it had a status less observed than was sweating, or flaring of the nostrils. But in folk-psychology, gem traders were said to watch the pupils of the buyer's eyes for signs of special interest. In academic psychology, the pupil was well-known mainly for the phenomenon of contraction when exposed to light; it was a favorite in the laboratory because so readily conditioned. Only a few decades ago, Eckhard Hess (Hess, 1975) and colleagues demonstrated with unmistakable evidence what those shrewd jade dealers had noticed. The pupil dilates when one sees what is interesting, attractive, and lovable, such as when a mother sees an infant or when a man sees a beautiful woman. Even more relevant in this latter case, when her pupils are dilated, her face looks softer, more beautiful, and above all, his pupils will dilate in response. Neither (unless they are trained observers) is likely to be aware of this. It just happens. It is involuntary. It is a routine, though seldom-recognized, example of the theory of empathy, in action. Like blood pressure, heart rate, and ovulation, some individuals can sense pupillary reactions, and even control them, but for most, it is subliminal. Because the interactions of our pupils come from such an unrecognized source, some imagine it to be 'intuition' — a lazy as well as false explanation. The fact is, the information is clear and direct, replicable, and easily visible (especially in blue eyes).

Ideas about 'intuition' confuse and mislead, as do other lures such as metaphors and myths. They are especially damaging to our less-obvious psychological realities, such as empathy. We say that someone 'speaks from the heart' if he is sincere, 'decides with her heart' if she seems romantic. Really, hearts do not speak. They inform, by clenching, racing, and so on, in response to some experience. A friend had his heart replaced with a pump. He still spoke with the same values, convictions, and sincerity as before. Where was his 'heart'? In the hospital garbage, long gone. But that was only his flesh-and-blood heart, not his 'real' heart. Perhaps he 'speaks from his pump'? That is no more likely and much less poetic. There is a 'psychological organ' we call 'heart'. It has a memory of heart experience, with functional autonomy, which is a functional equivalent of the flesh and blood organ. It is in this sense that empathy is an organ, as well as a form of intelligence. If it is an organ related to intelligence, it is organ-as-agency of intelligence (i.e., gathering information). Why this design? Perhaps it is an experience-seeking part of the therapist, or other humans, in the way that some other species or artificial models are heat-seeking or phototropic. Empathy is like a guidance system: it gets you to the airport but makes no decisions about what to do once you are there.

We may have doubts about these and other subtle 'ingredients' in spite of the evidence from such phenomena as the pupils of the eye. Electromagnetic? It sounds impossible. Yet it alters our cells and body chemistry. Try for yourself a crystal radio in an AM frequency. You act as an antenna. There will be tiny changes in the amplitude of your body. The crystal will change dimensions. You may hear music (or voices) with low-frequency headphones. Change your position or temperature, and the reception will change. Other such effects remain to be discovered, or uncovered (as with pupils), and while some will be false leads, some even too ephemeral to study, modalities now hidden will surface. However subtle, these mind-body interrelationships are more substantial than some notions of the physical world in which we place considerable confidence. The electron is only a theory. But it works so well, that is, explains so much (but not all) that it seems real.

Empathy, on the other hand, is not much of a theory, explains hardly anything, tells us nothing of the 'mechanisms', but it is an experiential actuality for many people, and generally considered an established fact. That 'fact' is so recently discovered and named that it seems new and fashionable. Without doubt it is primitive, quite ancient. Whole flocks of birds do it, bees do it, even recent PhDs do it. When domestic animals do it, humans call them 'smart'. When humans do it, they consider it elementary, from the heart, a sort of 'gut reaction', and a saving grace to counter the psychologists' suspicion of 'over-intellectualization'. This attractive subscribing to the 'wisdom of the body' is one-sided and unfortunate. Empathy should not be a denial of the brain. Some of our most advanced modern ideas may rely on empathy. Einstein's 'thought experiments' demonstrate the launching of an imaginary object into space, accompanied by the genius (as the archer goes with the arrow?) and upon return to earth, there is new understanding of time and space.

Does this exercise of empathy restore the supremacy of brain over body? Oddly, it cannot favor either, because, now we know, they are one. It is new but public knowledge that a part of the neural tube, forming in the neonate, is squeezed down into the lower cavity, creating the 'enteric nervous system' (Blakeslee, 1996, p. B5). The brain is not only that encased in the skull. A part, connected by the vagus nerve, is actually in the abdominal tissue. Biological study finds the same neurons and transmitters in each part, both formed by the original neural crest. When the theory of empathy is developed, it will support the restoration of the 'whole person' — an idea too long submerged by poorly informed mind-body disputes.

REFERENCES

Allport, F. (1937). *Social psychology*. Boston: Houghton Mifflin. (Original work published 1923.)

Anderson, R. & Cissna, K. N. (1997). *The Martin Buber — Carl Rogers dialogue: A new transcript with commentary*. Albany: State University of New York Press.

Armstrong, K. (1993). *A history of God*. New York: Ballantine Books.

Blakeslee, S. (1996, January 23). Complex and hidden brain in the gut makes cramps, butterflies and valium. *The New York Times*, pp. B5, BLO.

Brecht, B. & Weill, K. (1934). Ballad of Mack the Knife. On *Three Penny Opera* [record]. New York: Columbia MasterWorks.

Buber, M. (1933). *Between man and man*. London: Kegan Paul.

Goodman, G. (1988). *The talk book*. New York: Rodale Press.

Hess, E. H. (1975). *The tell-tale eye*. New York: Van Nostrand Reinhold.

Kirschenbaum, H. (1979). *On becoming Carl Rogers*. New York: Dell.

Kluver, H. (1966). *Mescal and mechanisms of hallucinations*. Chicago: University of Chicago Press.

Koch, S. (Ed.) (1959). *Psychology: A Study of a Science* (Vol. 3). New York: McGraw-Hill.

Mead, G. H. (1934). *Mind, self, and society*. Chicago: University of Chicago Press.

Murphy, G. (1947). *Personality: A biosocial approach*. New York: Harper and Brothers.

Perls, F., Hefferline, R. F. & Goodman, P. (1951). *Gestalt therapy*. New York: Julian Press.

Rogers, C. R. (1951). *Client-centered therapy*. Boston: Houghton Mifflin.

Sartre, J-P. (1956). *Self deception and falsehood*. In W. Kaufman (Ed.), *Existentialism from Dostoevsky to Sartre*. New York: Meridian Books.

Shlien, J. (1961). A client-centered approach to schizophrenia: First approximation. In A. Burton (Ed.), *The psychotherapy of the psychoses*. New York: Basic Books.

Stoehr, T. (1994). *Here, now, next: The origins of Gestalt therapy*. San Francisco: Jossey-Bass.

Vaihinger, R. (1924). *The philosophy of the 'AS-IF'*. London: Routledge Kegan Paul.

Wispé, L. (1994). History of the concept of empathy. In N. Eisenberg & J. Strayer (Eds.) *Empathy and its Development*. Cambridge, England: Cambridge University Press.

Worringer, W. (1948). *Abstraksion and empathy*. New York: International Universities Press. (Original work published 1908.)

CHAPTER 13

The Robert W. White School

(with Ronald F. Levant)

The Robert W. White School was set up in 1972 as a learning environment and therapeutic private school for public service. This is a 'special needs' day school, an alternative for adolescents, most of whom have been labeled as emotionally disturbed. They don't like that term and neither do we, but in fact they have much to be disturbed about. Those disturbing conditions of their lives are what we try to change, or at least counter, so that education can take place. We simply call them our 'kids' (so do they) and, though the first 30 had been excluded from 47 different schools, they often turned out to be talented and beautiful survivors of a world that has been less than welcoming to them.

Professor Robert W. White was one of the architects of that star-crossed program, Clinical Psychology and Public Practice, 'CP³' as it is known to those who have followed the recent history of the Graduate School of Education. At Harvard, Professor White developed the theory of competence as motivation, and the new school was named to honor him and to capitalize on the foundations of his theory. We believe that the development of any competence has general learning effects, that more challenging, novel, and highly valued competencies generalize to self-esteem, and that both cognitive and emotional growth stems from that. Self-esteem is the antidote for crippling shame of previous failures, and the fear of new learning ventures. Obviously we stress the factors of security, health, and strength since these, rather than deficiencies, are the base from which competence is gained.

Planned as one of several intended support and training bases for the CP³ Program, the Robert White School is now 'free-standing', an operation prized on

First published in 1974: John Shlien and Ronald F. Levant, 'The Robert W. White School', *Harvard Graduate School of Education Association Bulletin*, Fall 1974, Vol. XIX, No. 1, pp. 12–18. Reprinted by kind permission of The Harvard Graduate School of Education and Ronald F. Levant.

its own merits, and more widely related to the entire School of Education (and even to Harvard College) as a site for training and research. Aged two, it was an infant that had to grow up too fast, like the children it serves. They come from East Boston, Charlestown, Revere, Chelsea, Winthrop, the North End, and part of the West End.

The school is not yet of the community. Located in the Erich Lindemann Center in downtown Boston, the $15m building, of a style called neo-brutalism, is too expensive, too elegant, too intimidating; but we humanized our part of it, sometimes to the dismay of the management. It also has advantages: space is provided by the Department of Mental Health; there is nearby and friendly medical service for emergencies; the Superintendent, Dr. Gerald Klerman, is both our landlord and advisor; it is new, and that means (1) *fireproof* and with (2) *super adequate lavatory facilities* (as well as gym and swimming pool). Lack of 1 and 2 are by far the biggest obstacles to obtaining certification of a school in Boston, and certification is valuable to a private alternative school, especially if it wants to maintain public school connections for the eventual successful 'return of the excluded'.

The project also remains a Harvard-initiated and connected effort. The majority of its founders, and past or present board members: Robert White, Chris Dowell, Ted Sizer, John Shlien, Ron Levant, Charles Leftwich, Walter McCann, Blenda Wilson, have been Harvard affiliated. The staff has come largely from Harvard: one professor, five doctoral students, seven master's degree students, four undergraduates, and several volunteers. There are also graduates of MIT, Boston and Northeastern Universities, as well as some who held no degrees but were long-time residents of the communities with special qualifications. We're well aware of the risk of condescension, the ethos of the 'Christmas basket'. That isn't the way it happens. We aren't there for the quick fix and self-glorification. If Harvard has high quality to offer in an enduring program, to what better use could we put ourselves?

OUR KIDS

Our 1970 survey informed us that in Lindemann Center's 'catchment area' (a despicable term adopted by NIH [National Institutes of Health, Ed.] from sanitary engineering) with a population numbering 120,000, some 1,000 adolescents were in need of the services we planned. Within three months of our opening in 1972, court clinics, probation officers, and schools offered 150 referrals. Of these, we took 30, roughly in their order of arrival. Thirty boys and girls, most white, there by order of courts and authorities, scared and defiant, hopeful but skeptical, determined to be tough, new to us and for the most part to each other. They brought cliques, bigotry, a high degree of interest in drugs, sex, money, cars, entertainment — all those adult prerogatives — but seemingly little interest in school, where most had failed more than once, being on the average three years behind grade level.

It's a formula for excitement at best, trouble at worst. We had both. Within the first few months, not only did the kids fight each other, but brought knives, chains, and even a gun. Teachers were threatened, hit, kicked, burned, scratched, choked, cursed, and stolen from. Visitors entered at their peril, including police, who were punched in acts of daring for their invasion of what was becoming a protected turf. None of this violence was invented at the school. It was brought in from experiences outside — taught by adults. Within the year, teachers were also hugged, kissed, gifted, helped, loved and trusted — by the same kids.

After the first year, weapons were rarely seen. If carried, they are checked voluntarily with a counselor. They aren't needed for protection inside. Have we disabled these survivors of the jungle by domestication? It seems not so. Instead they need less to put all their wit and energy into war against the world — these 30 out of 1,000. Not that the world doesn't remain tough, tempting, and predatory. Fagin lives — runs a bait shop, a bar, a doughnut counter, deals in auto parts, radios, little girls, guns, any saleable piece of life or property.

Who are these kids? Socio-economically disadvantaged, of course, but also bearing streaks of genius. They are often bright, talented, and resourceful.

A girl hospitalized for nine years, from age seven, known as 'the animal' in the hospital.

'The worst school phobic in East Boston' (who comes on the train and has seldom missed a day in school).

A 16-year-old boy who reads at second grade level, has been in 19 foster homes, and has a plastic ear drum and kneecap.

It is more comfortable to return to statistics. About 70 percent of our families are not intact. Commonly, the one parent is an overwhelmed mother with as many as 13 children. Half live in housing projects, and three-quarters receive welfare assistance. Homes are often chaotic, tragic sudden death or injury are frequent and frequently witnessed by those survivors who are our students. Not that our kids have the most wretched lives in history. Their parents may have had harder times. They say they did.

Given all this, we start with a pupil-teacher ratio of 3:1. Intensive programs are expensive, but these teachers have to re-engage troubled kids in the process of learning; act as substitute parents where there is illness and distress; give individual attention to overcome initial inabilities in reading; be on hand to cushion violent interaction. As both staff and students become more experienced in their mutual work, the school can absorb more students, increase the size of classes, reduce the per pupil cost, expand the curricular offerings. Where a school of strangers needs to start with a 3:1 ratio, or even 1:1, a more mature one can operate with a 5:1, and eventually, we think, an 8:1 ratio. The ratio should not be fixed, but functional, changing with the balance of experienced and inexperienced people.

How big should we be? The answer is a function of staff capacity, not a fixed number. The whole unit should be no larger than the number of students who, with their families and supporting agencies, can be known intimately by half of the staff. That sets our maximum around 50.

If there should be more, they should be in separate schools. Those might be spin-offs, started by present staff out of their experience and training, or units integrated into public schools after teacher exchanges.

HOW MUCH SHOULD IT COST?

Money — how to get it and what to do with it — is a constant problem. We charge no tuition. A relatively small proportion of the funds come from private donors and foundations: primarily the Permanent Charity Fund, Godfrey Hyams Trust, Gardiner Howland Shaw Foundation. Public funding comes from the Departments of Special Education, Youth Services, Welfare, Office for Children, the City of Boston's Committee on Safe Streets, and NIMH [National Institute of Mental Health, Ed.]. A large proportion of our administrative staff time is devoted to requesting, appealing, negotiating, reporting, accounting, and evaluating for funding purposes — understandable and unavoidable, but a drain on energy that should go into service. Luckily, some prime administrative training results from the experience.

Both public and private funding sources are inclined to give planning grants, start-up funds, and 'seed money' in the hope that someone else will pick up the longer-term operational costs. This leads to a game of 'musical chairs' for sustained support, and must be one of the less valid reasons for the typically short life span of alternative schools. Entering our third year, we are at once thriving and precarious. That balance, as we see it, is the way it *should* be. An endowment is not part of our philosophy. Neither is permanence. We started, and will remain, a temporary institution, responsive to need. It is, however, a condition of risk, healthy, but vulnerable to untimely and sudden death through legislative or bureaucratic misfortunes.

How much should it cost? 'However much it costs' was the answer of the former Commissioner of Mental Health when we told him about the lives of some of our kids. More than Harvard tuition?[1] Yes, the per pupil cost has ranged

---

[1] Harvard tuition, though, is subsidized by many additional thousands of dollars per student via endowments.

from $3,000 to over $5,500. When the budget was painfully restricted in the first year, the staff voluntarily reduced their already modest salaries, which take two-thirds of the yearly income. As with all community mental health and other public service programs, there is the question of how much should go for the support of middle level professional salaries. Not only are our salaries modest (around $800 per month), but the range is narrow; the highest fulltime salary (the Director) is only 1 1/3 times the lowest. Still, the income of the staff is at the intermediate level (in Boston, read $14,000 for a family of four), while the kids and their families are at welfare and poverty levels. The consequent disparity in lifestyles and values — who wears jeans and prefers yogurt to steak — is noticeable.

We try to return some of the funds directly to the population they were designed to help. Partly for this reason, we put 15–20 percent of our total budget into direct student assistance. This includes money for food, clothing, transportation, medical and dental care, and recreation. In addition, students can earn up to $19.00 a week by attending classes and working at various jobs in the school or as teaching assistants. This sum is paid by check at the end of the week, not as immediate reinforcement à la 'behavior mod'. It is rather to provide some future orientation for kids whose experience makes them doubt tomorrow. It is also to provide an earned allowance, the only source of legitimate money for most, and to provide it in a weekly lump sum that enables some possibility of consumer education. That gets them to the bank, where one 13-year-old learned in two days to write his own last name as an endorsement, and where others start savings accounts for the first time in their lives. Imposing middle-class values? Most radicals have savings accounts, as do the masses of Russia and China.

Besides the direct student assistance, the budget provides for many services outside the school: family therapy and guidance, welfare counseling, summer programs, legal aid, emergency services of all kinds. Though it is a day school, after-hours work absorbs a large proportion of staff time, including midnight and weekend calls.

While direct student aid and extra-school services could be offset against the per pupil educational cost, those very offsets are a feature of our educational program. The question, 'what price Special Education?' remains. Will society pay that cost? One way or another, willingly or unwillingly, it does. Burglary and shoplifting, now 70 percent a juvenile offense, and the petty crime of the street hustler, have considerable costs, but also murder and bank robbery in our sections of the city are sometimes committed by 25-year-old youths — sometimes friends or acquaintances of our kids. What of those costs?

We have thought of diverting some funds to an experiment in which the welfare family income is supplemented by our per pupil cost. Of course we could not do it with state funds, but the cost of a single child in a residential school, if given to a poverty level mother and nine children, would double that family's income. It could buy more space, comfort, dignity, and nourishment. But if, as Bettleheim declares, love is not enough, money is not enough either. Along with concerns toward redistribution of income, our work tends toward a kind of 'emotional (i.e., non-monetary) communism'. For the staff it involves sharing our lives — our time, energy, living space, personal resources. Most citizens would rather share their dollars.

A CURRICULUM FOR WHAT?

The curriculum, aiming to provide the experience of competence in the service of self-esteem, can contain almost any subject, from whittling to electronics. Especially so when geared to the search for each child's genius and each teacher's specialities as they develop. Some of our subjects are offered because they are 'basic skills' (reading, writing), are required conventional wisdom (history), or analytic exercises (math), but some are there because students asked for them or teachers enjoy them. The roster of courses includes the core area subjects, transferable in the same credit system used by the Boston Public Schools — mathematics, social studies, language, arts, science. Plus — photography, electronics, skin diving, auto mechanics, arts, crafts, shop, music, dance, drama, sex education, consumer education, and juvenile law. As everyone knows, these subjects have important by-products. 'Curriculum' describes what is offered and how it is taught. It cannot predict all that is learned. Auto mechanics is a way of teaching math to a boy who wants to compute the cubic capacity of an engine, or to read a shop manual. Sex education deals with anatomy (the most interesting parts), with human relations, and moral values. Skin diving teaches confidence in a strange element, even to non-swimmers; makes the physiology of oxygen transfer, volume and pressure of gas, and other topics, vital to the boy or girl who wants to explore an underwater world in more than fantasy.

In the first two years methods are various. Whatever works, whatever captures the imagination, whatever makes for the right combination of challenge and comfort. Soma cubes, Polyhedra dice, geo-boards, pocket calculators, peer-teaching, traditional tables, or balancing the teacher's checkbook, as long as the method is servant to the learner. We subscribe to at least a two-factor theory of learning. Beyond that, methods are subordinate to the relationship. As we take on the mission of the laboratory school, we will test some practices, and we might invent a technique as esoteric as using biofeedback and audio-visual instruments for instance. But for the most part our successes come from the application of what is well known — love, attention, concern, respect. These cannot be exported like techniques.

Besides subject and methods, everyone wants to know about goals. Alternative schools must have individualized alternative goals. They must also have some general, multi-dimensional goals, e.g. 'to make life better'.

Goals ought also to fit the demonstrated reality of preferred lifestyles. Our kids are individualists, already habituated to a form of protest that got them thrown out of conventional schools — whether bored, scared, or rebellious. It is little use trying to fit them to the goal of factory work or perhaps even general industrial life. Nor do they display much entrepreneurial interest or talent. In that, they lack both examples and a capitalistic turn of mind. They seem to shun collectivist trends, and would be misfits as bureaucrats in America. The ethic of self-employment is probably most fitting, and if it is not to be illegal (burglary, and other forms they already know or have considered) we would do best perhaps to promote their training in skilled trades and crafts: piano tuner, musician, veterinarian, furniture maker, printer, teacher, beautician, auto mechanic, watch repairer. A curriculum for what, and goals for whom?

Finally, though the course offerings never explicitly say so, individual and group counseling, by all staff and sometimes by students, is part of every course. It goes on in the hallway, the classroom, the privacy of offices — whenever needed, usually on demand, seldom by appointment. It is a therapeutic school, with constant attention to attitudes and feelings related to behavior, Play therapy is often admixed with conversation, listening, and understanding. And with action. Sometimes, the counselor simply has to go outside the school with the child, and rearrange the environment.

STAFF, ORGANIZATION, PHILOSOPHY

More important than space, financing, or curriculum is the staff. In the beginning, the staff is the curriculum. They present themselves in the context of a subject. Although kids are willing to learn a subject, they want to know, 'who is that person?' or 'who am I in relation to him/her?'

The regular staff and volunteers are usually young, 30 or under, except for the professor, called 'White Owl' and considered ancient. Being young, the staff cannot have had many years of teaching experience, but is highly educated. They are dedicated, idealistic, mostly unmarried and usually childless, and, in every case, devoted to the kids. Being mortal, they want the normal objectives of life: a career, security and affection, and a sense of personal growth and competence. To the extent that the school can provide for these objectives, the staff can provide a growth-facilitating need-satisfying milieu for the students. The school therefore makes great effort to create conditions for:

1. enabling staff members to cope with a very demanding job and to enable

personal and professional growth;

2. staff communication remaining open, honest, and non-manipulative;

3. the development of shared goals and procedures for operation of the school.

Specialization is only partial. Generally, everybody does everything. All participate in administration, budgeting, nursing, proposal writing, janitorial work, teaching, and counseling. This lack of clear division of labor goes against the recommendations of our auditor's management system, and it may be less efficient, but it is more effective given our organizational philosophy.

There is probably much to be said for hierarchical structures, and iron chains of command, particularly in battle, storms at sea, building beehives or bureaucracies, or large organizations. Whatever the advantages, we prefer to do without them, or find them in other ways. Our way is a democratic sharing of the rewards, risks, and responsibilities of leadership. To fulfill one of the school's objectives, the opportunity for leadership rotates, and the director, a doctoral student, serves for a year or so until the next associate in line is ready, with each preceding and following director giving support. It works. Inconstancy may lead to some inconsistencies, but these give us a chance to compare and select the best of differences. As William James said, 'Consistency is the hobgoblin of little minds.' What we try to avoid is not inconsistency, or consistency — only little minds.

Philosophically, we find our roots in the educational theories of William James, A. N. Whitehead, John Dewey, Carl Rogers, and, of course, Robert W. White. And, on off days, Attila the Hun. Those are roots, but before we develop and prune our own branches, we have had to concentrate on making sure that the kids have breakfast — the beginning of each day's 'curriculum'. Actually, few schools anywhere have seriously considered the complex details of educational philosophy: human nature and purpose, theories of knowledge and of learning. That is not what the practical world asks of them. Most of our questioners, considering our population, assume our task to be less one of education, more the 'management of aggression', and essentially want to know, 'How permissive are you?' Compared to the outside world, we're gentle, and well aware of the self-discipline that takes. If harsh punishment were beneficial, these kids would be perfect. They've had it: broken bones, bruises and whipmarks, slammed into unconsciousness, handcuffed, tied in a blanket, burned, jailed. We do indeed set limits, but we try to make sure that these are for the kid's benefit at least as much as for our convenience. At the philosophical level of a simple declarative principle (spare the rod, accentuate the positive) our philosophy is, 'What we want for our own children, we want for these'. That philosophy both guides us and reveals our shortcomings.

THE FUTURE, 766, AND ALL THAT

We have made a beginning. It is an intensive experience in direct service responsibilities, very different (though not entirely separate) from the roles of theoretician, consultant, or critic. It has been necessary to be much more than a school in order to be a school. So far, we have demonstrated that our kids can (and many want to) successfully return to public schools in or near grade level.

It was always our view that alternatives should influence but not try to take over the traditional systems. According to original plans, we will produce what is expected of a university contingent — innovation, research, models, training, and dissemination — and, within the next five to seven years, dissolve into the community, taking on another form within the public school district. All of our planning then anticipated and now supports the 'Chapter 766' legislation in the Commonwealth of Massachusetts for the integration of children with special needs into the mainstream of enriched public education. It is a welcome vision.

Yet there are snares and delusions. The Area Superintendent of the public schools muses, 'There will always be a need for schools like yours.' Faster than injured children can be restored by special services, others are damaged by the corrosive aspects of the community itself. That is another problem. The 'community' as a healthy organism exists more as a fiction in the minds of hopeful advocates than it does in fact. We deal not so much with a psychological community as with a geographical province which suffers from racial, ethnic, socio-economic class, and temperamental divisions that make it not very receptive to its own excluded children.

Then, within our operation, we find that the whole set of ideas surrounding innovation, models, and policy change smacks of a certain arrogance. Constant demand for 'innovation' risks unsettled, hit-and-run interventions. 'Models' assume repetition — a Levittown of 'establishment alternatives' — and the more perfect the model seems, the more it becomes true that 'the best is the enemy of the good'. Policy orientation is an exercise in megalomania, exactly insofar as policy is set by people not involved in the realities of service delivery and who therefore dictate policy that cannot be implemented. Obviously, we find our practical experience thought-provoking in the service of reality testing. It convinces us that conceptually as well as literally, *special educational work must be planned and carried out on a human scale*, and that (1) that scale limits the measure of practical validity, and (2) is smaller than most of us like to think.

We have still much to learn about the life cycle of all kinds of alternatives. Is their essence the initial spirit of protest? Can they improve with age? Most do not last long enough to answer the question, due to some special vulnerability to hostile surroundings, or from inherent flaws equal to but different from those in the institutions to which they are alternative.

Organizationally, our alternative school is approaching early middle age. This year, Director Hayden Duggan will focus on educational tone and method. Henry Foley, scheduled to succeed as director, will probably bring to bear Professor Kohlberg's concept of a 'fair' school. Meanwhile, we will be trying to find the right balance of change and stability through fresh additions while more seasoned staff move to new careers.

In the planning stages, it seemed that the Robert White School was an end in itself. It is not. The real question becomes, what will happen to our kids as they move out into whatever life holds for them? They'll have friends — us — for the rest of our lives, a diploma, otherwise unlikely, some job training, and experience. For most, this is the last formal education and ours is a prep school geared to the complex informal education in their futures.

There is no proper happy ending to this report. Our work is both great fun and utterly serious. We live with a dilemma: a temporary institution and feelings of permanent concern for children already verging on an adult life that will be the ultimate test of our influence. That is beyond prediction. For the moment, while getting through adolescence is not getting through life, it is a crucial step and we have to be content with that.

Section 4

The Position of
Client-Centered Therapy

EDITOR'S INTRODUCTION

This section starts with the first part of the introduction to the book *Client-Centered Therapy and the Person-Centered Approach: New Directions in Theory, Research and Practice* (Levant and Shlien, 1984). This is John Shlien in his prime as he considers the future of Client-Centred Therapy. He urges the client-centred/ person-centred community of practitioners to stay true to their principles (cleanliness and 'good faith' are recurrent themes in his work) and he ends with a quote from Martin Luther King: 'We cannot achieve moral ends by immoral means'. I know that this sentiment resonates with the majority of practitioners in the person-centred tradition as therapists today are exhorted to return what Brian Thorne calls 'stress-fit work addicts' (Thorne, 1996) back to the fast-food joint after double-quick brief therapy according to a tick-box manual. Making the case for compassionate, humane therapy with a 60-year research tradition in the face of today's requirements for mechanised 'treatments' has never been more difficult nor has it been more desperately needed. I include this short piece to sustain everyone working to keep our approach alive.

John was particularly keen to have the book review which comprises Chapter 15 included. It is a passionate statement which not only helps position the Person-Centred Approach in contemporary helping psychology, but also represents his take on the history of the approach.

I know John clearly thought that the Wisconsin years nearly ruined Carl Rogers (see also pp. 125–6 this volume) professionally and personally. Did tensions in the Wisconsin project team change Rogers' views on theory and practice?[1] Was the move to California as smooth as we are sometimes led to believe? (For Rogers' own accounts see Kirschenbaum 1970; Rogers and Russell, 2002.) Events rarely run as smoothly as histories, oral or written, would have us believe. In his later years John knew that events would become distorted and mythologised through the imperfections of human memory, including his own. He simply wanted some of his thoughts available as a balance.

Chapter 16 was written for a presentation at the Third International Conference on Client-Centered and Experiential Psychotherapy (ICCCEP), held in Gmunden, Austria, 1994. It is an (unpublished) introduction to the paper titled 'Embarrassment Anxiety: A Literalist Theory' (Chapter 9, this volume) which was first published in the ICCCEP collection *Client-Centered and Experiential Psychotherapy: A Paradigm in Motion* (Hutterer, Pawlowsky, Schmid and Stipsits, 1994). I think it is the perfect endpiece.

It is another impassioned piece of writing in which John's enduring concerns are present: such themes as truth, transparency, self-deception and mental health, the future of client-centred therapy, strategies for its survival and flourishing and the relentless search for client-centered alternatives for the psychoanalytic concepts of transference ('an excuse') and the unconscious ('simply a monster').[2]

This chapter is largely the text of the talk as John abridged and adjusted it for possible publication — this section of the piece, however, never was. In the separate notes he used for the presentation on the day, he amplified points and made several robust comments in the margins which were edited out, probably for the sake of brevity and possibly to avoid litigation! For example, in one margin is written 'psychoanalysis, so is bad from the start'. Elsewhere he worried about 'political tactics' in the client-centered and experiential world.

I have included some of the 'lost' material from John's notes and comments in [square brackets] to indicate the interpolation of this additional material. Those readers who knew John will know that he was open and robust in public exchanges

---

[1.] For the most recent review of the possible effects of Wisconsin project on CCT theory and practice, see Lisbeth Sommerbeck's recent paper 'The Wisconsin Watershed — Or, The Universality of CCT' *Person-Centered Journal, 9,* (2) pp140–57, (2003). This paper was heavily influenced by John Shlien and contains many of his questions and thoughts about the Wisconsin Project.

[2.] In other notes, John wrote of 'the unconscious': 'The Client-Centered Position won't be fully established until our view of this concept is clear. We can by-pass it, or disregard the significalnce of the issue — but until we resolve the problems introduced by the idea, show how and what we have thought about it, we will remain a minor or immature factor in the world. Theory-wise, this concept is one of the great divides. Value-wise it is a concept from hell. There is no way to escape the need for interpretation. If this concept prevails, it justifies, even demands interpretation from a wiser person.'

of views with a wide range of people, rarely shying away from confrontation regarding theory or principles. I have tried to include only that extra material which adds to the theory or point of principle, or adds appropriate emphasis to convey John's obvious conviction and passion.

I can find no record of what John actually said at the conference, but with the text and the notes included here, the reader can be left in no doubt as to his thoughts and feelings. He had not tired of exposing the redundant 'intrenched esoterica' of therapy after 25 years. He finishes with a call to continue to develop credible, compassionate, phenomenological theory of our own. The net effect for me is certainly 'unease', but also inspiration for all those who hold the Person-Centred Approach at the centre of their work and life.

REFERENCES

Hutterer, R., Pawlowsky, G., Schmid, P. F. & Stipsits, R. (Eds.) (1994). *Client-Centered and Experiential Psychotherapy: A Paradigm in Motion.* Frankfurt: Peter Lang.

Kirschenbaum, H. (1970). *On Becoming Carl Rogers.* New York: Delacorte.

Levant, R.F. & Shlien, J.M. (Eds.) (1984). *Client-Centered Therapy and the Person-Centered Approach: New Directions in Theory, Research and Practice.* New York: Praeger.

Rogers, C.R. & Russell, D.E. (2002). *Carl Rogers, The Quiet Revolutionary: An oral history.* Roseville, CA: Penmarin Books.

Thorne, B. (1996). The cost of transparency. *Person-Centred Practice,* 4 (2), 2–11.

CHAPTER 14

'Introduction'

With Ronald F. Levant: pages 1–8 of the introduction to
the volume:
*Client-Centered Therapy and the Person-Centered
Approach: New Directions in Theory, Research and Practice*
Edited by Ronald F. Levant and John M. Shlien

PROBLEMS

Volumes such as this[1] appear every decade or so. In such a periodic review, recurring issues persist. One is the continuing debate on human nature: good or evil? This tends to be a 'projective' question: answers come from knowledge of self as well as conjecture about others, which may explain some of the durability and intensity of the debate. Here we take another look at it.

Client-centered theory is generally identified with the optimistic position, in which human nature is basically good: good when enlightened, good when free, or ultimately good. Whether human nature is ultimately good is an evolutionary question; we may not know until the world ends, by which time it would not matter. Whether it is basically good must be determined on the evidence of all that appears in human behavior. Evil must be taken into account. Rogerians are not blind fools, but neither do they want to turn the world over to the cynics, who already have the advantage of appearing to be the more realistic. Why so? That advantage is all too easy. Cynicism takes its scornful ease at the expense of idealism's efforts. Pessimists can't be disappointed or accused of bad judgment in case of failure. They hold a defensive position.

It is worthwhile to examine this position. First, that which we call evil (like that which we call violence) is that which hurts. Definitions of what hurts (and is

[1.] *Client-Centered Therapy and the Person-Centered Approach: New Directions in Theory, Research and Practice*. Edited by R.F. Levant and J.M. Shlien.

therefore evil) depend considerably upon our vulnerability or resistance to pain, as well as to others' intent to do injury.

'Harmless folk' are not considered evil. It appears, then, that the stronger need less protection, can bear more vulnerability, can afford idealism or dare to sacrifice for it. Cynicism comes from weakness, not realism. It is weakness in the face of pain, and since realism is a 'survival concept', pain is wrongly credited with more realism than is pleasure. To take the cynic's position is to feed on that wrong-headedness. In short, the world hangs together, as much as it does, because of what good there is in human nature.

The cynic doubts this logic, knowing as he does that people are motivated by reward and punishment. If true, what's the reward for goodness? Where is the reward in giving instead of taking? The answer makes sense only at a certain level of moral judgment. The answer is that virtue is its own reward. 'Virtue is its own reward?' It is beyond the comprehension of any cynic and not easily grasped by every idealist. The admiration of virtue is more than the pleasure of giving. It is a thing in itself. It is not the opposite of the position 'Making life hell for others is my greatest pleasure', either, and evil cannot be its own reward unless you can admire evil for itself — not for its style. There is really not much to be said for cynicism, except that it is self-protective. It may not subscribe to evil, but it denies good, it makes a false claim to realism, and its arguments are not especially sound.

At the same time, those who would use client-centered theory to support an idealistic view make a mistake when they point to our reliance upon the 'growth motive'. It is not the same thing. Growth is a 'positive' force, but it is neither good nor evil in a moral sense. Client-centered theory is *hospitable* to the idea of goodness; client-centered *therapy* has witnessed goodness produced at choice points in successful outcomes; but neither the theory *nor* the therapy can be held to prove the essential goodness of human nature.

Some changes in currents of thought lead us to a balanced perspective. People are capable of both good and evil, obviously. It is not clear that either one is naturally predominant. The first newer perspective is *interaction*. No longer does anyone argue for heredity or environment exclusively. Neither does one base an argument on humanity's hypothetical nature in isolation from social interaction. It is partly a question of what we, with *our* natures, do to, for, and with the person(s) whose 'human natures' are in question.

A second perspective is that of adjustable balance. There is no philosophical absolute, nor is any individual totally good or bad. Each one carries a double-entry moral ledger sheet, and the balance can change.

We are basically both good and bad, much as it is now commonly recognized that all are somewhat female or male. It is a matter of proportion. If good and evil are matters of behavior (how else would we know them?) as well as of hypothesized nature, behavior can and does change. Where evil was, there good can be. Who is evil can become good. That is what matters, rather than 'nature'. That change is something to which experience in client-centered therapy *can* testify. It need not be a fundamental assumption about nature, but only a working assumption about ways of being. What is fundamentally assumed is the *potential to change.* That is unequivocal. It underlies all belief in growth, education, and therapy. The change could be in any direction, but the prediction is that it will be in a positive direction. Does that guarantee a positive 'basic nature'? It does not. Unpredictability is one of our happily held assumptions about life and freedom. The establishing of certain conditions — such as a nourishing environment — has a predictable, encouraging, but not controlling, effect.

The 'flying circus' debates, such as Skinner (Rogerian man is determined to feel free) vs. Rogers (Skinnerian man is free to feel determined) have run their course. It may be that the debaters of the human nature issue should take their quest elsewhere. Client-centered therapy allows for everything but tries to promote the best. That is an uphill struggle and a risk, at a constant disadvantage. Effortless gravity is on the side of evil. Evil can always have the last word, wiping out opposition (because death is so final) where good must allow for a continuation of all possibilities. That is where client-centered therapy may have appeared to take a side on the human nature question, for it does choose life. It *is* on the side of life.

QUESTIONS ABOUT FUTURES

There are some questions about the characteristics and characters of this movement that might influence its future. Where is its current vitality? Is its center fading or only moving? At one time, it was in the universities. Research of the particular sort that met the needs of the blossoming system of therapy and the quantitative-experimental conventions of the institutions was the object and source of great energy. The theory needed development. The therapy needed outcome evaluation. Impact and respectability were gained thereby. Audio and, later, film recordings were made. They were lauded forms of leadership. Now everyone does it. The research that once seemed such a proud achievement is also now commonplace, and a source of criticism as well: no such research ever proves to anyone's satisfaction the absolutely irrefutable value and effectiveness of any psychotherapy.

In the beginning there was a wave of enthusiasm and a whole-hearted embracing of the fundamental ideas, at least for the purpose of a whole-hearted research. There was novelty, opportunity, a point of view that provided a welcome alternative and that appeared to be the democratic-egalitarian form of freedom and individuality in the field of mental health. The attitude was one of sincere commitment.

There is relatively little such commitment now. Students entering the field have a dazzling range of choices, presented in forceful competition. All claim to have some effectiveness and validity. How is one to choose? The general response is one of 'synthesis', 'integration', 'matching method to client needs and therapist's preference'. There are some examples in this volume. [See footnote 1, p. 204. Ed.]

The result is an eclecticism that tends to preclude the fully informed, fully invested commitment to any single mode. It leads toward incorporation of any chosen feature into the pragmatic mainstream of 'whatever works'. At least two problems stem from this. One is that 'pure forms' will disappear. Aside from nostalgia for classical types, the problem is that eclectics cannot test 'what works' because there will be confounded factors and effects. Research tends to come from a rather valiant belief and effort to confirm or deny a point. Those who use many methods will probably never discover *what* works, if they can study in a disciplined way whether anything is working at all. Research in this subject should (in order to have a fair chance of success) use only the most skillful and competent practitioners of a pure form. Neither the form nor the competence seems likely without the commitment. It is a formula for decline.

COHESION AND DISPERSION

Another factor is the urge of the practitioner (explicitly including those in this school of thought and in this volume) to be unique, find some expression of originality, develop some virtuosity. Rogers says they should; he does; it is reasonable in the service of progress and self-enhancement. The problem is one of centrifugal effect. There is no 'central committee'; no organization, formal or informal; and no stable center of information, communication, or membership. Subscribers to this system of thought may often recognize each other partly for what they are not (not behaviorists, nor psychoanalytic, etc.) though there are certain characteristics they and the system share.

For one, there are deliberately set limits to the power, authority, and status of the client-centered therapist. The therapist is always considered in relationship to the client; the relationship is one of service. The term 'empowering' is fashionable among those who feel they can bestow power. The intent is laudable in the interests of equalizing, so long as it is not demeaning in its magnanimity, and it is their own power they give. Rogers puts it a bit differently — the client-centered therapist 'never takes power away' (1977, p. xii). It is not an act of grace, but one of genuine respect.

Other orientations describe the therapist's role as 'surgeon', 'scientist', 'commander-in-chief', and, of course, doctor, with all that these imply about management and knowing best. Superiority is evident and considered necessary for the successful outcome of the operation, the battle 'for the sake of the patient'. The quite different role of the client-centered therapist is one of companion, fellow traveler, gardener — not servant, though serving, and certainly not master.

While these egalitarian modes have individual appeal for personal and political reasons, the renunciation of superior power is absolutely required by the implications of a central point *in the theory.* That is, the client is the very source, as well as criterion, of health and progress.

This is implicit in reliance on the growth motive as the prime cause. It states: (1) growth is a natural process; (2) the essential healing comes from within. The surgeon, then, may remove diseased tissue but cannot claim to grow the healthy tissue. Some think that Rogers brought an agriculturalist's leanings to his theory. Perhaps, though each of us, however citified, knows that farmers do not grow the corn; they may plant and cultivate, but the corn grows itself. It grows even where there are no farmers. So it is not a mistake when Rogerian therapy is called 'homeopathic'. This supercilious accusation was made in scorn, but it is true and a compliment. While these growth analogies may help the reader to understand the theory's base, they have a limit. Rogers means for the growth to lead to self-understanding, made possible because of a self-reflexive consciousness plants do not possess. The overall point is that this *theory,* independent of fair-mindedness or humility, dictates that the role of the therapist is to assist in another's inherent process.

Though power is limited, there are no limits to the possible levels of artistry, skill, and craft. But these are generally private performances. In the more public roles, Rogerians do not make the most of them. Our research, for instance, is not characterized by the 'flash of genius'. Not the sort that captures the imagination. Rather it is the painstaking collection and analysis of data, with some excitement, but without the glory of the instant revelation. When Rogers and his collaborators were preparing to publish the research in *Psychotherapy and Personality Change* [Rogers and Dymond, 1954, Ed.] at the University of Chicago, the dean of the division took note of the fact that it had been richly funded by prestigious sources (such as Rockefeller, NIMH [National Institute for Mental Health. Ed.]) and that it was in keeping with the highest standards of respectable research, rules of evidence, etc. He went on to remind the faculty senate of the occasion on which Freud's discoveries had been called by some scoffing Viennese colleagues 'a sort of scientific fairy tale'. 'What we need,' said the dean, 'are more scientific fairy tales.' He was wrong — we are suffocating from too many — but he was correct in realizing that this was not what he would get from the client-centered scientist. For a world wanting to be startled with revelations, such 'rigorous research' is disappointing and pedestrian.

So it goes. In client-centered writing, you do not find the literary flair, historical and mythological allusions, not the arcane; seldom the exotic or even erotic. No Ratman, or Wolfman — just homely Mr. Lin, or Mrs. Oak. Never called brilliant, or clever; occasionally eloquent but more often admired as lucid, plain-spoken, sensitive. The overall tone is more than mundane, but far less than glamorous. Not that either style has any bearing on truth or value. It does have some bearing on who is attracted to this orientation.

The 'dispossessed' rarely choose the Rogerian approach, though well they might, since it offers at once the dignity for others that they seek for themselves. Usually, though, if they have any opportunity to choose at all, more authoritarian orientations seem to suit better. Power, not the renunciation of it, may be the initial goal of the powerless. On the other hand, neither is this viewpoint a favored choice of the rich, aristocratic, elite, sophisticated. It lacks hauteur. We have known a few wealthy adherents, sometimes Quakers who are discreet about money and costliness but who have a quiet passion for friendly persuasion. Nor is this for those foaming with ambition. Rogers once said that those seeking fame and fortune would have more success if they did not attach themselves to him.

That leaves the middle class — not to be confused with second class, for many are as intelligent as can be found. But not arch, not wily, not artful. Middle class, or déclassé, and middle American in culture. Mild-mannered, unassuming, not weak, and, in fact, stronger than some more aggressive sorts, but able to bear their vulnerabilities. Students at the University of Chicago once made up a caricature regarding the problem of 'what is in the black box': Freud said he would pry it open through symbolic analysis; Skinner said there was nothing in it; and Rogers said that it wasn't polite to ask.

For reasons besides the inherent force and appeal of its ideas, this native movement spread rapidly in response to opportunities now disappearing. First, there was the Veteran's Administration, expanded on so vast and sudden a scale that training and employment became available for more psychologists than existed. In VA hospitals, psychologists who began providing adjunct services to psychiatry (testing; vocational counseling) soon began to fill the gaps caused by shortages of psychiatrists. Thus they became 'clinicians' doing 'psychotherapy'. Second, universities received a flood of graduate students and began to train many for those vacant professional positions in psychology. Student counseling centers were installed in dozens of colleges and universities, creating additional demand for graduates from training centers in universities. Client-centered therapy was well positioned to prepare candidates to fill these vacancies. Doctoral graduates could immediately enter senior academic and clinical positions. It was a multiplier effect. Third, the field of pastoral counseling had long been seeking a way to enable its ministry to combine theology and psychological therapeutics. (See Chapter 18 [see footnote 1, p. 204. Chapter 18: 'Rogers' Impact on Pastoral Counseling and Contemporary Religious Reflection' by Robert C. Fuller. Ed.])

Freud had declared that religion had no place in psychoanalysis, and some religionists replied in kind. Rogers, who had personal connections with liberal Christian theology, offered a practical alternative that enabled the field of pastoral counseling to grow through psychological instruction in the denominational seminaries.

As this is written, the situation is reversed. Vacancies in the psychological professions are fewer, and the production of doctoral-level psychology graduates far exceeds the demand. Private practice is the self-employment solution often chosen, and all forms of psychotherapy are soon to be in harsh competition with the medical profession and each other — a situation somewhat foreign to the origins of the movement.

Finally, there are two other perennials.

One is the challenge forever thrown to the permissive philosophy. What would you do if . . . e.g. your child is crossing a busy street, suicide is contemplated, etc.? Emergency is a real problem, and one does what one must according to the acceptable limits of risk, which depend a good deal on strength and vulnerability as well as long-term effects. There is a special debating tactic in such challenges: take one step not in keeping with your philosophy, and you lose the whole of it. Such a challenge appears in Chapter 14, where Hackney and Goodyear (p. 295) [see footnote 1, p. 204. Ed.] (themselves not of a client-centered persuasion, but participating in a comparative study of supervisors including Rogers) note that Rogers did not address the issue of 'vicarious liability' for ultimate welfare of supervisee's clients, citing the *Tarasoff* case of the threatened homicide as the instance of emergency. The basic answer comes from the lawyer-philosopher Roscoe Pound: 'Hard cases make bad laws', We recognize that if all practice is geared to safeguards against extremes, it is the ruination of the open society. Curfews do reduce crime, but when emergency rules, democracy dies. It is an authoritarian strategy for control, not necessarily based on the welfare of the client as first consideration but on the fault-free status of the therapist. It remains a problem, and it is everyone's. The costs and benefits need to be weighed and reweighed constantly and for each particular instance.

The second is a means/ends problem. Some who use techniques abhorrent to client-centered therapists justify intrusive or domineering ways as being for the ultimate good of the client. Interestingly, some who hold client-centered philosophy in contempt borrow its techniques (such as reflection, tentative understandings) to open up the client in early sessions for deeper probes later. The client-centered position recommends its own way throughout, holding with John Dewey that 'Means are ends at lower levels'. One never knows when the 'end' arrives. Really, the end is, for this moment, right now. It is not only that, as Martin Luther King put it, 'We cannot achieve moral ends by immoral means', but that the immoral means is at that very instant an immoral end. It may be the only end your client will ever experience. It is simply inimical to client-centered therapy to act on a 'You may not like or understand this now but you will thank me for it later' basis, not only for the sake of consistency, but especially because 'means are ends at lower levels', and we do not assume the opportunity of a hypothetical forever.

REFERENCES

Rogers, C.R. (1977). *Carl Rogers on Personal Power: Inner strength and its revolutionary impact.* New York: Delacorte.

Rogers, C.R. & Dymond, R.F. (1954). *Psychotherapy and Personality Change.* Chicago: University of Chicago Press.

CHAPTER 15

Theory as Autobiography
The man and the movement

VOLUME I, THE READER

A few years before his death, Carl Rogers began this selection from 16 books and 290 articles covering nearly 60 years of distinguished professional life. He left the material in the trusted hands of these editors, both authorized biographers, who organized 33 pieces into a valuable portable library.

Topics range from recollections of personal life to theories of knowledge, therapy, personality change, education, marriage, aging, political and philosophical positions, research summaries, and his final passion, peace and international relations. Excerpts from recorded case material illustrate his earliest published interview (1942, complete with footnoted blunders) and one of his last, in 1986, for a striking comparison.

Though not arranged in chronological sequence, the essays are a history of influential ideas, a great man, and a movement. Continuity is carried by what Rogers calls his 'one seminal idea' (p. 43), frequently repeated. Simply put, people have vast inner resources for self-understanding and self-directed solutions if they feel heard and understood in a facilitative relationship of warmth and acceptance. There are three other repeated themes to which he is permanently devoted: growth as motive; freedom to choose; and communication as clear, deep, and open as possible.

Contrasts come mainly in changing therapist behaviors, all supposedly consistent with theory. An example starts in his 1942 description of the value of recorded interviews. Thanks to these, 'therapy need no longer be vague, therapeutic

First published as a review of Kirschenbaum, H. and Henderson, V. L. (1989). *The Carl Rogers Reader*. Boston MA: Houghton Mifflin. And Kirschenbaum, H. and Henderson, V. L. (1989). *Carl Rogers: Dialogues*. Boston MA: Houghton Mifflin. In *Contemporary Psychology*, 1992, Vol. 37, No. 10. Reproduced with permisssion.

skill need no longer be an intuitive gift' (p. 218). The veil of mystery will be removed, research investigation enabled, and teaching and learning improved in 'a process based upon known and tested principles, with tested techniques for implementing those principles' (p. 218).

The program implied in this 1942 statement from Ohio State was developed at the University of Chicago, where Rogers worked with many colleagues from 1945 to 1957 in what he called his most productive professional period. As a champion of egalitarian ideals in a post-World-War-II environment where democratic values were prized, Rogers spoke eloquently for attitudes of warmth, respect, genuineness (or honesty) with dignity, safety, and freedom for the client — all in the service of understanding the client's internal frame of reference.

The work drew worldwide attention, attracted thousands of students, and garnered university and foundation support. Counseling centers and clinical applications spread, and research production was enormous. That, together with his theoretical work, brought Rogers his most cherished honor, the American Psychological Association's Distinguished Scientific Contribution Award (for research which this book tells us he later criticized as of doubtful worth and motive).

The academic culmination of his theory was his statement of the 'Necessary and Sufficient Conditions' (Koch, 1959), excerpted here as Chapter 17. It now seems laboriously formal and overreaching, applying to any type of therapy, any population, and many areas of life. Couched in 'if-then' terms, it constructs a deterministic proposition, leaving no apparent room for the will of the client. In the next two decades, rich essays on 'A Human Science' (Chapters 18 and 19) broke free of this rigidity.

With his eminence and the success of the movement, he could have moved anywhere. Curiously, there is nothing in this first volume to tell us where that would be (University of Wisconsin) and no mention of work during the anguished next 'seven years he wished he could forget' (Kirschenbaum, 1979, p. 275).

NOT NECESSARY BUT SUFFICIENT?

Instead, it is suddenly California, 1986, the era of the person-centered approach. Rogers unbound and without academic ties is now free to search without constraints, to delve into psychic phenomena, to write for popular audiences, and to address the Encounter Movement. He need not be a therapist, exactly; he could be a facilitator or simply a person. Empathy has long since become more than a 'condition'; it is a way of being. A new condition, not a model but a personal quality called 'one more characteristic', appears in the wings and Rogers writes,

when I am at my best . . . when I am closest to my inner, intuitive self,

> when I am somehow in touch with the unknown in me, when perhaps I
> am in a slightly altered state of consciousness in the relationship, then
> whatever I do seems to be full of healing. Then simply my *presence* is
> releasing and helpful . . . Or, 'almost always helpful'. (pp. 137, 148)

This is a far cry from the 'tested techniques' of 1942. Therapy may now indeed
be an 'intuitive gift'. Some mystery is returned. He no longer tries to teach but to
illustrate something he cannot always call into play. It may even be inimitable.

In the California culture, the role of the healer is highly appealing, and
Rogers was encouraged there to move in that direction, a guru in spite of himself.
His fame preceded him in every interview. He was also indeed a great listener,
now serving 'a force beyond himself' *(Dialogues,* p. 74). (I have, with many others,
witnessed his rapt attention, though it did not seem like an altered state.)

IF YOU REMEMBER, THE FACTS ARE FRIENDLY

How did we get here from Chicago? The journey was made by way of Wisconsin,
where Rogers went as a professor of psychiatry and psychology, with great
opportunity, ambition, and new colleagues to test his theory and practice with
hospitalized patients. The first mention of this location appears, perhaps
inadvertently, in the introductory chapter of the companion volume, *Dialogues,*
which was put together entirely by the editors, without Rogers and after his
death.

This chapter was rewritten, circa 1964, by Rogers with the assistance of two
associates. Lacking his usual fluent clarity, the wording is uneasy and hesitant. It
both suggests and denies change:

> A number of years ago, I tended to refer to these attitudes in relatively
> loose, general terms as the therapist's belief in the worth and dignity of
> the individual and the therapist's capacity to provide a relationship of
> safety and freedom in accord with his basic respect for his client . . .
> [Now we] have advanced more specific thoughts about these conditions.
> (pp. 10–11)

Whether truly advanced or more specific is debatable. If language did tighten
(though still defined by the earlier terms), theory relaxed. A core problem shows
in the discussion of one of the three 'essential ingredients', unconditional positive
regard. 'He [therapist] prizes the client in a total, rather than a conditional way.
He does not accept certain feelings in the client and disapprove of others' (p. 13).

A page later comes a different opinion, so contradictory as to suggest a different
theory, and perhaps a different author.

> Our recent experience in psychotherapy with chronic and unmotivated schizophrenics raises the question whether we must modify our conception of this condition. Very tentatively it appears to me at the present time that, in dealing with the extremely immature or regressed individual, a conditional regard may be more effective in getting a relationship under way, hence therapy under way, than an unconditional positive regard. It seems clear that some immature or regressed clients may perceive a conditional caring as constituting more acceptance than an unconditional caring. The therapist who expresses the theme, 'I don't like it when you act in such and such a way: I care for you more when you act in a more grown-up fashion', may be perceived as a 'better parent' than one whose caring is unconditional. (pp.14, 15)

Plainly, this is not complete acceptance. Unconditional regard proved to be something the therapists were unable or unwilling to provide. The definer 'unconditional' was cast off, leading to a final hedge: 'Though our work has changed in a number of significant ways it is a matter of some interest that we have seen no reason to alter in any basic way our conception of the relationship' (p. 31).

Not only is this a matter of interest but a matter of concern. For example, where is it written that the therapist should be perceived as a parent? The real question is what to do when a vaunted project is failing, when patients are not voluntary, self-initiated clients with free choice but are unwilling and unresponsive. Should we declare that the therapists are inadequate, that the population is unsuitable, or that the theory is wrong? Is the test too severe? Should the practice be changed in a way that violates the theory? Should the theory be changed to accommodate the practice? Really, it was a watershed for the man, theory, and movement — a point when both means and ends were bent out of shape. With that denied, how could they recover?

The remainder of the second volume is the *Dialogues* themselves, beginning with Buber, whose very definition of 'dialogue' makes this exchange a profound and memorable experience. Tillich is another formidable intelligence. His concept of 'a love which is listening' (p. 77) surely expresses Rogers, who is drawn to say that as a therapist, he feels 'in tune with the universe, with forces operating through me' (p. 74).

Skinner, as humanistic as any, meets Rogers as an old friend (this is not one of the previously published debates). They have surprising understanding and appreciation of each other and depart anticipating some unspecified change. Polanyi voices conceptions of science most compatible with those of Rogers' later period. Bateson and Rogers rightly consider their meeting a fiasco and try later to mend it through correspondence.

May and Rogers exchange letters in a reprise of the human nature: good-versus-evil issue, which is featured throughout these conversations. Like most participants, both Rogers and May have an informed theological background. As psychotherapists, their different predispositions and experiences lead them to differing testimony, and we are left with traditional theological conclusions to this issue. It seems strange that as psychologists they never considered developmental stage theory or even the convention of individual differences. Apparently nature must be universal, all or none.

In separate pieces, Rogers displays a forceful style of analysis in his reviews of Neibuhr and of 'The Case of Ellen West'. Both volumes, especially when taken together, will richly reward close reading.

REFERENCES

Kirschenbaum, H. (1979). *On Becoming Carl Rogers.* New York: Delta.

Koch, S. (Ed.) (1959). *Psychology: A study of a science* (Vol. 3). New York: McGraw-Hill.

CHAPTER 16

Untitled and Uneasy[1]

Let me begin with the circumstances of my title and of the invitation to come here. The invitation was a surprise. I am not exactly a member in good standing in this conference. But it came from a friend, Reinhold Stipsits, and it was for a meeting two years hence. Surely one can think of something in two years. In fact, too many things. So I agreed, if the presentation could be listed as 'Untitled #1'. First, to give me some freedom of choice, and second, to imitate the artists I have always envied, with their paintings 'Untitled #1, 2', etc.

Still, there is the matter of 'uneasy'. Do I belong here? I don't belong here. I did not belong in Leuven [the first ICCCEP in 1988, Ed.], and realized that within a few days — a realization that grew as time passed. My interest had been aroused by the words 'client-centered' in the announcement. Midway through the conference, someone said to me on the stairway (Garry Prouty, it was), 'Doesn't seem very client-centered, does it?' It was just what I had been thinking. Later, a string of other events strengthened this impression — up to the present moment.

Not to speak of these concerns would be to knowingly acquiesce, and that means to conspire in my own destruction, so it is of personal importance to me, and I hope will raise questions of concern to all of us.

Then I will tell, insofar as time allows, about some ideas that I wish I were able to offer for such a meeting as this, and then one new theory of anxiety as a concrete suggestion for discussion.

First, here is a declaration of principles from which I presently work:
1. All theory is autobiographical.
2. No theory is universal. If it claims to be, it exaggerates, and has a totalitarian tendency.

[1.] Originally the previously unpublished introduction/first part of the paper 'Embarrassment Anxiety: A literalist theory' presented at the Third International Conference on Client-Centered and Experiential Psychotherapy (ICCCEP), held in Gmunden, Austria, 1994.

3. The client is unique, is the *main* factor in success, *and must have the right to fail*, as well as to succeed. [Some clients have hardly any other way to assert themselves, other than to fail. JMS] (This is not to excuse the therapist [although entirely too much attention is give to the *performance* of the therapist. JMS].)
4. In the history of ideas, every choice has personal motives.
5. The main human problem is: *how to lead an honorable life*. (More than to be fully functioning, well adjusted, successful, etc.)
6. My objectives are clarity, and cleanliness.

Of the members of our host committee[2] I knew two — Reinhold Stipsits and Robert Hutterer. The paper by Hutterer on our 'identity crisis' seemed to me to be a brilliant and judicious analysis, and it is good to see that it has finally been published (Hutterer, 1993). His quotation of Carl Rogers' 1951 statement, 'The truth is not arrived at by making concessions . . .'(p. 8), is very much to the point. I was equally challenged by Stipsits' weighing of the fundamentalist and the eclectic positions. On that score, neither suits me. I believe that everyone should learn the fundamentals, but 'fundamentalist' sounds dangerously narrow and rigid. With eclecticism, I have no problem. I simply despise it as being no point of view whatever, yet even worse than no position at all.

But if one does have a position, it helps the aim of clarity to know what that is. My choice is the 'Literalist' position. A position that calls for explanations based on natural, observable events. It tries to avoid the deliberately arcane, mysterious and ornamental modes of analysis. When I say that I am for clarity, I mean the refinement rather than the blurring of distinctions. I am for cleanliness as an 'experiential' event. You can feel it. Dirt happens. Cleanliness requires an act of will. Then, it follows, I am for separation, certainly not for false 'community', and for a number of reasons. One is what Americans call 'truth in advertising'. The public should know what to expect, be able to make an informed choice. Second, I am for 'pure forms' insofar as they can be developed. This is partly to enable true research. No mixture of methods can inform us as to which qualities have an effect on which outcomes. Further, the kind of pragmatism that says, 'whatever works' is not for me. Such pragmatists have no principles, only instruments, and by no means access to all available instruments, either!

I feel very fortunate to have had sufficient success with my chosen method, and not need to search for another, because this method, client-centered, seems to me to be the only *decent* one. If it does not work for someone else, they have reason to seek elsewhere. What I hope is that they will do what they want to do, and *call it what it is*. It is simply not acceptable to pour new wine into old bottles,

---

2. ICCCEP organising committee. [Ed.]

especially since it is the *labels* that are the sought after objects. (In the Bible, it was originally goat skins, not bottles, and there was a different rationale for using new containers — namely, the old skins cracked and leaked.)

By no means am I the only one so concerned — Mearns and Thorne wrote in 1988,

> We are little short of horrified by the recent proliferation of counselling practitioners, both in America and in Britain, who seem to believe that by sticking the label 'person-centred' on themselves they have licence to follow the most bizarre prompting of their own intuition or to create a veritable smörgåsbord of therapeutic approaches which smack of eclecticism at its most irresponsible. (p. 2)

In 1986, John K. Wood had already noted,

> Most people repeat vacuously the cliché: 'I believe that Rogers's conditions are necessary, but not sufficient.' Some of Rogers' closest colleagues use hypnosis, guided fantasies, paradoxical statements, dream analysis, exercises, give homework assignments and generally follow the latest fads to supply their missing deficiency (p. 351).

[Let me tell you of some of the history to which I was a witness. When this point of view was called 'non-directive' (certainly an awkward term) there was much concern about the image it suggested, i.e., as having *no* direction. The intent, then, was to indicate that there is indeed direction, but that the direction is prompted and determined *by the client*. It was never intended to mean 'therapist directed'. Never. JMS]

What troubles me especially is that one cannot readily tell whether these activities are thoughtless incongruities of theory and practice on the part of people who are simply looking for shelter, or whether they are part of a calculated political tactic — what is called in American financial circles, 'corporate raiding', i.e., capture the brand name, make it subsidiary, insert your new product into the old market (they *look* similar) — soon most people won't know the difference. Perhaps this is not an arrogant takeover, but an innocent and jolly 'open house', many mansions, hospitality. In that case, I can only ask, is it true generosity to give away what does not belong to you?

In the brochure announcing the publication of selected proceedings from the Leuven meetings, I read,

> It [the book *Client-Centered and Experiential Psychotherapy in the Nineties*. Ed.] does not represent a single vision but gives the floor to the *various sub-orientations* [my emphasis, JMS]: classic Rogerians; client-centered therapists who favor some form of integration or even eclecticism; experiential psychotherapists for whom Gendlin's focusing is a precious

way of working; client-centered therapists who look at the therapy process
in terms of information-processing; existentially oriented therapists . . .

Nice to be included, even though reduced from the *original* to a *sub*-orientation.
'Classic Rogerians', I suspect means, as in 'classic cars' — needs restoration, deserves
to be in a museum. I suspect because, elsewhere I have read that these newer
practices 'evolved'. It is true; one can read of the Wisconsin period that there were
'increasing' variations and deviations from non-directive modes, that these 'grew'
in frequency, etc., but where is it written that they represent 'evolution'? That
implies a higher form, better product, does it not? And what is the evidence for
this judgment? I think it is just a preference. What is this larger vision? Making
room for *what*? [What *is* the meaning of this 'evolution'? What is its direction?
What do all these have in common? Is anything excluded? JMS]

I ask partly because, during the Leuven meetings, I went into the coffee
shop, and there was introduced by Gene Gendlin — a friend for many years —
to a young man of whom Gene said something like, 'and he's an MD, a psychiatrist,
and (sounding aggrieved) we can't even make room for him'. 'Yes,' said the Dr
'and I give client-centered shock therapy to my patients, and they appreciate it,'
I thought to myself: (a) 'My God, this is a nightmare'; (b) 'since when are we so
crazy about psychiatrists?' and (c) 'what is this "making room", what is going on
here?' [I later thought a lot about this man. Was he trying to make more humane
the use of a tool he had been taught to use? Or was he using 'client-centered' as a
cover, to take the curse off something he knew to be cruel? JMS]

So I hurried away, and now add this to the list provided by John Wood. And
I am truly horrified. I do know that there is the possibility of such a thing as
'person-centered interrogation'. It has been thought about by intelligence (that
means 'spy') agencies, but all that is just a perversion of the meaning of client-
centered. I really would like to recommend to you a respectful consideration of
the meaning of 'classic'. It has grace and beauty, stands the test of time, sets
standards of comparison. Classical does not equal primitive — it looks quite
good after modern grotesque.

Two other incidents affected my feeling about these matters. Reinhard Tausch,
a man for whom I feel respect and affection, though we differ on many issues,
came to Gmunden for a visit. In a conversation, he asked, 'Do you think that
Rogerian psychology will die?' I don't know. It may sicken, but not die, and that
is worse. Sicken because, as a host, it is invaded by pirates and parasites. A day
earlier, Gerald Pawlowsky, with great kindness and courtesy, drove us from the
airport to Gmunden. He was talking about his work with a psychoanalytic group
in Vienna, and I was thinking, what fun, a psychoanalytic group in Vienna, but
how does he put that together with Rogerian ideas, and he said, 'I like the person-
centered people because they don't fight so much.' Probably that is true. I think

that we are a nation of sheep. I think that we may stand quietly, watching our own disintegration with the silence of lambs. I think it would be better to fight more openly, and to know why. I believe that many people here do not say what they think. I *know* it.

Understand that when I talk about cleanliness, and distinctions, and separations, I am not talking about such criminal outrages as 'ethnic cleansing'. This is not a matter in which our land, homes, families, lives are threatened. It may be territorial in a psychological sense, but if we are wise enough, we know that such space is unlimited. So we are only talking about our souls, spirit, or about what is honorable. If we cannot stand up for that, then the answer to Tausch's question is, yes — we are in a morbid state already.

One reason we are in such a state is that we never have forged an independent position on some crucial 'theoretical' matters. One of these is the question of the unconscious. It is the Great Divide and the ultimate source of psychoanalytic power. 'We are all equal before the throne of the Unconscious', said Freud, but that is to indoctrinate us as equally helpless. The experts, you know, are more equal. They have the ear of the court. Maybe, like the Wizard of Oz, they *are* the court. It is a concept from hell. I mean that partly as a joke, because it is easily translated into 'the devil made me do it'. But it also related to the mechanism of denial: I didn't do it; I don't remember, etc. As one of your own great philosophers put it, 'My memory says I did it; my conscience says I could not have. Memory yields.'[3] And we should add, sanity fades. So does morality.

It is a concept from hell on other grounds. For one, if it is true, if 'the Unconscious' really exists, the need for analytic interpretation of symbolic behavior is relatively well justified. Not absolutely, but relatively. And, from hell because it can never be totally disproved. It has all sorts of strategic and tactical advantages. But until we resolve this difficult problem, we are weak. At least, that is my view. Rogers tried to by-pass it, partly by reliance on the concept of 'levels of awareness' — a good start, but logically vulnerable, and he was under pressure during most of his later life in California to succumb to the ideas of 'intuition' and unconscious. [These 'treasures', the 'pure gold' of transference and the unconscious itself, come from the same zone. We had better think about alternative explanations for both, not only because it is a great challenge — to a theory that has captured the imagination of the world (certainly of most psychologists) — but because we will have a sense of intellectual immaturity until we go through this exercise. Another reason is that the concept of the unconscious justifies, almost demands, the interpretation of 'experts'. As a negative (*un*conscious), it is difficult to fully refute. JMS]

[3.] F.W. Nietzsche (1866). *Beyond Good and Evil.* Most translations have something similar to 'I have done this, says my memory. I could not have done this, says my pride, and remains adamant. Eventually my memory yeilds.' [Ed.]

It was my hope to present work on this problem for this conference. I wish that I were not so alone with it. Tangentially, it is what I was attacking in my 'countertheory of transference' paper, which I think has made little impact — although it has been translated into eight languages and Rogers said it was one of the few papers written by another that he wished he had written himself. In case you have never heard the idea, it was a 'literal' exposition of the role that understanding plays in evoking feelings of love (positive transference) towards the therapist, and the role that misunderstanding plays in the evoking of hate. Those are natural consequences, both in and out of therapy. [Of course it is just an idea, it had no new technique attached. JMS]

Of course, 'literal' cannot satisfy the psychoanalytic world, which holds that 'transference' is an 'unconscious' process. [Theoretically true, but hard to imagine now when everyone is waiting expectantly for it. Wolberg calls transference, 'one of the treasures of the unconscious'. JMS] For those who like the idea, what argument can persuade them to give it up? [Not only is it a line of defense for the therapist, but a dramatic pleasure. JMS] It is a thrill! I have had analyst-clients who told me so. [As Freud said, 'There is an incomparable fascination in a woman of high principles who confesses her passion'. That, I consider literal. But to a therapist who cannot take responsibility for having provided the conditions that promote this confession, 'transference' is an excuse, and even has an additional benefit — excusing arcane practice from a protected and superior position. JMS] And it is quite possible to cultivate transference if that is your desire. Even in our own community, the literalist point of view is not well received. Perhaps that is because we have never developed the alternative explanations.

And perhaps we don't even want them. In that respect, we are too much like the rest of the world. When my 'countertheory of transference' was republished in our *Person-Centered Review* journal,[4] several people of various persuasions were invited by Editor David Cain to comment. One psychoanalyst complemented me on my 'charming naïveté', saying, 'Yes, John, there is a transference.'[5] This is a snide witticism [a 'smiling insult'] and side-steps the argument completely. The phrase comes from an old editorial headline, reprinted every Christmas, to answer the letter a little girl wrote some decades ago, asking, 'Is there really a Santa Claus?' The answer begins, 'Yes, Virginia, there is a Santa Claus', (literally, a lie) and goes on to explain the spirit of the holy season. But we might in turn say, 'Yes, Santa Claus (whoever you are behind your mask or desk), there *is* a Virginia and *she wants to know*. You have your reasons for not answering truthfully. What are they?'

---

4. *Person-Centered Review*, 2 (1), 1987. Reprinted as Chapter 8, this volume. [Ed.]
5. Response by H. Greenwald to 'A countertheory of transference', published in *Person-Centered Review*, 2 (2), 1987, p. 165. Reprinted in Cain (2002). [Ed.]

I go to such length to tell you this because literal questions want literal answers, which are often hard to get. It is the *myth* that has charm, not so naïve as *sinister*. I have seen my efforts at literal explanation similarly dismissed by members of our own society, one saying, 'Yes, John . . .' and another saying, 'Well, transference has been around for a long time . . .'

[This reply to a child's question is republished every year (as is the idea of transference). They do have something in common: there is a Santa Claus, but he is not real. He is a fake, a sort of lie, created and maintained by parents, the merchants and the children. And the lie offers benefits; it can be used to punish as well as reward, is the occasion for reciprocity and gift-giving (but not every day) and is related in a sort of commercial way to the adoration and cherishing of children (but not every day). A tradition that is hard to question, but a lie nevertheless. It masks the truth, that is, the literal truth. The question is, what do *we* want? Literal truths or symbolic representations?

Another critical reviewer said I reminded him of the man searching for his keys under the lamp post, 'because that's where the light is'. My intention *is* to bring light into the 'dark' places of transference and the unconscious, if we must play with these stupid metaphors. Isn't that what client-centered therapy is all about? JMS]

If anyone would like to work with me on the problem of the unconscious, help will be welcome. Meanwhile, I present one more 'literalist' essay. Once more unto the breach.[6]

REFERENCES

Cain, D.J. (2002). *Classics in the Person-Centered Approach.* Ross-on-Wye: PCCS Books.
Hutterer, R. (1993). Eclecticism: An identity crisis for person-centred therapists. In D. Brazier (Ed.), *Beyond Carl Rogers.* London: Constable.
Mearns, D. & Thorne, B. (1988). *Person-Centred Counselling in Action.* London: Sage.
Rogers, C.R. (1951) *Client-Centered Therapy.* Boston: Houghton Mifflin.
Wood, J.K. (1986). Roundtable Discussion. *Person-Centered Review. 1* (3) pp. 350–1.

[6.] Then followed John's presentation of 'Embarrassment Anxiety: A literalist theory'. (Chapter 9, this volume.) [Ed.]

Appendix

Memorial Minute on the Life and Work of

John M. Shlien, Ph.D.

April 6, 1918 – March 23, 2002

We mark with light in the memory the few interviews we have had,
in the dreary years of routine and of sin, with souls that made our
souls wiser; that spoke what we thought; that told us what we knew;
that gave us leave to be what we inly were.
R. W. Emerson, Divinity School Address, 1838

We gather as a community of friends and scholars to pay tribute to the life and work of John M. Shlien. For 35 years of insightful teaching and research and then active retirement, he was our colleague at Harvard University. Before that, for some of us, he was a mentor, colleague, and even therapist at the University of Chicago. We gravely miss John's presence, his probing queries, his wise counsel, his understanding, his determined efforts to make life better in intimately human ways, through teaching and writing, and through public policy. As a teacher, he made us wiser. As a psychotherapist, he freed us to speak and be what we inwardly knew.

John's approach to life was poised, serious about things that matter, playful with ideas, loyal to friends, kind, encouraging to those in difficulty, and steadfast in his commitments. Those commitments particularly involved a relentless quest to understand what enabled constructive personality change to occur. He examined what constitutes social policies in education, urban planning, and employment that foster fulfilling human development. In pursuit of those goals he was also engaged in administering effective academic and service programs in both Chicago and Boston.

As a scholar, John's theoretical and research interests were firmly centered in psychology, especially personality psychology and psychotherapy. He also brought to bear new methods of empirical research concerning the process and outcomes of psychotherapy, research which was much needed in refining our specific knowledge of how therapeutic relationships actually bring about personal growth or 'personality

Published in the *Harvard University Gazette* May 15, 2003. Reproduced with kind permission of the authors.

change'. He stood out as one of the pre-eminent leaders of the 'Client-Centered Therapy' movement (now more often referred to as the 'Person-Centered Approach'), and he was particularly adroit at interweaving experience and research from clinical settings into the ongoing development of theory in that field.

John came to these interests by a natural, though rather distinctive, route. After being born and growing up in Kansas City, his academic and professional interests developed in social anthropology and the sociology of knowledge as well as in psychological research. He completed his military service in World War II between 1942 and 1945 in the Selection and Validation Program of the Psychological Research Unit of the U.S. Army Air Force. He later (1949–50) had a Civil Service job as Chief Examiner and Director of Test Construction in Chicago. Pursuing advanced studies at the University of Chicago in the late 1940s, he worked on anthropology in the emerging interdisciplinary program named the 'Committee on Human Development'. Eventually this led to the completion of his Ph.D. in that same program in 1957, but by that time his interest had shifted to psychotherapy research and practice, and his dissertation entailed 'An Experimental Investigation of Brief, Time-Limited, Client-Centered Therapy'. His thesis demonstrated that time-limited therapy (e.g. 20 sessions) could have just as profound and lasting consequences on personality change as much longer unlimited therapy protocols.

It was actually in the process of interviewing professionals regarding the sociology of knowledge through the Committee on Human Development that John Shlien met Carl R. Rogers, the psychologist who developed the theory and practice of Client-Centered Therapy. At first Carl's quiet manner as well as the therapeutic techniques of listening and clarification of feelings seemed disarmingly simple — no ponderous analytic procedure nor working through of a complex 'transference' relationship as in psychoanalysis. But the undeniable effectiveness of the client-centered approach became quickly apparent to John; and it was, needless to say, far less expensive for clients. (The term 'client' was used rather than 'patient' in order to underscore the locus of initiation of change and the fostering of personal insight, as preferable to the implication of a more compliant and dependent status of 'patient' in a medical model.) Carl Rogers soon became a very important mentor and friend of John's. They shared a profound respect for the inherent capacity of individuals, even under severe psychological stress or neurotic anxiety, to work through confusing and frightening webs of emotional bewilderment, and to regain healthy and constructive growth, given a safe context of genuine therapeutic support.

Much of the early work of the client-centered therapists was undertaken at the Counseling Center at the University of Chicago. John began his own work there in 1950 as an Intern, and soon became the Services Coordinator in 1952, then later (1955–57) a Research Associate and Staff Counselor. It became his special responsibility to document through clinical research procedures clear evidence of the psychological changes that occurred when the 'necessary and sufficient conditions' of constructive personality change were provided, thereby demonstrating the validity of the new theories of psychotherapy within the client-centered perspective. Carl Rogers became very indebted to John and others for this scientific validation. John took on more administrative responsibility at the Counseling Center when Carl Rogers left for Mendota State Hospital in Wisconsin to test the viability of the client-centered model of therapy with individuals who had been diagnosed with psychotic disorders.

Other colleagues at the Counseling Center carried on statistical work (Jack Butler), theoretical writing (Laura Rice), therapy supervision and training (Gene Gendlin), but John Shlien rather uniquely maintained involvement in all of these areas, while at the same time teaching actively, and for a period of time (1963–67) administering the clinical program as Chairman of the Interdepartmental Committee on Clinical Psychology and Director of Clinical Training.

His professorial appointments advanced through Assistant (1957–61) and Associate Professorships (1961–64), to Full Professor in the Department of Psychology and the Committee on Human Development from 1964 to 1967. He was a teacher much admired by both students and colleagues at the University of Chicago.

In 1967, John Shlien came to Harvard University, receiving an appointment as Professor of Education and Counseling Psychology in the Harvard Graduate School of Education. This came at the time when a new interdisciplinary program was being considered that would build on knowledge and research in psychology and psychiatry, but shift away from a clinical emphasis on the treatment of pathology (illness) to the proactive design of better systems of community development and institutional planning that would enable people to thrive in more healthy ways in the first place. It was conceived as a movement from individual therapy toward public policies that would support psychologically positive growth and community interaction. The program was designated 'Clinical Psychology and Public Practice', and was supported by the Divinity School, the Medical School, the Graduate School of Arts and Sciences, and the Graduate School of Education. John Shlien was one of the key framers of this program and helped bring together other significant colleagues like Chester (Chet) Pierce (medicine), Richard (Dick) Rowe (education), Ira Goldenberg (community development), and William (Bill) Rogers (divinity). The philosophy of the program, somewhat analogous to the client-centered approach, was that facilitating 'grass roots' changes in the interests of local communities, rather than centralizing power in top-down political control and mandated planning, would bring greater fulfillment to those whose lives were affected. The program set out in an 'action research' mode to both initiate and study such changes. An interdisciplinary curriculum was built to support a strong and innovative doctoral program in Clinical Psychology and Public Practice.

In 1972, as a major experiment in action research, John Shlien created the 'Robert W. White School' at the Erich Lindemann Community Mental Health Center in downtown Boston. The idea was to develop with students, especially those who had failed or been expelled from public school mostly for mental or behavioral problems, and with teachers, a 'curriculum' that would positively engage kids, draw on their unique talents and interests, and build a real community of learners. Measuring success in this effort was difficult, but in spite of frustrations, the school did have a very constructive effect in the lives of many young people. It established a model of program development that could be used in smaller and more focused ways in other public and private schools.

The Clinical Psychology and Public Practice program, physically located in Nichols House at HGSE, attracted many extraordinarily talented students with strong interdisciplinary backgrounds and deep convictions about constructive social change along with pushing the frontiers of knowledge about such change. Some students went on to become community organizers, institutional mediators, entrepreneurial consultants, advocates for under-represented minorities; some became psychotherapists; some writers, professors and researchers in both academic settings and public policy 'think-tanks' or governmental settings. All were touched and in important ways changed by their interactions with John Shlien. In recent months, several have given explicit voice to the magnitude of that influence: for example Neill Watson, now Clinical Psychology Chairman at the College of William and Mary, and Ronald Levant, now Dean of Nova Southeastern University's Center for Psychological Studies (*Boston Globe*, 4/3/02).

John's intellectual contributions within psychology were varied and in many respects profound. He would frequently introduce nuggets of insight about human consciousness that forced students and colleagues to rethink theories that had previously seemed well-established. But unlike most major university professors, he never published a major volume of theoretical or research findings. He did not codify any 'new' theory of personality or of social change. We believe he could have, but perhaps he was too impatient and restless of imagination to settle on a fixed configuration of theoretical ideas. Clearly, he was always eager to follow new avenues of awareness, and very respectful of the complexity and potential self-deceit of any strict formulation of the mind's permutations.

The writing that he did undertake showed both brilliance and courage. He was, for instance, intrepid about taking on the task of dismantling one of the primary tenants of traditional psychoanalytic theory: the idea of 'transference'. Although the 'working through of the transference', i.e. analyzing the emotional and historical psychodynamic content of complex psychosexual feelings presumably 'projected' or 'displaced' onto the analyst by the patient, was central to the work of psychoanalysis; John Shlien effectively countered the theory by showing that such a concept as 'transference' shielded the analyst from real feelings that emerged between patient and doctor, or analysand and analyst, or client and therapist. In his words, 'Transference is a fiction, invented and maintained by the therapist to protect himself from the consequences of his own behavior.' John developed an historical and psychological argument to support his contention by carefully reviewing the classic cases of J. Breuer with 'Anna O.', and of S. Freud with his early female patients. The sexual overtones of these cases were revealed in private correspondence, and in several instances interrupted therapy. Yet clustering the sexual content within the concepts of transference and counter-transference disguised a potent reality while ironically doing so in the name of unraveling disguises. This is not to say John dismissed completely the presence of displaced feelings or 'transference' phenomena in therapy — or real life — but he showed the error of making this the central feature of the therapeutic enterprise. The truly central feature for him was understanding, empathetic understanding — complex, realistic, at the pace of the client, honest, caring. And at this, he was a master.

Another instance of his perceptive writing concerned the psychology of secrecy. He cited the astute observation of the British statesman R.H.S. Crossman: 'all secrecy corrupts; semisecrecy corrupts absolutely' (a paraphrase of Lord Acton's dictum about absolute power). John went on to unravel both the intra-psychic and interpersonal corrupting consequences of half-truths. 'Things do not fit as a whole, but neither can the right and wrong parts be separated from the intentionally sticky wrappings. The mind-numbing outcome is "learned ignorance"' (1981). Again in this exploration, John analyzed Freud's case of 'Dora' and the function that secrets and the unravelling of secrecy played in therapy — and the part they could have played. In an eerily contemporary vein, both Crossman and Shlien point to the public policy temptations and disasters of semisecrecy, noting the obsession after World War II with 'security' and 'intelligence' telling us something about 'the alluring but false meanings of secrecy. Strong, honorable, and humane security and intelligence do not come from secrecy, but we are misled to think that they do, and we are weakened (corrupted) thereby.' This work was, by the way, contemporaneous with the writing on *Secrets* by S. Bok at Harvard (1982).

The area where John could have written far more than he did was in 'phenomenology'. The concept was compelling to John because it pointed to the possibility of understanding (at least partially) the inner phenomenal world of the other. How do things look, taste, feel to another from within his or her own unique perspective? What are this person's hurts, bewilderments, premonitions, leanings, struggles to undo the learned 'half-truths'? This is, in a sense, the central task of a psychotherapist — or of a community development convenor — or of a good politician. Phenomenological sensitivity often leads to compassion and the initiation of self-directed change. The links with the philosophy of Husserl could have been explored. And the implications for research on these aptitudes of transcending the self in empathy for another could have been great. John talked about this, but alas his writing on phenomenology was minimal.

John retired from the Harvard faculty in 1984. During most of his tenure at Harvard he and his wife, Helen, lived in a handsome contemporary home in Wayland, MX. But after retirement, they maintained their residence in Cambridge for at least half of each year, the other half being in Big Sur, CA. John's associations with students and colleagues continued. He used his more open schedule to travel and lecture, primarily in Europe, on the principles and applications of client-centered or person-centered theory. On some occasions, these trips involved impressive international conferences of professional psychologists, one important example of which was at the University of Leuven, Belgium, where John and his students were key participants and presenters.

In this review of John's life, we should give special honor his personal affection for his family. His marriage to Helen was a bond of nearly 60 years! He admired her strength, intelligence and independence, her care for the children, and her keen artistic and business sense. Helen was always involved in the art world, and for a period ran an excellent gallery in Boston.

They had three children, David, Andrea, and Laura, all three of whom now live in California. There are five grandchildren and three great-grandchildren. John loved all of them greatly.

John was also artistic and fun-loving. He shared with Helen a knowledge and love of contemporary art, and their home was filled with interesting, and some very valuable, paintings and sculpture. John admired the sculptural form of automobile design as well, and the enjoyment of driving sports cars. Jaguars were his favorite, and he owned with pleasure XK 140, XK 150, and XKE convertibles. He also had a wonderful sense of style and color in the silk scarves, wool sweaters and blazers that he wore. He always had a distinguished and calm 'presence'.

John was not a conventionally religious person, but he certainly had a sense of the ineffable, the mystery of the transcendent, and a wonder — verging on awe — at the richness of essence and existence. He once attended a discussion on religion between Bruno Bettleheim and Paul Tillich. He reported finding Bettleheim quite plausible in laying out Freud's view from *The Future of an Illusion* that the urge toward religious belief was a 'projection' of a longed-for father. Tillich replied, 'But what is the screen?' 'Not a weighty reply, to my way of thinking', John wrote, 'but increasingly I realized that "it" cannot be nothing' (1984). He was a seeker.

So to this fine teacher, scholar and friend, we pay our final respect. A teacher of teachers, a therapist of therapists, a researcher for searchers, an inquirer among those who asked some of the deepest queries of life. Our admiration and appreciation for John Shlien is great. With sadness and many levels of humble identification, we bid him farewell.

Respectfully submitted,

William R. Rogers, Formerly Parkman Professor of Religion and Psychology, Harvard University.

Michael J. Nakkula, Marie and Max Kargman Assistant Professor in Human Development and Urban Education Advancement, Harvard Graduate School of Education.

Chester M. Pierce, Professor of Education and Psychiatry *Emeritus* Harvard Medical School, Harvard Graduate School of Education.

Index

PCCS Books

The largest list of Client-Centred Therapy and Person-Centred Approach books in the world

Client-Centred Therapy and the Person-Centred Approach
Essential Readers
Series edited by Tony Merry

Client-Centred Therapy: A revolutionary paradigm
Jerold Bozarth

Experiences in Relatedness: Groupwork and the person-centred approach
Colin Lago & Mhairi MacMillan (Eds)

Women Writing in the Person-Centred Approach
Irene Fairhurst (Ed)

Understanding Psychotherapy: Fifty years of client-centred theory and practice
C.H. Patterson

The Person-Centred Approach: A passionate presence
Peggy Natiello

Family, Self and Psychotherapy: A person-centred perspective
Ned L. Gaylin

Contributions to Client-Centered Therapy and the Person-Centered Approach
Nathaniel J. Raskin

Rogers' Therapeutic Conditions: Evolution, Theory and Practice
Series edited by Gill Wyatt

Volume 1: Congruence
Gill Wyatt (Ed)

Volume 2: Empathy
Sheila Haugh & Tony Merry (Eds)

Volume 3: Unconditional Positive Regard
Jerold Bozarth & Paul Wilkins (Eds)

Volume 4: Contact and Perception
Gill Wyatt & Pete Sanders (Eds)

PCCS Books

The largest list of Client-Centred Therapy and Person-Centred Approach books in the world

The Tribes of the Person-Centred Nation: A guide to the schools of therapy associated with the PCA
Pete Sanders (Ed.)

The Client-Centred Therapist in Psychiatric Contexts: A therapists' guide to the psychiatric landscape and its inhabitants
Lisbeth Sommerbeck

Steps on a Mindful Journey: Person-centred expressions
Godfrey T. Barrett-Lennard

Learning and Being in Person-Centred Counselling (second edition) A textbook for discovering theory and developing practice
Tony Merry

Person-Centred Practice: The BAPCA Reader
Tony Merry (Ed)

Trust and Understanding: The person-centred approach to everyday care for people with special needs
Marlis Pörtner

Classics in the Person-Centered Approach
David J. Cain (Ed)

Client-Centered and Experiential Psychotherapy in the 21st Century: Advances in theory, research and practice
Jeanne C. Watson, Rhonda N. Goldman & Margaret S. Warner (Eds)

Pre-Therapy: Reaching contact-impaired clients
Garry Prouty, Dion Van Werde & Marlis Pörtner

Voices of the Voiceless: Person-centred approaches and people with learning disabilities
Jan Hawkins

Freedom to Practise: Person-centred approaches to supervision
Keith Tudor & Mike Worrall (Eds)

Journals

Person-Centred Practice
The journal of the British Association for the Person-Centred Approach

Person-Centered and Experiential Psychotherapies
The journal of the World Association for Person-Centered and Experiential Psychotherapy and Counseling

---

Visit our website for news of the latest releases www.pccs-books.co.uk

UK customers call 01989 77 07 07 for discounts